the
SEVEN
SECRETS
JOHN
HAGEE

Charisma
HOUSE
A STRANG COMPANY

Most STRANG COMMUNICATIONS/CHARISMA HOUSE/SILOAM products are available at special quantity discounts for bulk purchase for sales promotions, premiums, fundraising, and educational needs. For details, write Strang Communications/Charisma House/Siloam, 600 Rinehart Road, Lake Mary, Florida 32746, or telephone (407) 333-0600.

THE SEVEN SECRETS by John Hagee
Published by Charisma House
A Strang Company
600 Rinehart Road
Lake Mary, Florida 32746
www.charismahouse.com

Unless otherwise noted, all Scripture quotations are from the New King James Version of the Bible. Copyright © 1979, 1980, 1982 by Thomas Nelson, Inc., publishers. Used by permission.

Scripture quotations marked KJV are from the King James Version of the Bible.

Scripture quotations marked NIV are from the Holy Bible, New International Version. Copyright © 1973, 1978, 1984, International Bible Society. Used by permission.

Cover design by Rachel Campbell

Library of Congress Cataloging-in-Publication Data

Hagee, John.
   The seven secrets / John Hagee.
       p. cm.
Includes bibliographical references.
   ISBN 1-59185-237-4 (hardback); 1-59185-818-6 (paperback)
   1. Success--Religious aspects--Christianity. I. Title.
BV4598.3.H33 2004
248.4--dc22

                    2003024350

05 06 07 08 09 — 987654321
Printed in the United States of America

*This volume is lovingly dedicated to my wife,
Diana Castro Hagee, who has made my home and
ministry as the days of heaven on earth.*

Contents

v

CHAPTER ONE

A Successful Life Is for Everyone

E VERY person on earth wants to be successful in life, but the question that haunts humanity is this: "What is success?"
Success is for EVERYONE!
Success is for YOU!
Success is for you NOW!

You must believe you *can* succeed if you *are* to succeed. If you believe you can or you believe you can't, you're right! What your mind can conceive you can achieve. God wants you to succeed. And He promises to help you through His advice in the Bible: "This Book of the Law shall not depart from your mouth, but you shall meditate in it day and night, that you may observe to do according to all that is written in it. For then you will make your way prosperous, and then you will have good success" (Josh. 1:8). If you're not successful, it's not God's fault!

Every person reading this book is unique. When you were born, the genius of God exploded and made a person that the world has never seen before and will never see again. You were born to do good. You were born to succeed in life. You were born to bless others' lives. You have unlimited potential, but you must learn how to release it to reach your destiny.

However, you don't stumble into success any more than you stumble into the gates of heaven. Success is not an event; it's a lifelong journey. You cannot possess what you are unwilling to pursue. Success comes to those who plan, to those who prepare, to those who are persistent, and to those who are willing to endure pain to achieve their goals.

You cannot possess what you will not pursue.

Success escapes the majority of Americans. Ron Blue, author of *Master Your Money*, states, "According to the Office of Social Security, only 2 percent of Americans reach age sixty-five with two hundred dollars in the bank."[1] Think of it! After working for forty-five years, 98 percent of Americans are not able to save twenty dollars per year.

I ask you again, what is success? Ask this question to the next ten people you see. Then listen closely to what they say. They will stutter, look off into the distance, and finally stumble to give a vague definition to a simple question. If you ask ten people, you will get at least twelve different answers. I know; I've asked ten people, and their responses were amazing.

I've had intelligent people look me directly in the eye and joyously announce:

- Success for me is when I retire!
- Success for me is reaching the goal I've set for myself.
- Success for me is when the last child leaves home and the dog dies.

Maltbie D. Babcock, a pastor and author of the well-known song "This Is My Father's World," states a true principle that few people realize: "One of the common mistakes and one of the costliest is thinking that success is due to some genius, some magic, something or other which we do not possess."[2]

Unfortunately, success for many men would be to have a body like Hulk Hogan's, a golf game like Tiger Woods', a brain like Albert Einstein's, and the wealth of Bill Gates. Success for many women would be to have the beauty of Catherine Zeta-Jones, the grace and poise of Jacqueline Kennedy Onassis, and the compassion of Mother Teresa.

Every person has his or her own definition of success. I will give you mine at the end of this chapter. First, let me clear the emotional and intellectual fog by stating what success is not.

I
SUCCESS IS NOT MONEY

If you think success is money, consider these facts of life:

Money can buy you a palace of breathtaking splendor, filled with priceless works of art by Rembrandt, Monet, Picasso, or Michelangelo. Money can fill your house with the finest furniture and your garage with luxury automobiles, *but money cannot buy you a home filled with love and respect from the people who live there.*

Money can buy the finest physicians in an hour of sickness, but money cannot buy the God-given gift of health.

Money can buy you a bed of solid gold, but money cannot buy you one minute of rest or inner peace.

King Solomon, the richest monarch in ancient Israel whose horse stables had gold-plated hinges on every door, said, "Whoever loves money never has enough money; whoever loves wealth is never satisfied with his income" (Eccles. 5:10, NIV).

Solomon is not the only man who realized that money does not buy rest or inner peace. Centuries later, Benjamin Franklin, one of America's founding fathers, said, "Money never made a man happy yet, nor will it. There is nothing in its nature to produce happiness. The more a man has, the more he wants. Instead of its filling a vacuum, it makes one. If it satisfies one want, it doubles and trebles that want another way. That was a true proverb of the wise man; rely upon it: 'Better is little with the fear of the Lord, than great treasure and trouble therewith.'"[3]

In 1923 a group of the world's most successful financiers met at the Edgewater Beach Hotel in Chicago. Collectively, these tycoons controlled more wealth than was in the United States Treasury at that time. Year after year newspapers and magazines had been printing their success stories and urging the youth of the nation to follow their examples.

Twenty-seven years later, let's see what had happened to seven of them.

- ◆ Jesse Livermore, the greatest bear on Wall Street, committed suicide.

- ◆ Leon Fraser, the president of the Bank of International Settlement, also committed suicide.

- ◆ Ivar Kruegar, the head of the world's greatest monopoly, committed suicide.

- ◆ Charles Schwab, the president of the largest independent steel company, lived on borrowed money the last five years of his life and died penniless.

- ◆ Arthur Cutten, the greatest wheat speculator, died abroad insolvent.

- ◆ Richard Whitney, the president of the New York Stock Exchange, was released some time ago from Sing Sing Prison.

- ◆ Albert Fall, a member of a president's cabinet, was pardoned from prison so he could die at home.

All of these men had learned how to make money, but not one of them had learned how to enjoy a successful life.[4] Money cannot buy you one minute of rest or inner peace. Nor can money buy you lasting success. How many of us have even heard of one of these seven men or their accomplishments?

Money will attract legions of people to you,but money cannot buy you the treasure of one true friend.

Christina Onassis, as the daughter of Aristotle Onassis, was one of the richest women in the world. Yet she had to hire people to play tennis with her, to go swimming with her, and to go to supper with her. She had a fortune so vast she couldn't possibly spend it in her lifetime, yet she lived a lonely, sad, and empty life.

It was my great pleasure to have a personal and private audience with Elvis Presley when he was at the pinnacle of his legendary world-wide fame. I liked Elvis and loved his music. He was and always will be the "King."

Elvis had more luxury cars than he could drive. He had jets, motor-cycles, diamonds, and a gold-plated telephone. One of his Cadillacs had a fourteen-layer paint job, some layers of which had gold flakes in the paint. Yet I had never before met a man who lived such a lonely life.

Money will attract people to you like bees to honey, but money cannot buy true friends. They will be takers, not givers. As soon as your money is gone, they will be also.

Money will buy books, but money cannot buy brains. I have attended and graduated from two wonderful universities. The first was Trinity University in San Antonio where I made the dean's list while playing right guard and linebacker on the university's football team. I received my master's degree from North Texas State University.

A beautiful prayer tower was erected in the center of the Trinity University campus. Every day the chimes in that prayer tower echoed across the campus, reminding every student of the time, every hour on the hour. That beautiful prayer tower had to be locked with an iron gate.

Why?

Some students who could not achieve the academic dreams of their wealthy fathers climbed the stairs of the prayer tower and leaped to their deaths. Money will buy books, but money cannot buy brains.

Money will buy you food, but money cannot buy a healthy appetite.

Have you ever thought that the empty plate on your family's table was beautiful? Most women see a dirty plate as something to wash, a chore to be completed.

An empty plate only becomes beautiful when you have a sick child, suffering with a deadly disease like cancer, and you watch this precious child lose his or her strength and vitality day after day after day. You fix the finest foods you possibly can prepare and watch your beloved child push these dinners away, nauseated by the sight.

As the pastor of a church of eighteen thousand members, I have on several occasions sat at a family table and watched a mother cry because her child refused to touch the delicious food on the plate. Every member of the family would encourage the child, "Eat just one bite for me." The child's response? Only a weak shaking of the small head, followed by Mom's silent tears.

The next time you see a dirty plate on your table, take time to thank God for the food He has given and the appetite to want it. Money can't buy that.

Money can buy a crucifix around your neck, but money cannot buy a Savior in your heart.

On one occasion a very gracious and beautiful Hispanic woman in her midforties was brought to my office by her sister for urgent counseling. The woman had every reason to be excited about her life.

She had a husband who loved her dearly and provided handsomely for her and their two healthy children. Both young people were doing very well in their academic and athletic activities in public school. After asking enough questions to establish a personal profile, I asked this very simple question: "Tell me, how do you see your life and your future?"

What gushed out of her mouth was a poisoned stream of emotional and mental suffering. Her world was perpetual darkness on a meaningless journey that was totally void of joy or peace. She lived in a physical world of material abundance, but what she described was the suburbs of a living hell.

Dangling about her neck was a large, diamond-studded cross. She had this cross around her neck but no Savior in her heart. Most people would describe her physical world as heaven—she described it as hell.

Money can buy a church pew with your name engraved on it in gold script, but money will not buy you a ticket to heaven.

Success is not money.

2
SUCCESS IS NOT REACHING A GOAL

I have been a minister for more than forty-five years, and I've heard legions of people boast of reaching a long-sought goal and then sit down and die. Reaching their goal destroyed them.

People often say, "My goal is to retire." To me, retirement is when you sit on the porch and watch the sun set if you can stay awake that long. Retirement is a rut, which by any other name is a grave with both ends kicked out.

There's one horrible fact about retirement you should always remember: You can never take a day off! Before retiring from your job, stay home a week and watch daytime television. Retirement could be a great joy if you could figure out how to spend time without spending money.

I repeat: Reaching a goal can destroy you via stagnation and the illusion of accomplishment. I believe in goals as long as they do not become gods. Goals must be targets and not terminal destinations. Successful people are motivated to exceed their goals!

*One of the most important lessons in life
is that success must continually be won and is
never finally achieved.*

—CHARLES EVANS HUGHES

On Mother's Day of 1975, at the age of thirty-five, I became the pastor of the Church of Castle Hills. This A-frame church was comprised of twenty-five desperate souls deeply in debt and spiritually disillusioned. The former pastor had become a hopeless alcoholic. In a drunken rage he shot his wife. His picture had appeared on the front page of a San Antonio newspaper for attempted murder.

That A-frame church, with a seating capacity of about three hundred, was a disaster looking for a place to happen. There was only one difference between that church and the *Titanic*. The *Titanic* had a band.

The first time I met with the leadership of the church, the senior member of the board said, "Let's set a goal of two hundred in Sunday school by year's end!" To him this was success, and when you have twenty-five disillusioned people, deeply in debt with no money in the bank, most would agree with him.

I did not! I sensed that this goal would become the church's god. They would see it as a terminal destination, not a target.

Yet I knew why this board member felt that two hundred in Sunday school was a decent goal. As this man spoke, I looked around and saw a building that looked more like a bomb shelter than a sanctuary. The paint was peeling inside and out. The carpets had holes deep enough to be bunkers. The pews needed to be refinished, and half the lights didn't work. Those that did flickered off and on. The church interior looked like a B-grade movie set for a Halloween house of horrors. And this guy stood in front of me, swinging his arms like a windmill as he waxed eloquent about a goal of two hundred people in Sunday school!

I looked at this zealous believer and managed to say, "Let's not set any goals just yet. They may keep us from reaching our destiny."

The shocked board member looked at me with a gaping-open mouth and extended his hands heavenward in utter disbelief! His pastor lacked vision.

By that year's end our Sunday morning attendance was well over five hundred. In three years we built a new sanctuary that would seat sixteen hundred and filled it three times on Sunday. We had to start a Saturday night service for those who could not get in on Sunday morning.

That "goal of two hundred" has grown to become Cornerstone Church, a church of eighteen thousand active members who are making an impact on the city of San Antonio, our nation, and the world via radio and television. Had we set a goal of two hundred, 90 percent of that congregation would have folded their arms, sat down, and turned into Bible-toting mummies once we reached that goal. Their speech would have reflected their thinking: "We've arrived!" "This is as good as it gets!" "We reached our goal!" Had I agreed to a goal of two hundred, they would have become resentful when I insisted we could do better.

Again, goals are good, but goals are not gods! Goals must be targets, not terminal destinations.

Success for many people is nothing more than fantasy. They fantasize, "Someday my dreams will come true. Someday my ship will come in." Listen up! Ships don't come in; they're brought in.

Many people live on a fantasy island called, "Someday I'll." They say things like, "Someday I'll retire!" "Someday I'll reach my goal!" "Someday I'll get married!" "Someday I'll be successful!"

Are you living there? Are you looking for a place in your personal or professional life where you can level off and stagnate at a destination that will be the last stop before the graveyard? If so, your goal has become your god.

One of my favorite poems of all times is "Someday I'll." Read it thoughtfully and ask yourself if you're living there or want to go there.

SOMEDAY I'LL

There is an island fantasy
A "Someday I'll" we'll never see
When recession stops, inflation ceases
Our mortgage is paid; our pay increases
That Someday I'll where problems end
Where every piece of mail is from a friend
Where the children are sweet and already grown
Where all the other nations can go it alone
Where we all retire at forty-one
Playing backgammon in the island sun.

Most unhappy people look to tomorrow
To erase this day's hardship and sorrow
They put happiness on "lay away"
And struggle through a blue today
But happiness cannot be sought
It can't be earned; it can't be bought
Life's most important revelation
Is that the journey means more than the destination.

Happiness is where you are right now
Pushing a pencil or pushing a plow
Going to school or standing in line
Watching and waiting, or tasting the wine
If you live in the past you become senile
If you live in the future you're on Someday I'll
The fear of results is procrastination
The joy of today is a celebration.

You can save, you can slave, trudging mile after mile
But you'll never set foot on your Someday I'll
When you've paid all your dues and put in your time
Out of nowhere comes another Mt. Everest to climb
From this day forward make it your vow
Take Someday I'll and make it your Now![5]

Success is not money, and success is not reaching a goal.

3
SUCCESS IS NOT POWER

Adolf Hitler had absolute power over Germany in one of history's most brutal and bloody dictatorships. His demonic dreams dragged the world into a global bloodbath as his Nazis systematically slaughtered six million Jews with a brutality that numbs the mind.

On April 30, 1945, Hitler blew his brains out, hiding in his bunker with a handful of fellow Nazi fanatics. He ordered his body to be burned to prevent the Germans from mocking his corpse as the Italians had mocked Mussolini, who was hung upside down.

Hitler had absolute power, but he was not successful.

Saddam Hussein ruled Iraq for decades with the iron grip of terrorism. He had the power of life and death over millions of Iraqis; he amassed a fortune of billions; he built a series of elaborate mansions for himself and members of his family while the children of Iraq starved. He had absolute power, but Saddam Hussein was not successful.

Now his torture rooms, rape rooms, and assassination chambers are finished! His reign of terror is over, extinguished through the courageous leadership of President George W. Bush and the heroics of America's armed forces.

Bill Clinton went to Washington, D.C., pledging to give the American people the most ethical administration in American history.

Did he fulfill that pledge? Walk with me through the years of Bill Clinton's leadership. First there was Travelgate, where faithful and loyal employees were fired without cause so that Clinton loyalists could have their jobs. Then there was Cattlegate, where Hillary invested a pittance and made over one hundred thousand dollars. Then there was Filegate, where the federal government screened over nine hundred files of private citizens considered hostile to the Clinton administration. You might remember that Chuck Colson went to prison for mishandling one file. No one in the Clinton administration was ever charged with even a misdemeanor for this horrendous abuse of power.

Next there was the Whitewater Scandal, which was endless. All of this was laced with President Clinton's sexual misconduct with Jennifer Flowers, Paula Jones, and Monica Lewinsky.

When America's embassies in Africa were attacked, President Clinton fired missiles into an abandoned terrorist camp, only destroying sand dunes, so he could get his sexual exploits with Monica Lewinsky off the front pages of America's newspapers. He cut the military budget and refused to respond to any terrorist threat to this nation. His administration was America's holiday from history.

Then came September 11, 2001, the bitter fruit of Bill Clinton's eight years of retreating from international terrorism. This horrendous day was a tragedy America will never forget, but few will remember why it happened: A president who had the power of this great nation behind him refused to use this power to defend the people of America. History will judge him to be one of our most unsuccessful presidents. Clinton's leadership spawned the most corrupt, deceitful, and power-hungry administration in recent American history.

Long ago, the apostle Paul stood, bound in chains, before Felix, a Roman governor. Paul reasoned with Felix about the "righteousness and judgment to come" (Acts 24:25). The Bible record states that Felix shook so violently he could hardly sit on the throne. He had the absolute power of the Roman Empire behind him, yet he shook before a prisoner in chains who successfully described his faith in Jesus Christ and the truth of what his Savior had done.

Yes, Felix had power, but power is not success. Two thousand years later we call our sons "Paul" and our cats "Felix."

Success is not money or reaching a goal. Success is not power.

4
SUCCESS IS NOT DETERMINED
BY YOUR CIRCUMSTANCE

Some of the world's greatest men and women have been saddled with disabilities, but they have managed to overcome them. Cripple a man, and you have Sir Walter Scott. Lock a man in a prison cell, and you have John Bunyan. Bury a man in the snows of Valley Forge, and you have George Washington. Raise a man in abject poverty, and you have Abraham Lincoln. Subject a man to bitter religious prejudice, and you have Benjamin Disraeli. Strike a man with infantile paralysis, and you have Franklin Delano Roosevelt. Burn a man so severely in a schoolhouse fire that the doctors say he will never walk again, and you have Glenn Cunningham, who set a world record in 1934 for running a mile in 4 minutes and 6.7 seconds. Deafen a genius composer, and you have Ludwig van Beethoven.

The world is not interested in the storms you encountered, but they want to know: Did you bring in the ship?

Have a man or a woman born black in a society filled with racial discrimination, and you have Booker T. Washington, Harriet Tubman, Marian Anderson, or George Washington Carver. Make a man the first child to survive in a poor Italian family of eighteen children, and you have Enrico Caruso. Have a man born of parents who survived a Nazi concentration camp, paralyze him from the waist down when he is four, and you have the incomparable concert violinist Itzhak Perlman. Call a man "a slow learner," "retarded," and write him off as uneducable, and you have Albert Einstein.

Success is not found in your circumstance.

Success is overcoming your circumstance.

Helen Keller was born blind and deaf, yet she graduated with honors from college. Margaret Thatcher, England's first—and only—woman prime minister who joined with President Ronald Reagan to crush communism and bring down the Berlin Wall, lived upstairs over her father's small grocery store. For a while her childhood home had no running water and no indoor plumbing. Michael Jordan, who is doubtless the greatest basketball player to ever walk on the court, was cut off the team in high school. Bill Gates, the billionaire who founded Microsoft, was a college dropout. Golda Meier, Israel's first—and only—woman prime minister, was a divorced grandmother from Milwaukee.

Success is not determined by your circumstance.

5
SUCCESS IS NOT "HAVING IT ALL"

Anyone who tells you that you can have it all is lying. Russian author Leo Tolstoy tells the story of a rich man who was never satisfied. He always wanted more, more, more. One day this rich man heard of a wonderful chance to get more land. For a thousand rubles he could have all the territory he could walk around in a day. But he had to make it back to the starting point by sundown or he would lose it all.

This wealthy man arose early and set out. He walked on and on, thinking he could get just a little more land if he kept going further and further. But he went so far, he realized he must walk very fast if he were to get back in time to claim the land.

As the sun got lower in the sky, he quickened his pace. Then he began to run. Finally he came within sight of the starting place, so he exerted his last energies, plunged over the finish line, fell to the ground, and collapsed. A stream of blood poured out of his mouth, and he lay dead. His servant took a spade and dug a grave. He made it just long enough and just wide enough and buried the avaricious man.

The title of Tolstoy's story is "How Much Land Does a Man Need?" He concluded by saying, "Six feet from his head to his heels was all he needed." You can't get it all or keep it all. Success is not having it all.

You can be anything you want to be, but you can't be everything.

You can be a brain surgeon or a rancher, but you can't be both. You can be a master salesman or a scratch golfer, but you can't be both; as your golf score goes down, so will your sales.

Did you see the movie *City Slickers* with Billy Crystal and Jack Palance? The story line of the movie is that Billy Crystal is having a midlife crisis. He is failing at his job for which he is infinitely qualified. His marriage is about as exciting as watching paint dry. He and his two friends go out West for a two-week cattle drive to discover themselves.

At a critical moment in the film, Billy Crystal and Jack Palance, a crusty old cowboy, are riding horseback side by side. Jack Palance looks over at Crystal and asks with his raspy voice, "How old are you?"

Crystal responds in his nervous tenor voice, "Thirty-nine."

Palance stares holes through Crystal's head and responds, "Yeah? You all come out here about the same age with the same problems. You spend fifty weeks a year getting knots in your rope, and you think two weeks out here will untie them for you. None of you get it!"

Palance pauses, and Billy Crystal nervously looks at the leathery face of the legendary cowboy, waiting for words of wisdom to get his lackluster life in high gear.

Finally, Palance speaks. "Do you know what the secret of success in life really is?"

"No, what is it?"

Palance, a homemade cigarette dangling from his lips, holds up his index finger and says, "It's this!"

Crystal incredulously inquires, "Your finger?"

The crusty old cowboy stays with his theme. "One thing! Just one thing! You stick to that, and everything else don't mean nothing."

"That's great, but what is that one thing?"

Palance pulls the cigarette out of his mouth and snarls, "That's what you've got to figure out."

Success is not having it all. Success is knowing the one thing in life that God has assigned you to do and doing it with all of your heart, soul, mind, and body. Let us never forget the words of the apostle Paul, "One thing I do…" (Phil. 3:13).

Success is not money or reaching a goal. Success is not power. Success is not determined by your circumstance, and success is not "having it all."

6
SUCCESS IS NOT MAINTAINING
THE STATUS QUO

The status quo is stagnation! Our goal at Cornerstone Church is to be as good as we can be every day, every hour, every minute. If we're not progressively improving, we're stagnating, which is death by another name. Any department head who is satisfied with being "as good as we were last year" will not be here next year.

Three years ago I looked at the growth charts of our church, which we keep with excruciating detail. Every usher has a clicker in his hand and counts the people in the pews as he takes the offering in his section. We know exactly how many people come to church at Cornerstone every time we open the doors. Those numbers are entered into our database for weekly, monthly, quarterly, and annual analysis.

We do the same for our home Bible study groups. Several years ago, as I analyzed the past three years of our growth, I could clearly see that our home Bible study groups had flat lined, even though the sanctuary was packed to the walls on Sunday morning.

I restructured the entire infrastructure of Cornerstone Church from top to bottom. No sacred cows were spared. Programs and personnel who were not producing were terminated. It was a spiritual earthquake! It was painful yet extremely productive.

The measure of success is not whether you have a tough problem to deal with, but whether it's the same problem you had last year. Do not complain about what you permit!

We began an intensive leadership training program called the Government of Twelve, a concept that comes from the Word of God. You see, twelve in Scripture is the number of government.

When God wanted to form a nation that would be eternal, He built it around twelve tribes. Those twelve tribes formed the nation of Israel. That nation has endured the slavery of Egypt and the cruelty of Pharaoh. That nation has survived Haman's murderous plot to exterminate the Jews in Persia. That nation survived when Herod slaughtered innocent children by the thousands, trying to prevent the life and ministry of Jesus Christ. That nation survived when Titus and the Roman legions tried to destroy Jerusalem in A.D. 70, killing at least five hundred thousand Jews.

Israel survived a second Roman attack in A.D. 135 under Hadrian. Rome hated the Jews because the Jews were monotheistic. The first commandment declares, "Thou shall have no other gods before me," and the Jews died by the thousands at this time, defending the honor of God's name. Yet Israel, that government of twelve, survived.

Then came seven Crusades. The crusaders came from Europe after they received the pope's blessing. Believe it or not, before the crusaders left Europe, the pope forgave any sinful act they might commit en route to, or returning from, Jerusalem. The crusaders were not holy men. The truth of history is they robbed and raped the Jews from Europe to Israel. Whole cities of Jews were slaughtered because they would not convert to a Christianity that carried a cross and a razor-sharp sword, which the crusaders held at Jewish throats, demanding they convert or die. And the Jews died by the thousands, yet Israel survived.

The nation of Israel has survived the Babylonians, the Romans, the Greeks, the Persians, the Ottoman Empire, the British Empire, and the living hell of the Holocaust. On May 15, 1948, the Jews of the world returned to Israel as Zion was reborn in a day, according to Isaiah 66:8. They came speaking sixty-six languages and were forged into a nation of might and majesty by the hand of God. The survival of Israel is living proof that a righteous God sits on His throne and determines the affairs of men.

We chose a government of twelve because the number twelve is ordained by God, and this government of twelve tribes survived overwhelming trials and persecution.

We also chose the concept of the Government of Twelve because Jesus in the New Testament began with twelve disciples. When you read the Book of Revelation, you see twenty-four elders bowing around the throne of God. Twelve of them represent the Old Testament church and twelve represent the New Testament church.

In forming the Government of Twelve at Cornerstone Church, I chose the best twelve husband-and-wife teams in the church. After teaching them a core curriculum I designed, I asked each of my twelve to choose twelve additional leaders. Then I taught this second generation of twelve the same core curriculum. The process was repeated over and over again, until we had almost eight hundred teams who were ready and willing to give spiritual oversight to the members of Cornerstone Church. Previous to this, we never had more than one hundred twenty home Bible groups.

To reach the port of success we must sail, sometimes with the wind and sometimes against it—but we must sail, not drift or lie at anchor.

—OLIVER WENDELL HOLMES

The result? The church exploded into spiritual, numerical, and financial growth that was far greater than anything we had ever seen before. As I type this manuscript, our financial growth is up almost 30 percent in the worst economy since the Great Depression. Our Sunday morning attendance packs out our auditorium of five thousand seats, our prayer chapel, and the multipurpose room.

Why did this happen?

Because the leadership of Cornerstone Church refused to be satisfied with maintaining the status quo—and God blessed our endeavors. Every day we are trying for continuous improvement in every department. We accept the fact that there is a better way to do everything we're doing, and we're looking for it every day. We know that success is not maintaining the status quo.

The Toyota story

Just a few months ago, Toyota Motor Corporation announced that they were coming to San Antonio to build an $800-million manufacturing plant for pickup trucks. It was wonderful news for our city.

When the global auto maker made their announcement, Fujio Cho, Toyota's president, said, "There is an important word in the Toyota vocabulary that you'll hear a lot in coming years—*kaizen*." *Kaizen* means "continuous improvement," a process that is integral to every area of Toyota business.

The philosophy of "continuous improvement" isn't a Japanese philosophy but a Toyota corporate concept that has helped the company succeed around the world. This concept transcends culture and industries.

I was born in 1940, and as a child the memories of World War II live vividly in my mind, including the pain of Pearl Harbor and the horror of Hiroshima. After the war, the words *made in Japan* were synonymous with questionable quality in workmanship. Not now!

Today when I go to the mall to shop with my wife, I do not see the Hudsons, Studebakers, Nashes, Kaisers, and Packards—the cars I saw in parking lots as a child. Today I go to the mall and see Nissans, Toyotas, Hondas, Datsuns, Isuzus, and Lexuses.

I am well aware that America helped Japan rebuild its factories and economy following the war, but there's much more to the story than Uncle Sam's helping hand. Japan's success is far-reaching. Among the nations of the world, Japan has the lowest infant mortality rate, the lowest rate of violent crimes, the highest percentage of literacy, the longest average life span, and the highest education level among their youth. Overpopulated and with limited resources Japan comes on like David taking on Goliath. Japan has not maintained the status quo.

There is no poverty that can overcome diligence.

—JAPANESE PROVERB

By the 1980s, Toyota had become the world's third largest motor vehicle maker, behind only General Motors and Ford. How? Through the philosophy of *kaizen*, which means "continuous improvement."

Have you accepted the status quo, or are you looking for continuous improvement?

Remember, success is not maintaining the status quo.

7
SUCCESS IS NOT AVOIDING CRITICISM

How do you respond when you receive criticism from your spouse or your employer? Does criticism emotionally waste you? There are three ways to avoid criticism:

- ◆ Do nothing!
- ◆ Be nothing!
- ◆ Say nothing!

Success is not avoiding criticism, because this is impossible. Success is learning how to receive criticism without fear as you replace your defense mechanism with honesty, love, forgiveness, and a sense of humor. The trouble with most of us is that we would rather be ruined by praise than saved by criticism.

Criticism is one of God's finest shaping tools. In the hands of an expert it can transform us from self-centered individuals into people who live and act like Jesus. But most of us have failed to realize that criticism can be beneficial. We run in terror from the man or woman coming down the sidewalk with sandpaper, steel wool, and a sharp chisel.

It's difficult to understand, but God just may have sent that Pharisee to polish you until you reflect the glorious image of Christ.

I'll admit that criticism from a friend is much more difficult to receive than criticism from enemies. If your enemy criticizes you, you can shrug him off. But if criticism comes from a friend, it's going to keep on coming until the matter is settled.

There are two kinds of criticism: justified and unjustified. How do you tell the difference?

Criticism that is justified has at least a measure of truth in it. An Arab proverb states, "If one person calls you a donkey, forget it. If five people call you a donkey, buy a saddle."

Let me give you a personal illustration of justified and unjustified criticism.

When I first started preaching at the age of seventeen, my pulpit mannerisms were a mirror image of what I had observed in the Assemblies of God, the denomination in which my father served as an ordained minister for fifty-three years. I paced the platform like a caged lion. I fell into the linguistic trap of trying to sound anointed even if I wasn't.

It sounds like this: "If you-aah...want to be saved-aah...all you have to do-aah...is confess your sins-aah!"

This is not the anointing; it's a bad habit. But I didn't know that at the age of seventeen.

One day the senior pastor of a very successful church where I was preaching a two-week revival took me to lunch. After we placed our order, he asked, "Why do you constantly race from one side of the platform to the other while you're preaching?"

I was dumbfounded! I responded with a litany of names of preachers who burned up the carpet in every sermon.

The pastor was not impressed.

I was imitating what my father's denomination labeled as the finest preachers in America, I told this man.

"They are not your role model. What you have to say has so much substance you don't need the cheap theatrics. When Jesus presented the Sermon on the Mount, He sat down and preached. He didn't run like a house cat with its fur on fire. Slow down, John! The substance of your message is *the message*."

This constructive criticism instantly changed my pulpit mannerism. That day the racetrack routine died.

The secret of success is to do the common things uncommonly well.

—JOHN D. ROCKEFELLER

Now, let me give you an example of unjustified criticism. Remember, unjustified criticism is criticism that contains no truth. This is a painful story but absolutely true.

Several years ago I hired a man to work for John Hagee Ministries. This man was no stranger to me. I had attended college with him and the woman who became his wife. He was an ordained minister. I considered him a friend of forty years standing.

After he had worked for John Hagee Ministries for about a year, I noticed a distinct change in his attitude. Little did I know the seriousness of the problem.

Then I received an urgent long-distance call from the president of a Christian college, stating that this employee had made some of the most vicious remarks concerning me personally that he had ever heard pour out of another man's mouth.

"What did he say?" I asked.

"He said you were an alcoholic who was drunk most of the time. As a matter of fact, he said he prepared your sermons when he wasn't dragging you out of one bar after another."

I was stunned!

"Is that all he said?" I tried to laugh it off, but I felt a German mad coming on.

"No, he also said you sent your wife to California to get abortions when she got pregnant!"

That sent me over the edge. You can attack me all you like; I'm a big boy with a tough skin. If you attack my wife or children, I'm coming after you with all guns blazing.

I hung up the phone. (Not really—I slammed the phone down.)

I sat in my office until I could talk without shaking with rage and then drove over to our television center. I walked into this "friend's" office, slammed the door, and said, "Let's talk!" Then I repeated what had been said to me.

This employee denied every word! This man I had known for forty years lied so masterfully I wondered if the college president who called me could have been mistaken.

When two people I trust tell me something that is totally contradictory, I ask God to reveal to me who's lying. I prayed the words of James 1:5: "If a man lacks wisdom, let him ask."

Two weeks later I received a call from a television partner in another state, saying that he had talked to this same employee, who told him exactly what had been told to the college president.

Now I knew who was lying.

I asked the television partner to engage this employee in a telephone conversation and tape it. He did. The tape was mailed to me, at which point I contacted my attorney, who drafted the most Draconian cease-and-desist letter in the history of jurisprudence.

The employee was fired!

I sent him and his attorney a copy of the cease-and-desist letter, which stated in part that he "knowingly had lied, and if he, his wife, or any member of his family" ever did so again they could expect to be sued in a court of law and the letter would be used as evidence to determine their guilt.

Against the advice of his attorney, the fired employee signed the cease-and-desist letter. The lying stopped instantly!

If I took the time to tell you a fraction of the absolutely unfounded criticism (a.k.a. lies) Diana and I have endured over the years, it would fill the pages of this book and several more. I encourage every reader when you hear a rumor about your pastor or someone with a national television ministry to "try the spirits to see if they be of God!" You would have a hard time believing the number of liars and deluded psychotics who carry Bibles and call themselves Christians.

Unfortunately, unjustified criticism has plagued human beings for centuries.

One day Henry Ward Beecher, one of the greatest preachers in American history, went to the pulpit to preach. The house was packed. As the highly acclaimed orator placed his Bible on the pulpit, he found a blank sheet of paper with one word written on it: "Fool!"

Beecher's keen sense of humor seized the moment. He lifted the paper for all to see, and then his booming voice filled the church as he thundered, "Generally I receive letters from people who write the letter and forget to sign their name. This letter is uniquely different. The person has signed his name and forgotten to write the letter."

Unfortunately, many people are all too ready to criticize others. After forty-five years in the ministry, I can tell you with considerable authority that I have met some people who have a critical spirit and could make Jesus "cuss" on any given day. A person with a critical spirit is someone who has divorced hope and married despair.

Often criticism comes to you from people who are simply envious of you. You should remember that crows pick only at the best fruit. When someone says, "I hope you won't mind my telling you this," you can be sure you will.

When you are criticized unjustly, forget it!

Jesus did!

When the Pharisees accused Him of being possessed by Satan (Mark 3:22), Jesus realized He was not dealing with rational criticism. Instead of listening to their criticism, He called it what it was: blasphemy. Jesus refused to become a dumping ground for their garbage. You do the same!

But remember to listen when the criticism is justified.

My dear friend Jamie Buckingham, one of the most gifted authors of our generation, wrote several books describing the life of Kathryn Kuhlman. Jamie wrote in his book *Coping with Criticism*:

> For a number of years, until her death in 1976, I worked off and on with Kathryn Kuhlman as a writer. Although Miss Kuhlman was very sensitive to criticism, she never let it deter her from her goal. Instead, she used it to help her get there, always seeming to make the very best out of even the harshest criticism.
>
> Shortly after she went on nationwide television with her weekly program, she received a letter from a public school official in the little town of Iredell, Texas.
>
> "I love you and love your program," he wrote. "It would have been much better, however, if you didn't have to spend so much time tugging at your skirt trying to pull it down over your knees. It was really distracting. Why don't you wear a long dress instead?"
>
> Kathryn read the letter. "You know, he's right," she said to her secretary. She never wore another street-length dress on her television program. A lesser person would have responded with anger or passed it off as just another senseless remark. But she was not that sort of lesser person. She heard. She coped. She let it help her toward her goal of communicating. All of which was possible because there was no root of bitterness to give a bad taste to everything that came into her life, which presented another viewpoint.[6]

Kathryn Kuhlman took criticism that held an element of truth and used it to make her ministry even more unique than it already was. You do the same!

Dr. James G. Carr, a management psychologist, points out that a major deterrent to gaining information about ourselves lies in our own natural reluctance to discover anything about ourselves that is less than flattering. When we erect defenses against our own inadequacies, when we try to hide our faults from ourselves and others, we close the doors to a vital source of self-knowledge and therefore deny ourselves the necessity of spiritual growth.

Stop hiding from the truth. Every one of us can improve what we're doing and the way in which it's being done. Criticism may be the key that opens the door to self-discovery. *Selah*!

Success isn't any one of these seven myths. Instead let me give you a true definition of success from God's Word in the Bible.

GOD'S PORTRAIT OF SUCCESS

If you want a picture of a successful life as heaven measures it and God views it, don't look for it in the glaring lights and blaring bands on Broadway. Don't look for it in Washington, D.C., or in the United Nations. Listen, rather, for the sound of water splashing into a basin, while God incarnate, in a humility that made angels hold their breath, sponges the grime from the feet of His undeserving disciples in the upper room. "He who is greatest among you shall be your servant," Jesus said (Matt. 23:11). This is true power, and this is absolute success in life.

What do you think of when you hear the word *servant*?

Do you see someone on the social registrar between Chicken George of *Roots* and the millions of nameless migrants who flood into America from Mexico? Do you see someone who is pathetic, without will, or purpose? Someone who is bent over, crushed in spirit, and lacking in self-esteem? Someone who is weary and soiled, wearing ragged, wrinkled clothes?

Unfortunately, our false definition of the word *servant* is expressed in the sarcastic beatitude of J. B. Phillips, who wrote a paraphrase of the New Testament:

> Blessed are the pushers…for they get their way.
> Blessed are the hardboiled…for they never get hurt.
> Blessed are they who complain…they get all the attention.
> Blessed are the blasé…for they never worry about sin.
> Blessed are the slave drivers…for they get results.
> Blessed are the greedy…for they get what they want.

Contrast this with the definition of some of Christ's devoted followers. For instance, how did the apostle Paul, the man who converted the Gentile world of his age, introduce himself? "Paul, a bondservant of Jesus Christ, called to be an apostle, separated to the gospel of God" (Rom. 1:1).

How about James, the half-brother of Jesus and a leader in the church in Jerusalem? "James, a bondservant of God and of the Lord Jesus Christ" (James 1:1).

Peter, upon whom Christ built His church? "Simon Peter, a bondservant and apostle of Jesus Christ" (2 Pet. 1:1).

And John, the Revelator, who put his pen to parchment to tell the world the things that would come upon the earth. Listen to his introduction of himself: "The Revelation of Jesus Christ…to His servant John" (Rev. 1:1).

Finally, how did the Lord Jesus Christ, who sits at the right hand of God, introduce Himself? "For even the Son of Man did not come to be served, *but to serve*, and to give His life a ransom for many" (Mark 10:45).

The similarity in these introductions is obvious. And some Christians wish that they could echo this humility. Ruth Calkin, author and poet, expressed that wish in her poem "I Wonder":

> You know, Lord, how I serve you with great emotional fervor in the limelight. You know how eagerly I speak for you at the women's club. You know how I radiate when I promote a fellowship group. But how would I react, I wonder, if you pointed to a basin of water…and asked me to wash the calloused feet of a bent and wrinkled old woman…day after day…month after month…in a room where nobody saw…and nobody knew. I wonder? Do you also wonder?

I ask, "How do you introduce yourself?"

Thirty years ago it was my high honor to sit beside Corrie ten Boom at the Fleming Revell luncheon for their authors in Dallas, Texas. Corrie had just written the smash hit *The Hiding Place*, which later became a film by the Billy Graham Evangelistic Association. It was a luncheon I shall cherish for a lifetime.

I sat beside this precious saint of God, pounding her with questions concerning how the Nazis had thrown her family into the living hell of the Holocaust for the crime of hiding the Jews Hitler wanted to murder. I listened to every word and was bathed in the sweet spirit of this Dutch Holocaust survivor.

I never met anyone who had a greater love for the Jewish people or the state of Israel. With sparkling eyes and distinct Dutch accent she told me to always remember the debt of gratitude every Christian owes to the Jewish people.

They were the chosen people, the apple of God's eye, who gave us the precious Word of God. Every verse, chapter, and book were written by the seed of Abraham. Remember that the patriarchs we adore—Abraham, Isaac, and Jacob—were Jewish. What sense does it make to praise the dead Jews of the past and hate the Jews across the street?

Remember that it was the Jewish people who gave us Mary, Joseph, and Jesus. Jesus kept the feasts of Israel and will return to earth as a Jew to rule an eternal kingdom that will never end. When He comes, He will restore His church and restore Israel as the center of the universe.

Corrie ten Boom was the keynote speaker for several thousand guests who were in attendance. Finally, the master of ceremonies called everyone to attention and introduced Corrie by reading from several typed pages of accolades that were accurate and phenomenal.

When Corrie rose to walk to the lectern to speak, thousands quickly stood and filled the auditorium with thunderous and extended applause. No one who attended that luncheon will ever forget the first sentence that came out of her mouth.

"I thank you for your kind words, but I prefer to be introduced as Corrie ten Boom, a servant of Jesus Christ."

I ask again: How do you introduce yourself? Take a moment in the next few days to consider this: A man wrapped up in himself makes a very small package.

Finally, let's look at a man who proves that success can be for everyone.

THE RED McCOMBS STORY

B. J. "Red" McCombs was born October 19, 1927, in the dusty west Texas town of Spur. Red's father walked off the farm as a nineteen-year-old farm boy to become an apprentice mechanic. With a third-grade education, he slept on a dirt floor for two years and applied his bright mind to the principles of automobile mechanics. The owner of the garage gave him meals and tobacco money. Red's father became a master mechanic who worked for the Ford garage on what was at the time called *motor cars*.

When Red was a freshman in high school, his teacher told him that to master the art of public speaking he should listen to the only radio station they could get in Spur, Texas, a station that originated in Lubbock. He did so faithfully.

Red learned well and led the school's parliamentary procedure team, which supervised the Robert's Rules of Order contest. And as a member of the FFA he ran the beef cattle judging team.

Red's first entrepreneurial effort came at the age of ten when he started sacking roasted peanuts and selling them to cotton pickers. Red said, "It was a great learning experience for me. In my first few sacks I put too many peanuts in the little sacks and ended up with a milk bucket full of nickels, but all I did was break even. Then I got a second batch of sacks and put in half as many peanuts, rolling the sack up. I sold out without one customer complaint, and half the nickels in the milk bucket were mine. This was my first lesson in marketing using capital that my father was furnishing."

Red left Spur for a two-year stay at Southwestern University in Georgetown where he played tackle on the football team. From Southwestern he went to Texas University in Austin, and from there he went to law school for two years.

At the age of twenty-two, Red left Austin for Corpus Christi where he started selling cars for a dealer named George Jones. Red became an instant superstar.

"I was at the George Jones dealership for three years, and during those three years I learned immediately that the average salesman was selling ten cars a month, and I was selling a car a day—thirty per month."

Red saved his money, mortgaged his home, and moved his wife, Charlene, and their children into a two-room rented house. He laid every chip he had on the line and went for broke, starting his own used car business in 1952 at the age of twenty-five.

One year later Mr. Hemphill, Red's immediate boss at the George Jones Dealership in Corpus Christi, moved to San Antonio to start a new Ford dealership. Five years later Hemphill asked his superstar salesman from Corpus to join him in San Antonio. The new dealership was called Hemphill-McCombs, located on San Pedro Avenue.

The secret of a successful life is to be like a duck, smooth and unruffled on the top but paddling furiously underneath.

Red fondly remembers the genesis of his career. "Within eighteen months of coming to San Antonio I went from owning two used car lots in Corpus Christi with a total of five employees to having Ford dealerships in San Antonio, Houston, and Dallas with two hundred fifty employees. The collar was off and the horse was running!"

Within a few short years Red McCombs built the sixth largest automobile dealership in America, an automobile empire owned and operated by a boy from Spur, Texas, who sold peanuts to cotton pickers and whose father slept on a dirt floor as an apprentice mechanic.

Then Red's entrepreneurial instincts were drawn to professional sports. He bought the San Antonio Spurs in 1972 and owned them for five years. He then purchased the Denver Nuggets in 1980, and after six years sold them to buy the San Antonio Spurs for the second time in 1988. Five years later he sold the Spurs again.

The Minnesota Vikings came on the market, and world-famous author Tom Clancy and his investment group made an offer to buy them. After months of negotiation, Red was successful in 1998 in his quest for the Vikings, which he still owns.

In San Antonio we have a saying, "If you see Red mounted on a sway-backed mule in the Kentucky Derby, put your money on Red because he'll find a way to win."

How did a boy selling peanuts reach such staggering heights of success? He looked at adversity like a lion looks at a juicy steak. He overcame the obstacles. He leaped over every hurdle of opposition with a positive attitude and a heart that remains compassionate and generous. He and his gracious wife have given millions to universities, charities, churches, and noble causes. He walks with presidents and prime ministers but has not lost the common touch. Red McCombs is a Texas legend that will only grow as he races into the sunset of his life.[7]

People like Red McCombs prove that success is for everyone. All you need is the power to succeed. And I will give you my secrets for success in seven steps. In fact, throughout this book on success I will use the number seven. I've done this because seven has particular power in the Bible.

THE POWER OF SEVEN

I have been a scholar of the Word of God for forty-five years and have been especially attracted to the study of biblical numerology. There's a message in Bible numerology, just as there is in the written Word.

I have been particularly interested in the number seven, which is the number of perfection. Think about how this number appears throughout the Bible. There are seven days of creation in Genesis. There are seven feasts in Israel, which prophetically reveal the future. Jacob served seven years for each of his two wives. There were seven cows and seven ears of corn in Pharaoh's dream, reflecting prosperous years and years of famine.

The tabernacle, which was designed by God in every minute detail, had seven pieces of furniture that portrayed the path of redemption from the shedding of blood to the ark of the covenant in the holy of holies. Seven priests with seven trumpets circled Jericho seven times in the Book of Joshua, and the walls came tumbling down.

In the Book of Revelation there are seven churches, seven lampstands, seven stars, seven seals, seven horns, seven Spirits of God, seven angels, seven trumpets, seven crowns, seven plagues, and seven bowls of wrath.

This book is *The Seven Secrets*. Each of these seven secrets of a successful life has seven principles of application that produce forty-nine Bible truths that will release God's Year of Jubilee in your life.

I have learned each of these seven secrets of success along the way as my ministry increased throughout the years. God Himself guided and provided from the first day of my Christian walk. I pray that these forty-nine divine truths produce a prosperous harvest above and beyond your wildest dreams.

I believe success is for you.

Success is for you NOW!

CHAPTER TWO

Secret One: The Mystery and Power of Your Mind

An Empire of Unlimited Resources and Attitudes

YOU are a king or queen in a kingdom of unlimited power and potential: your mind. Your ability to achieve a life of staggering success or live a life of unspeakable squalor and disappointment depends on one single choice.

That single choice is made every hour of every day you live.

That single choice determines your joy, your peace, the quality of your marriage, your professional success, the happiness and well-being of your children, and, most importantly, the destiny of your soul.

That single choice will determine your stress factor. It will determine your ability to turn hate into love, rejection into accomplishment, and fear into triumph.

That single choice is *how you choose to react to what has been done to you in the past or is being done to you right now.* Your attitude will determine your success in life.

Dr. Viktor Frankl, a Jewish physician, endured the hell of the Holocaust by this single principle. The Nazis killed his family, placed him in a concentration camp, starved him, beat him, and cut off his hair to shame him. His name was forgotten, and in its place his arm was tattooed with the symbol for political prisoners.

When the horror of the Holocaust mercifully ended, Dr. Frankl was not seething with bitterness or a compulsive inner rage that demanded revenge. He was not broken or bowed by the Nazi hell he had just endured. When asked how he managed to endure such vicious and inhuman treatment with such a positive outlook on life, he said, "Everything can be taken from a man but one thing: the last of human freedoms, to choose one's attitude in any given set of circumstances, to choose one's own way."[1]

On September 11, 2001, Americans watched in horror as nineteen Islamic terrorists flew hijacked commercial jets into the Twin Towers as missiles of death. We watched in utter disbelief as the flames of the inferno engulfed the upper floors, and our beloved citizens of New York City leaped to their deaths to prevent being burned alive. And the horrendous attack continued as the Pentagon was hit and United Airlines Flight 93 crashed in a field in Pennsylvania. 9/11 was America's new day of infamy, the day the war on international terrorism began.

While I was in New York City, I visited ground zero. I stared in disbelief at the massive canyon where the Twin Towers formerly stood as the symbol of America's economic strength. Three thousand people died there. It is a moment in time I shall never forget.

And how did New Yorkers choose to respond to this savage and senseless act of terrorism?

A sign on one edge of ground zero boldly proclaims their response to the world. It reads, "The human spirit is not measured by the size of the act but by the size of the heart." That's the attitude terrorists will never conquer. That's the attitude God calls us to adopt.

The Bible is the road map for the mind and has much to say concerning what we allow ourselves to think. This book is not only the world's bestseller; it is also man's best purchase. In fact, the Bible is the constitution of Christian civilization. The Bible says, "Whatsoever things are true, whatsoever things are honest, whatsoever things are just, whatsoever things are pure, whatsoever things are lovely, whatsoever things are of good report…think on these things" (Phil. 4:8, KJV).

You have to make up your mind. How are you going to face the day? There are only two kinds of attitudes—good ones and bad ones.

PROFILE OF AN ATTITUDE

Let me give you my definition of an attitude in a series of four statements:

Your attitude is an inward feeling expressed by outward behavior. Your attitude is seen by all without you saying a word.

Your attitude is the advance man of your true self. The roots of your attitude are hidden, but its fruit is always visible.

Your attitude is your best friend or your worst enemy. It draws people to you or repels people from you.

Your attitude determines the quality of your relationships with your husband, your wife, your children, your employer, your friends, and God Almighty.

Unfortunately some of us choose to have bad attitudes, and some people are all too vocal about such attitudes.

One morning I checked my luggage at the airport in Washington, D.C., and saw mistletoe tied over the luggage rack. I asked the man behind the counter, "Why is that mistletoe tied to the luggage rack?"

He responded, "That's so you can kiss your luggage good-bye." That's an attitude—a bad one (although his words might be all so true).

Let me ask you: Does your face look like a reprint of the Book of Lamentations? Is someone always raining on your parade? If you inherited General Motors Corporation, do you feel that someone would outlaw cars? Is the bird that is singing outside your window a buzzard? If so, you have an attitude problem.

However, attitudes do not have to be permanent. Choose to change your attitude right now. Consider adopting these seven secrets of a good attitude.

I

YOUR ATTITUDE IS A CHOICE

You choose your attitude every morning when you get up. King David said, "This is the day the LORD has made; we will rejoice and be glad in it" (Ps. 118:24). If you woke up this morning and did not find your picture in the obituary column, get happy. Choose to have a good attitude as soon as you get up.

On one occasion I took my watch to the jeweler to be repaired. He examined my watch and asked me this question, "Reverend Hagee, when do you wind your watch?"

I thought for a moment and then responded, "There is no particular time. I just do it when the watch slows down."

The jeweler looked at me, leaned on the counter, lowered his glasses, and said, "If you'll wind your watch first thing in the morning, it will be able to withstand the shocks you put it through during the day."

I never forgot that simple sentence. The Bible says, "And those that seek me early shall find me" (Prov. 8:17). When you adjust your heart and soul early in the morning to the will of God for your life and choose His thoughts and His mind-set, your day is guaranteed to be successful.

What kind of attitude did you choose this morning? Was it, "Good morning, Lord," or, "Good Lord, it's morning"?

A positive attitude is a choice that some people make, despite their problems. Not too long ago, Barbara Walters of ABC News interviewed the movie star Christopher Reeve, who had been thrown from a horse and had become an instant paraplegic. The interview was one of the most powerful and inspirational interviews I have ever seen on secular television.

Christopher Reeve sat in a wheelchair, totally paralyzed from his neck down. The man who played Superman could not lift his hand, could not feed himself, and could not perform the simple task of breathing without the help of a machine. What was his and his family's response to his dilemma?

His wife, Dana, touched his forehead, looked into the camera, and said, "This is what you are, not your body." She was affirming that Christopher Reeve was still the man she had married. You are what you think, she was saying, not what your body is capable of doing. Her attitude was a choice.

The past is past—not present!

The best thing you can do to guarantee your success in life is to forget the past. The apostle Paul gave some of the greatest advice a mortal can accept when he said, "Forgetting those things which are behind..." (Phil. 3:13).

Have you had great success? Forget about it. Were you salesman of the year last year? Forget about it. Did you make the honor roll last semester? Forget about it! Did you win the country club golf championship last year? Forget about it! Stop looking at where you have been, and start looking at where you can be. Don't park by yesterday's accomplishments or yesterday's failures.

You must remember it is impossible to succeed without experiencing failure. A man who never failed is a man who never accomplished anything.

When Polish pianist Paderewski first chose to study piano, his teacher told him his hands were too small to master the keyboard. Yet the fire in Paderewski's belly to become a celebrated pianist drove him to overcome this limitation. He became a world-renowned pianist.

When the great Italian tenor Enrico Caruso first began to study voice, his teacher told him his voice sounded like the wind whistling through the window. Showing an attitude that conquered adversity, Caruso became one the greatest tenor singers on earth.

Jesus Christ could have written a book titled, *The Seven Secrets of Failure*. The storyboard of the chapters would read something like this:

1. Society calls My birth illegitimate.

2. I was born into a hated minority, the Jews, who experienced brutal political oppression.

3. The recognized church called Me a heretic, a drunkard, and a demonized outcast.

4. The state called Me an insurrectionist too dangerous to live.

5. One of My closest friends sold Me out to the government for thirty pieces of silver.

6. I was tried and convicted without a fair trial.

7. I am the Creator of heaven and earth, but I was treated like a criminal.

Jesus Christ experienced all these failures so that He could sit in heaven and be our advocate with the Father. He could say, "I sat where they sat, and I felt what they felt. I was once a human being who had to face adversity, rejection, and betrayal." His response to His suffering and ours? "Be of good cheer; I have overcome the world" (John 16:33).

The past is past—not present!

Unfortunately, we must admit that we spend far too much of our time fretting over what I call "spilt-milk items," the moments in life that can't be changed. Rather than giving attention to the most important assignment we have every morning—the choice of our attitude—we waste our creative energy over things that cannot be changed.

The spilt-milk items

The greatest waste of energy in America is not electricity or natural gas. It's the emotional and intellectual energy we waste fighting the inevitable situations of life. We must clearly understand: We cannot change some things in life.

> You cannot change the death of a loved one. The Bible says, "For as it is appointed for men to die once…" (Heb. 9:27). It's a fact: One out of one dies.

> You cannot change the fact that one day in your life your spouse told you, "I want a divorce."

> You cannot change the foolish choices of your grown children. Your daughter chose to marry a man who is an absolute loser. Your son chose to marry a woman who has absolutely no spiritual or emotional stability. You cannot change your grown children's choices.

When you fight the inevitable situations of life you grow bitter and resentful. You get ulcers. You become twisted, negative, and hateful. Some people actually die because of their inability to move beyond these inevitable situations.

Major F. J. Harold Kushner, an Army medical officer held by the Vietcong for over five years, cites an example of such a death. Among the prisoners in Kushner's POW camp was a tough, young Marine, twenty-four years old, who had already survived two years of living hell as a POW in relatively good health.

The reason for his endurance was that the camp commander had promised to release the young man if he cooperated. Since this had been done before with others, the Marine turned into a model POW and became the leader of the camp's thought reform group.

However, as time passed, the young Marine gradually realized that his captors had lied to him. Once the full realization took hold, he became a zombie. He refused to work and rejected all offers of food and encouragement; he simply lay down on his cot in a fetal position, sucking his thumb. In a matter of weeks he was dead.

Caught in the vise grip of lost hope, life became too much for this once-tough Marine. Once he surrendered to despair, there was nothing left for him to do but lie down and die.

Have you surrendered to despair because of your past or the inevitable situations in your life? Stop it! The greatest days of your life are before you.

The past is over. Stop living life looking in the rear-view mirror. Look forward. Press on! The best is yet to be. God never consults your past to determine your future.

God never consults your past to determine your future.

Consider Moses, the lawgiver and liberator of Israel. Moses, to whom God chose to give the Ten Commandments for the Jewish people. Moses, who wrote the first five books of the Bible. Moses, whose name is known all over the face of the earth four thousand years after he died.

Remember that this same Moses was a murderer. He was listed in Egypt as public enemy number one. He was a fugitive from justice who fled to the backside of the wilderness and lived for forty years as a shepherd, herding sheep in the blistering sun. With the chisel of adversity, God was shaping Moses' life to liberate the Jewish people.

Moses did not allow his past to determine his future. He invaded Pharaoh's majestic marble hall and shouted, "Let my people go!" The nation of Israel was born when one man refused to stop struggling to achieve his divine destiny.

Or consider King David, the young shepherd boy who killed the giant Goliath of Gath. This was the greatest military victory in Israel's history. Later David rose to the pinnacle of power and led Israel to what historians call *The Golden Era*.

But remember that David committed adultery with Bathsheba and murdered her husband in cold blood. Yet God said of David, "He's a man after my own heart" (Acts 13:22). God did not allow David's past to determine his future.

Are you paralyzed by your pitiful past? Is there a dark chapter that leaves you captivated by shame and incapable of moving forward? If God forgave and used Moses and King David, the Lord will do it for you. Get this thought in your mind and repeat it until it is etched into your brain: The past is over!

I want to teach you one of the most therapeutic phrases in human speech. I have taught it to my congregation over the years, and the results are positively miraculous. Everyone goes through adversity, rejection, and reversal. The phrase to remember in times like these is this: "Get over it!"

Have you been hurt? Get over it!

Have you been criticized? Get over it!

Have you been betrayed? Get over it!

Have you failed? Get over it!

It would be impossible to estimate the number of jobs lost, the promotions missed, the sales not made, the marriages ruined, the churches destroyed by whiny, thumb-sucking, pity-pot people without grit, focus, or fortitude.

In 1 Thessalonians 5:18 the apostle Paul wrote, "In everything give thanks." In reversal, give thanks. In heartache, give thanks. In dungeons of despair or diadems of delight, give thanks. In pain, in poverty, or in prosperity, give thanks. "Be thankful to Him, and bless His name. For the LORD is good; His mercy is everlasting" (Ps. 100:4–5).

God is greater than the criticism you are facing. He is greater than the giants you are facing. He is greater than the mountains you are climbing. He is greater than the burdens you are carrying.

Look at the Bible record of men who chose to focus on the silver lining, not the black cloud. These men did not curse the darkness; they lit a candle and the darkness vanished. They specifically chose their attitude.

At the age of eighty, Joshua and Caleb were climbing the mountain to fight the giants standing between them and the Promised Land. Together, they shouted, "Give me this mountain!"

Remember that years before they had come into the Promised Land with a committee of twelve spies, ten of whom said, "It truly flows with milk and honey…but…we are not able to go up against the people" (Num. 13:27, 31). In the Hebrew language the word *but* cancels out everything that is said prior to it in a sentence structure.

The *but* of these ten men canceled out the promises of God and made the Israelites captives of their fear. And God judged Israel by allowing every person twenty years and older to die in the wilderness because they refused to accept what God clearly said was theirs.

How many of the promises of God are you canceling out by saying, "I know that's God's will for my life, *but*…" "I realize this new job is a fantastic opportunity, *but*…" "I'm confident the person God has brought into my life is to be my spouse, but…"

I have considered preaching a sermon titled "Everybody Has a But."

Stop saying, "I could, *but*…"

Start saying, "Today I will…"

Stop hiding from success because you're afraid you'll fail. Failure is necessary. Stop fearing risk. Have faith in God, and step forward to reach for the stars.

Everything in life involves risk:

- To laugh is to risk appearing the fool.
- To weep is to risk appearing sentimental.
- To reach out for another is to risk involvement.
- To expose feeling is to risk exposing your true self.
- To place your ideas and your dreams before a crowd is to risk their rejection.
- To love is to risk not being loved in return.
- To live is to risk dying.
- To hope is to risk despair.[2]

Take a risk! Climb out on the limb where the fruit is. Stop living life hugging the tree trunk and whining because other people get the fruit. Reach for the brass ring, and stand in the winner's circle.

Your attitude is a choice.

2

YOUR ATTITUDE DETERMINES YOUR ATTAINMENTS

I have preached a sermon titled "Miracles Come in Cans," which was inspired by the words of the apostle Paul who said, "I can do all things through Christ who strengthens me" (Phil. 4:13). The person who reaches great heights is the person who has an "I can" attitude, which permits him to accomplish great attainments. Glenn Cunningham is an inspiring example.

Born on a Kansas farm and educated in a one-room school, Glenn lived a tough and difficult existence as a boy. He and his brother were responsible for keeping the school's fire going. One morning when the boys poured kerosene on live coals, the stove blew sky high. Glenn would have escaped, but his brother had been left behind. Rushing back to help, he suffered terrible burns, as did his brother. His brother died, and Glenn's leg sustained severe damage.

The story does not end here, however. Glenn had long dreamed of setting a track record. Through a period of discouragement, disappointment, and threatened meaninglessness, he somehow kept going. More than that, he made up his mind that he would walk again—and he did! That he would run again—and he did! That he would discipline himself—and he did! That he would master the mile—and he did! That he would break the international record—and he did!

Glenn Cunningham achieved worldwide fame as the "Kansas Flyer," setting world records in the mile run (4:06.8) in 1934 and 800 meters (1:49.7) in 1936. He received the coveted Sullivan Award in 1933 as the country's top amateur athlete, finished fourth in the 1932 Los Angeles Olympics at 1,500 meters, and won the silver medal in the 1936 Berlin Olympics. In 1938, when Cunningham ran his fastest mile in 4:04.4, he owned twelve of the thirty-one fastest mile times on record. Glenn Cunningham was inducted into the National Track and Field Hall of Fame in 1979.

Glenn Cunningham purposed in his heart, and his resolve had the power to transform the ugliest circumstances into the richest blessings. Glenn Cunningham had an "I can" attitude.[3]

Perhaps you're not reaching your objective in your job because you lack motivation. You've tried and failed, so you've quit trying. Have you really tried your best? On your job...in your marriage...with your education...with your children? Why don't you try one more time? This time give it all you've got. Purpose in your heart.

Your attitude determines your attainments. And that attitude is reflected by your speech.

The power of your words

The Bible says, "Death and life are in the power of the tongue" (Prov. 18:21). What you say has a strange and powerful way of becoming reality. I believe that when a person says, "I wish I were dead," he or she-invites the spirit of death to invade his or her life.

When an unhappy wife says, "My marriage is a failure," she has pronounced the doom of this relationship.

When a pregnant mother says, "I don't want this baby," she is pronouncing the termination of her pregnancy or a curse upon the life of a child yet to be born. Speech is that powerful.

Words are as common as blossoms in the springtime, yet how mighty they are to wound the spirit of a human being. The wounds of a sword will quickly heal while the wounds of the tongue will fester forever. Are you permitting your speech to destroy your future?

Stop saying "if" and start saying, "I will by God's grace." Stop saying, "It's impossible," and start saying, "For with God nothing will be impossible" (Luke 1:37).

Stop saying, "I don't know the right people," and start saying, "I know Almighty God, and through Him all things are possible."

Stop saying, "I'm not educated." Start saying the words of the apostle James: "If any of you lacks wisdom, let him ask of God" (James 1:5).

Stop saying the words, "I'm too old." Moses was eighty years old when God called him to ministry. He died at one hundred twenty and walked to his own funeral.

It's true. Your attitude determines your attainments. Compare the life of Doubting Thomas to the life of the apostle Paul. Doubting Thomas studied under Jesus' teaching for three and one-half years. Thomas saw the miracles of Jesus feeding five thousand out of a boy's sack lunch. He saw Jesus walk across the raging waters of the Sea of Galilee toward the twelve disciples, who were terrified that they were going to drown. He heard the Lord speak, "Peace be still," and immediately the waters became like glass.

Thomas heard Jesus command demon spirits to come out of the demoniac of Gederah, and Thomas saw those evil spirits enter swine, who ran down the slope into the Sea of Galilee. Thomas was there when Jesus prayed the prayer, "Lazarus, come forth," and a dead man walked out of his grave.

Doubting Thomas saw all of these miracles, and yet when Christ went through His trial, Thomas instantly doubted that Jesus was the Son of God. Even after the other disciples had seen the risen Lord, Thomas said, "Unless I see in His hands the print of the nail...I will not believe" (John 20:25).

Thomas deserved the nickname "Doubting Thomas," and he's been known by that name throughout the ages. His accomplishments were very meager because he embraced doubt instead of faith in Jesus Christ. He definitely had an attitude problem.

Compare Thomas's life to that of the apostle Paul who was born about 1 A.D. as Saul, "a Jew, born in Tarsus of Cilicia…of the stock of Israel, of the tribe of Benjamin, a Hebrew of the Hebrews" (Acts 22:3; Phil. 3:5).

Saul never met Jesus! He never had the opportunities that Doubting Thomas had to see the miracles, to hear the Sermon on the Mount, or to see the dead walk out of their graves.

In fact, at first Saul was convinced that Jesus Christ was a fraud. When Stephen preached that Jesus Christ was both Lord and Savior and had risen from the dead, Saul considered this absolute nonsense. The very idea enraged him.

Saul pursued Stephen vindictively, stirring up enmity, dissension, and jealousy, insulting Jesus as a fraud. He restrained neither his hot temper nor his biting sarcasm.

Unfortunately, Saul's Pharisees had a stronger weapon than insult. If they could twist Stephen's words to sound blasphemous, they could sentence him to death. Soon they said, "We have heard him speak blasphemous words against Moses and God" (Acts 6:11). The Pharisees dragged Stephen before the seventy-one judges of the Sanhedrin.

Two years earlier Jesus Christ had stood in this same hall before these same men. Now Stephen gave a testimony of Jesus Christ that enraged the Sanhedrin. Stephen threw caution to the wind when he saw a vision of the Son of Man standing at the right hand of God as he was speaking to the judges (Acts 7:56). The Bible records that everyone "saw his face as the face of an angel" (Acts 6:15).

The people dragged Stephen out of the city and stoned him to death. Acts 7:58 records, "And the witnesses laid down their clothes at the feet of a young man named Saul." This is the man who became Paul, the father of the New Testament church.

Later, on the road to Damascus, God blinded Saul with a bright light like the noonday sun, which caused Saul to fall from his horse.

The voice from heaven said, "Saul, Saul, why are you persecuting Me?" Saul answered that question with a question of his own: "Who are You, Lord?" And the voice from heaven responded, "I am Jesus whom you are persecuting."

Saul was led by the hand into Damascus and was three days without food, sight, or water. Then in a vision the Lord told Ananias, a devoted Jewish Christian who lived in Damascus, to "arise and go to the street called Straight, and inquire at the house of Judas for one called Saul of Tarsus" (Acts 9:11).

I believe Ananias looked toward heaven and said, "God, You've got to be kidding! You want me to go pray for the man who has murdered Your followers and imprisoned others? He's a living devil."

God's answer is recorded in Acts 9:15. "Go, for he is a chosen vessel of Mine to bear My Name before Gentiles, kings, and the children of Israel."

How many times is it true that the most difficult people you know are the people with the most potential? God often blesses you with people who irritate you to remove a weakness in your character. Remember, it's the irritating grain of sand the oyster turns into a pearl.

After Ananias prayed for Paul, Paul received his sight. He arose from that place and carried the gospel of Jesus Christ throughout the Mediterranean basin. Everywhere he went, the New Testament church was established.

Paul became the author of thirteen books in the New Testament. This man talked with angels. The people of his time bowed before him, believing he was a living god. Paul was even given a guided tour of heaven and knew he could never describe the New Jerusalem. He simply wrote, "Eye has not seen, nor ear heard, nor have entered into the heart of man the things which God has prepared for those who love Him" (1 Cor. 2:9).

To this day Paul's book to the Romans is considered a theological masterpiece, the cornerstone of Christianity. Martin Luther read this book, and one single verse—"The just shall live by faith" (Rom. 1:17)—birthed the Reformation.

All of this was accomplished by a man who never met Christ in the flesh, while another man, Doubting Thomas, who lived with Jesus, who ate with Him, who touched Him, and who prayed with Him accomplished virtually nothing. Your attitude determines your attainments.

3

YOUR ATTITUDE DETERMINES YOUR EMOTIONAL HEALTH

When we began our church in San Antonio in October of 1966, I was the pastor, the janitor, the guy who cut the grass, the youth director, the choir director. There were days I felt like ripping my phone right out of the wall.

The first winter I decided to take the youth of our church skiing in Colorado. As I walked into the beautiful ski lodge, nestled in tall trees that were covered with snow, I saw a sign on the desk of the owner that said, "The man who can make me angry can kill me."

After the owner of the ski lodge had gotten all the information he needed about our group, I asked him about the sign.

He folded his hands, looked directly at me, and said, "The story of that sign is this. My brother-in-law was one of the most successful businessmen in Colorado. He had just purchased a brand-new Cadillac and had driven it less than one mile when someone hit him, denting the front fender. My brother-in-law got out of his car screaming, ranting and raving like a madman. Suddenly he dropped dead in the middle of the street. From that day until this one, I have lived by the motto on this desk: The man who can make me angry can kill me."

Are you killing yourself?

The American Association of Psychiatry says that one in every four Americans is not emotionally well. If you get in a group of four and the other three look all right, it's you!

It is a fact: Your attitude controls your emotional health. Your attitude is an inward feeling, expressed by outward behavior.

4

YOUR ATTITUDE OVERCOMES ADVERSITY

All of us experience adversity. Life can be a grindstone, chipping away at our existence. A grinding stone makes a diamond shine with radiance, but this same stone can reduce solid rock to dust. Life can grind us down or polish us, depending upon the stuff we're made of. Are you made of the right stuff?

If what you're doing doesn't produce resistance, what you're doing is not worth doing. Consider these facts:

- Without the resistance of water, ships can't float.
- Without the resistance of air, planes can't fly.
- Without the resistance of gravity, men can't walk.

Adversity is opportunity to those who possess the attitude of the New Testament believer, which I've seen expressed by members of our congregation.

San Antonio is a military town. There are five military bases here, and we are fiercely proud of all the men and women who serve the United States in the armed forces, but the Vietnam War was an especially difficult time for our city and our nation.

I'm reminded of the time when Billy came home from Vietnam. His mother knew he had been injured, but she didn't know how badly. She went to the train depot, expecting her son to get off the train on crutches, wounded but able to be healed. She waited and waited as all the other soldiers got off. Then she finally saw her son being pushed toward her in a wheelchair. He was a quadriplegic.

She looked at him in disbelief and screamed, "My God, Billy, that war has taken everything from you!"

Billy looked directly at his mother and said with total conviction, "No, Mother! It didn't take away the joy that God has given me. I still have that joy."

Attitude overcomes adversity. Again let's consider some elementary facts:

- A rubber band is effective only when it's stretched.
- A turtle gets nowhere until it sticks its neck out.
- Kites rise against the wind, not with the wind.

Attitude overcomes adversity.

The process of struggle develops your character, your strength, and your mind.

When I was last in Israel, we went to Hebron to the house of the potter. There I saw a man making pottery just as ancient Israelis had made pottery thousands of years ago, at the time when Jeremiah wrote, "I went down to the house of the potter" (Jer. 18:3).

I watched the potter spin the wheel with his feet and use his skilled hands to shape the clay that was to become the perfect vessel. When his talented fingers felt imperfection in the clay, he would take the clay and smash it, reducing it again to nothing, extracting the imperfections.

Then he would start shaping the vessel again, and if he felt another imperfection, he would crush the clay again. *Wham!* On this particular day, the potter started over three different times. After smashing the pot the third and final time, he placed the pot in the blazing fire. Turning to us, he said, "I leave it in the fire until it's done."

I asked him, "How do you know when it's been in the fire long enough?"

He looked at me and said, "I leave it in the fire until I can pull it out, tap it on the top edge, and hear it sing."

I have never forgotten that single statement. Whenever God has crushed me to remove my imperfections, I have always remembered He gives me the chance to sing at the top of my lungs. If I don't sing in the face of adversity, He places me in the fire again. *Wham!* Yet God does not place me in the fire to torment me. He places me in the fire to perfect me. Peter wrote, "Think it not strange concerning the fiery trials you go through" (1 Pet. 4:12). Go through them singing.

In ancient Israel when the refiners were perfecting gold they would bring the metal to a boiling point. With a fine screen, they would skim off the dross, the imperfections found in the gold. Then the gold would be placed in the fire again, and the process repeated until it became fine gold. This process only stopped when the refiner could extract the gold and see his face in the gold itself.

When God can place you in the fire and pull you out and see His own glorious image in you, your fiery trial will end. But as long as you're resentful and bitter and stomp your feet in protest, God will continue to place you in the fire until the imperfections and the dross are removed. Your attitude determines how long you stay there. Your attitude can overcome your adversity.

Charles Steinmetz, the electrical genius who was one of the founding fathers of the colossal General Electric, was crippled from birth. His body was grotesque; he was a hunchback, and he was so short in stature, he looked like a dwarf.

Steinmetz's mother died before he was one year old. His father was comparatively poor, but his dad was determined that young Charles would have as thorough an education as possible. Charles couldn't run and play games as normal boys did, so he made up his mind that he would devote himself to science. He set this goal: "I will make discoveries that will help other people."

When Steinmetz immigrated to the United States, he could not speak a word of English. His face was swollen from the cold he had endured on the boat passage. His sight was defective. His clothes were shabby. The port authorities were tempted to return him to his native Switzerland.

But Charles stayed, and even found a job that paid him twelve dollars a week. There he showed amazing abilities. The infant company, General Electric, quickly realized that Charles Steinmetz was one of the greatest experts in the world in the field of electricity. His career was marked by unparalleled research and development.

When Steinmetz died in 1923, one writer said, "This deformed hunchback had the mind of an angel and the soul of a seer."[4] Though he was twisted and dwarfed in body, Charles Steinmetz was a giant in mind and spirit.

A friend of mine who lived in Schenectady, New York (the original corporate home of G.E.), for about ten years heard over and over again about Thomas Edison's brilliant protégé, Charles Steinmetz, but she never heard that he was dwarflike or crippled. His accomplishments, not his stature, outlived him. His attitude overcame adversity.

Why do we get discouraged? Because we count our blessings on our fingers and our miseries on our calculators.

Yet the storms of life are intended to make us better, not bitter. Count it all joy! No flower can bloom in paradise that is not transplanted from Gethsemane. God will look you over on Judgment Day, not for medals or degrees, but for scars.

The attitude that overcomes adversity conquers murmuring and grumbling.

The trap of murmuring and grumbling

The Bible warns against murmuring and grumbling. Consider these two verses:

> Do all things without complaining and disputing.
> —PHILIPPIANS 2:14

> Behold, the Lord comes with ten thousand of His saints, to execute judgment on all, to convict all who are ungodly among them of all their ungodly deeds....These are grumblers, complainers, walking according to their own lusts...
> —JUDE 14–16

Complainers are on God's judgment list. We murmur about our homes when three million Americans will sleep tonight in cardboard boxes. We complain about things we don't have. Yet, in the next hour, ten thousand children will starve to death around the world.

The *Chicago Tribune* carried the story of a child in the ghetto who was taken to the hospital with pneumonia. Her home had neither heat nor blankets. When the nurse brought in a glass of milk for the ten-year-old girl, she extended her bony hands toward the glass of milk and asked the nurse, "How deeply may I drink?"

"What do you mean, honey?" the nurse asked.

The ten-year-old girl responded, "In my house, no one can have one whole glass of milk by himself. Father draws a line on the glass, and we have to stop drinking there. How deeply may I drink?"

The apostle Paul wrote in Philippians 2:14, "Do all things without complaining." Our generation needs that message. It's virtually impossible to complete a day without falling into the trap of grumbling, complaining, and whining. The biblical fact is this: When Israel murmured, God sent snakes to bite them. If God did that today, most churches would look like a reptile house next Sunday.

Life is full of things that prompt us to grumble. You know it's going to be a rotten day when your car horn goes off accidentally and remains stuck as you follow a group of Hell's Angels on the freeway. Or when your boss tells you not to bother to take off your coat. Or your income tax check bounces. I've had quite a few such days.

On one occasion I was caught in a massive traffic jam at the red light on Loop 410 and Blanco Road. That light is a five-minute light. Parked right in front of me was a little old lady, staring through the windshield at the traffic light like a bird dog staring at a convoy of quail.

The light went from red to green, and she did not move. I couldn't believe it! The light went from green back to red, and we sat there another five minutes.

Now I'm grinding my teeth severely enough for molar dust to fill the car. Would you believe it? The light went from red to green, and she did not move a second time! *Surely this is the Great Tribulation John wrote about in the Book of Revelation*, I thought.

I lost it! I honked my horn. I smacked my hand against the dash. I screamed at the top of my lungs, "Drive it, lady, or park it, but not here and not now!"

At this awkward moment of emotional release I glanced to my right and saw a car full of my church members. They all waved, laughed, and said, "Hello, Pastor Hagee. See you're having a wonderful day."

Caught in the act of grumbling!

Yet, the attitude that overcomes adversity refuses to murmur or grumble or to play the blame game, which has become quite popular in the United States.

The blame game

You refuse to take responsibility for who you are and for what you've become. It's someone else's fault. Your parents failed you. Your Boy Scout leader didn't give you enough cookies when you were nine years old, and that's why you've become a psychopathic liar. The government wouldn't give you a grant for the underwater bubble blowing class you wanted to attend.

Listen up! You need to take charge of your life or someone else will. If you don't accept responsibility for yourself, there is no hope. Why? Because change is not possible until you accept responsibility for yourself. If you empower other people to control your destiny, there is no change. You cannot change them. You can only change yourself.

When we blame others, we extend the differences between us and the other people. We poison our relationships. When we blame ourselves, we multiply our guilt. When we blame God, we cut off our only source of power.

Consider these statements:

> Blame never affirms; it assaults.
> Blame never restores; it wounds.
> Blame never solves; it complicates.
> Blame never unites; it separates.
> Blame never smiles; it frowns.
> Blame never forgives; it rejects.
> Blame never builds; it destroys.

Until you develop the attitude that overcomes adversity and stop blaming yourself, your parents, your Boy Scout leader, God, and others, you will never live one happy day.

Your mind is like a computer—junk in, junk out. If you think about every offense that has ever come your way, your mind will be corrupted for life. But if you choose to "pack up your troubles in your old-kit-bag, and smile, smile, smile," hell can't beat you.

Let me urge you to take charge of your thoughts, your marriage, your future, your destiny, and your eternal soul. Let your mind feast upon the pure Word of God, which produces positive change.

Your attitude can overcome adversity.

5
YOUR ATTITUDE DETERMINES
THEIR ATTITUDE

In every relationship of life your attitude toward other people will determine how they respond to you.

For instance, your attitude determines the quality of your relationship with your children. A number of years ago I was in the M. D. Anderson Hospital in Houston, one of America's foremost cancer clinics. I was there for two days, visiting a teenage girl, a member of Cornerstone Church who had cancer.

I saw a very handsome father who was going to chemotherapy with his six-year-old son. The father was a tall, broad-shouldered man with a head full of black curly hair and a radiant smile. His tender glances at his son made it obvious that the son was the apple of his father's eye. And you could tell that the son was just as devoted to his dad. Each time they walked past me, the son firmly held the father's hand, radiating confidence that everything was going to be all right because his dad was right there with him. This beautiful boy was taking chemotherapy and had lost all his hair from chemo and radiation.

The next day as the father walked past me I noticed he was totally bald. His little boy stopped and looked at me. "My father cut his hair off so he would look like me," the child told me.

That's the attitude that makes your home like the days of heaven on earth. In every relationship your attitude toward other people will determine how they respond to you.

Are you in business for yourself? Your attitude toward your customers will determine their attitude toward you. Industrial-research has discovered the six reasons why people quit going to business establishments.

- ◆ 1 percent die.
- ◆ 3 percent move away.
- ◆ 5 percent develop other friendships.
- ◆ 9 percent leave because someone beats your price.

- ◆ 14 percent are dissatisfied with the product.
- ◆ 68 percent quit because of an attitude of indifference toward them by some employee.

Your attitude toward your customers will determine their attitude toward you.

Teddy Roosevelt, the twenty-sixth president of the United States, said, "The most important single ingredient in the formula of success is knowing how to get along with people."[5] John D. Rockefeller, one of the richest Americans, said, "The ability to deal with people is as purchasable a commodity as sugar or coffee, and I will pay more for that ability than any other under the sun."[6]

Jesus Christ said, "Whatever you want men to do to you, do also to them" (Matt. 7:12). I repeat: Your attitude toward others determines their attitude toward you.

How is your attitude toward your spouse? Your children? Your employer? Your customers? Your employees?

Years ago children used to collect Coke bottles and return them to the grocery store for money. Then there came a bottle with a strange slogan: No deposit; no return! If you put nothing in, you get nothing back!

Look at those four words! No deposit; no return.

Life is like that—your marriage, your children, your job, and your relationship with God. No deposit. No return!

Your attitude toward God will determine His attitude toward you.

What is your attitude toward Jesus Christ? I often wonder if believers today know the real Jesus Christ of Nazareth. In the twenty-first century, we have efficiently cut off the claws of the Lion of Judah, certified Him as "meek and mild," and recommended Him as a household pet for pious old ladies.

To those who knew Him, however, He in no way resembled a milquetoast personality. They knew Him as a dangerous firebrand. Yes, He was tender to the unfortunate, patient with honest inquiries, and humble before heaven, but He insulted the established church and angered the local clergy whom He called hypocrites. He terrified the Roman government. Anyone who could feed five thousand out of one sack lunch, who could heal the sick and wounded, who could raise the dead, could marshal an army of zealots who might overthrow Rome in ancient Palestine.

Jesus referred to King Herod as "that fox" (Luke 13:32). He ate with prostitutes and sinners and was looked upon as a "glutton and a winebibber, a friend of tax collectors and sinners" (Luke 7:34).

The Lord insulted indignant tradesmen and threw them and their belongings out of the temple. He showed no proper deference for wealth or social position. When confronted with theological traps, He displayed a paradoxical humor that offended serious-minded people.

What is your attitude toward Jesus Christ? Do you see Him as that pious household pet you control on a leash or as a man who could raise the dead and feed five thousand with five loaves and fishes? Your attitude toward Him will determine His attitude toward you—and your ability to believe in His help.

Let me ask you this question: If you don't go to God's house, why should He come to yours? A pastor was once asked to define faithful attendance at worship, and this was his reply: "All that I ask is that we apply the same standards of faithfulness to our church activities that we would in other areas of life." That doesn't seem too much to ask. The church, after all, is concerned about faithfulness. Consider these examples:

If your car started one out of three times, would you consider it faithful? If the paperboy skipped Mondays and Thursdays, would he be considered faithful? If you didn't show up at work two or three times a month, would your boss call you faithful? If your refrigerator quit a day now and then, would you excuse it and say, "Oh, well, it works most of the time."

If your water heater greeted you with cold water one or two mornings a week while you were in the shower, would it be faithful? If you missed a couple of mortgage payments in a year's time, would your mortgage holder say, "Oh, well, ten out of twelve isn't bad"? If you missed worship and only attended meetings often enough to show you were interested but not often enough to get involved, are you faithful?

I have often thought about having a "no excuse" Sunday at Cornerstone Church. To encourage both the faithful and unfaithful to attend church, the following notice would be placed on the church lawn:

> Cots will be placed in the vestibule for those who say, "Sunday is my only day to sleep."

> Murine eye drops will be available for those with tired eyes from watching TV too late on Saturday night.

There will be steel helmets for those who say, "The roof would cave in if I ever came to church."

Blankets will be furnished for those who think the church is too cold, and fans for those who say it is too hot.

We will have hearing aids for those who say, "The minister speaks too softly" and cotton for those who say, "The preacher's too loud."

Scorecards will be available for those who wish to list the hypocrites present.

Some relatives will be in attendance for those who like to go visiting on Sundays.

There will be TV dinners for those who can't go to church and cook dinner also.

One section of the church will be devoted to trees and grass for those who like to seek God in nature.

The church will be decorated with both Christmas poinsettias and Easter lilies for those who have never seen it without them.

What is your attitude toward church and your relationship with Jesus Christ? If you don't go to God's house, do you expect Him to remember you? The Bible warns against "forsaking the assembling of ourselves together" (Heb. 10:25).

Over forty-five years of ministry I have discovered that the people who enjoy life and their relationship with God possess an attitude of gratitude.

The power of an attitude of gratitude

An attitude of gratitude is the key to releasing the supernatural power of God. Do you need a miracle in your health, your business, your marriage, or in the lives of your children? The key is the attitude of gratitude.

Philippians 4:6 states, "Be anxious for nothing, but in everything by prayer and supplication, with thanksgiving, let your requests be made known to God." The attitude of gratitude is necessary to make other forms of prayer effective. In fact, without the attitude of gratitude God does not listen to your prayer. I encourage you to start your prayer time with thanksgiving, not a series of requests and demands.

The apostle Paul gives us an example of being thankful: "First, I thank my God through Jesus Christ for you all" (Rom. 1:8). Thankfulness comes first.

The attitude of gratitude is the key to releasing the supernatural power of God. Do you need to experience a miracle? Start by giving thanks!

The Bible tells the story of Jonah in the belly of the great fish. We might say this is the Old Testament version of *Jaws*. In the theater of your mind visualize what it's like to be in the stomach of this great fish. It stinks. It's slimy. You need not be Phi Beta Kappa in psychology to know that Jonah desperately wants out of this predicament. He has defied God's clear direction to go to Nineveh, and now he needs a major miracle.

For several verses Jonah prays and nothing happens. Then he says, "I will sacrifice to You with the voice of thanksgiving" (Jon. 2:9). At that moment, God supernaturally intervenes and brings a miracle to Jonah. The "great fish" turns toward the shore where he spits Jonah out on dry land.

Do you want-to experience God's supernatural power? Then stop complaining about your situation and start offering thanks to God for His miraculous answers.

Jesus fed five thousand with the attitude of gratitude. In John 6:11, the Bible says, "And Jesus took the loaves, and when He had given thanks He distributed them to the disciples, and the disciples to those sitting down." There was no-long bellicose, chest-pounding prayer with perfect iambic pentameter. Just simple thanks and a supernatural miracle.

Again, the power of thanks produced a supernatural miracle when Jesus raised Lazarus from the dead with the supernatural power created by the attitude of gratitude. The Bible says, "And Jesus lifted up His eyes and said, 'Father, I thank You that You have heard Me.'…Now when He had said these things, He cried with a loud voice, 'Lazarus, come forth!'" (John 11:41, 43).

Why did He call Lazarus by name? Because if He had not used Lazarus's name, every dead man on Planet Earth would have gotten out of his grave. Jesus was and is the resurrection and the life.

Lazarus walked out of his tomb. To the amazement of Mary and Martha he unwrapped his grave clothes. I can see members of the First

Church of the Frozen Chosen saying, "It's not possible that this is happening." "I don't believe this."

Do you need a miracle? Start offering the Lord a prayer of thanksgiving. He will open the windows of heaven for you. He will give you houses you didn't build, wells you didn't dig, and vineyards you didn't plant.

Begin praying like this, "Lord, I thank You for the trial I'm going through. I don't understand it, but I know You're too wise to make a mistake and too loving to be unkind."

Or, "Lord, I thank You for the business that has failed. I will not become bitter. Yet will I praise You, the glory and the lifter of my head. I know that You are leading me right now to the greatest opportunity of my life, because Your plans for me are greater than anything my mind could possibly conceive."

Or, "Lord, I thank You for that heartache. I thank You for this dark Gethsemane. I thank You for the night I prayed the night through with no hope in view. That was the night I heard Your voice, and I felt Your gentle touch. That was the night I found You to be the friend that sticks closer than a brother. That was the night You became my fortress, my high tower, my shield,-and my buckler. You alone are my God, my king, and my redeemer. I bless Your holy name."

Start praying like that, and God will move mountains to answer your prayer.

Are we so blessed that we no longer know how to be thankful? Are we so pampered and privileged we can't be grateful for the simple things God provides every day? I walk the halls of the hospital almost every day. I hear grown men gasping for breath, and I thank God that I can breathe without pain. I see people in wheelchairs, and I thank God that I can walk.

Do you take your health for granted? Then I challenge you to go to any hospital in your city today. There you will find people your age who will never leave the hospital alive, eyes that will never see another sunset, limbs that are twisted beyond medical repair, ears that cannot hear, minds that have snapped beneath the pressures of life. Then look up and say, "Thank You, God. Thank You for the blessing of health I so richly enjoy."

There was a sign on the end of the dressing room in the Jeppeson Stadium in Houston, Texas, where I dressed for every high school football game. The sign read: "I complained about having no shoes, until I met a man who had no feet."

Have you forgotten how to be thankful? Listen to this powerful, supernatural principle from the lips of King David. "Delight yourself also in the LORD, and He shall give you the desires of your heart" (Ps.-37:4).

Your attitude toward God and others determines their attitude toward you.

6

YOUR ATTITUDE IS CONTAGIOUS

Your attitude is contagious to the other members of your family, to your church, and to the business you're trying to run.

Look at the contagious attitude of the apostle Paul, who established the attitude standard for New Testament believers. Paul was stoned, beaten, and left for dead. He was shipwrecked and bitten by deadly vipers. He was criticized, slandered, and run out of town. He was imprisoned and forsaken by fellow believers.

What was his reaction? He did not stage a pity party and try to resign his post in the church. Rather, he put his pen to parchment and wrote, "In all these things we are more than conquerors" (Rom. 8:37). He encouraged Christians to "fight the good fight of faith" (1 Tim. 6:12). He said to "endure hardship as a good soldier of Jesus Christ" (2 Tim. 2:3). And he pointed them to the future: "For our light affliction, which is but for a moment, is working for us a far more exceeding and eternal weight of glory" (2 Cor. 4:17). That's the attitude that's contagious. Does this describe you?

Look around you! Analyze the conversations of people you know who lead unhappy, unfulfilled lives. They are the people who are too negative, too critical, and too argumentative. They are sarcastic and arrogant. They act like junkyard dogs from 9:00 in the morning till 5:00 in the afternoon. They have mastered the art of creative suffering. They cannot keep friends, a job, or a spouse. They are joyless toads, and I say with the apostle Paul, "From such, turn away!"

Your attitude is contagious. It breeds confidence or despair.

Consider the battle of David and Goliath. When Goliath came up against the Israelites, the forty thousand Israeli soldiers all thought, "He's so big we can never kill him." David looked at the same giant and thought, "He's so big I can't miss him." His attitude bred confidence.

Your attitude is contagious. I encourage you today to start saying aloud:

> I can do all things through Christ.
>
> —PHILIPPIANS 4:13

> All things are possible to him who believes.
>
> —MARK 9:23

> Whatever things you ask in prayer, believing, you will receive.
>
> —MATTHEW 21:22

> Why are you cast down, O my soul?...Hope in God.
>
> —PSALM 42:11

> In all these things we are more than conquerors through Him who loved us.
>
> —ROMANS 8:37

Your attitude is a choice; your attitude determines your attainments; and your attitude overcomes adversity. Your attitude toward others determines their attitude toward you. Your attitude is contagious.

7

YOUR ATTITUDE CAN OVERCOME ANY DISABILITY

During the Vietnam War, I was watching the classic Bob Hope show for soldiers abroad. As Bob Hope went through his-canned comedy routine, I watched two soldiers sitting in the front row in wheelchairs. Each man had one arm. They sat side-by-side, and when Bob Hope said something that was funny, they joined forces to clap for him. They were genuinely-happy and were not dismayed by the tragedy of being without an arm.

On November 8, 1970, there was a hard-fought game between the New Orleans Saints and the Detroit Lions. The game was nip and tuck, and it came down to the last final seconds to see who would win. The crowd gasped as they realized that the Saints were going to try a field goal of sixty-three yards. To try something that had never been done before in the history of man would certainly take a Goliath of a person. The crowd looked for a man with a size forty-five shoe and a chest as big as the back of a semi.

Instead a man ran out onto the field who had no fingers on his right hand, no toes on his right foot, and only half of his kicking foot. When Tom Dempsey kicked that ball, he set history for professional football. Tom Dempsey not only won a football game, he saw an obstacle and refused to be handicapped.

Most people wait for their circumstances to change before they decide to change their attitude. That's backward. Look at the things people quit because of circumstances. They quit jobs and business ventures. They quit the church. They quit marriages. They quit college. They're waiting for something in that relationship to change before they change. The truth is…if you'll change the way you think about your world, your world will change today.

Listen again to the words of the apostle Paul, "Whatsoever things are good, whatsoever things are true, whatsoever things are lovely, whatsoever things are of good report, think-on these things" (Phil. 4:8).

You are the absolute sovereign over a kingdom of unlimited resources—your mind. You and you alone determine your destiny by the choice of your attitudes.

CHAPTER THREE

Secret Two: The Seven Perseverance Principles

Keys to Being a Champion

O N my eighth birthday my mother, who was the guiding light of my life, began to teach me a word that would forever shape my life. That word was *perseverance*.

Her definition of *perseverance* was simple: "Those who persevere are the ones left standing when everyone else quits!" She would take her angelic hands, hold my face until her dark eyes penetrated my soul, and say, "You are my son, and quitting is unthinkable! You must learn that perseverance begins with perspiration."

I

PERSEVERANCE BEGINS WITH PERSPIRATION

On April 12, 1948, my eighth birthday, I walked into the small kitchen of our south Texas home, anxious to see what adventure this special day would bring. I sat down at the table and watched my mother fix a country breakfast of ham and eggs. Mom was a fanatic about anyone wasting time for any reason; she began speaking without stopping her work.

"Today I'm going to give you something for your birthday that will benefit you for the rest of your life!"

My imagination raced into overdrive. What could it be? A baseball bat that couldn't be broken? A new baseball glove? Not a Bible—I had two already.

This wishful odyssey echoing through the corridors of my mind ended abruptly as Mom said, "Today I'm going to teach you the priceless value of perseverance and work."

"How are you going to do that?" I responded. I knew my mother's dearest friends called her a workaholic, so I now approached her "gift" with trepidation. She often said to her four sons, "I only want you to work a half day every day, and I don't care which twelve hours you choose!" Fact is, Mother could have been a drill instructor in the Marine Corps.

As soon as I was old enough to reach the sink, she had me washing dishes. Born with a creative mind, I thought if I would drop a dish and break it, she might think the task too advanced for my pay grade. I did so! Her response? She calmly told me to sweep the glass off the floor and place it in the trash. Then she said, "When you get a job that pays money, I'll deduct the price of the dish!"

I quickly scrapped the drop-the-dish plan. Work? I started cutting the grass and ironing my school clothes when I was six. Perseverance? We used a Sears push mower for a two-acre lot of thick St. Augustine grass that would exhaust Arnold Schwarzenegger.

The difference between history's boldest accomplishments and its most staggering failures is simply the willingness to persevere.

On my eighth birthday I learned that those earlier lessons were only the beginning. "Today, I'm going to take you to Mr. Jodick's cotton farm and let you pick cotton," Mother stated.

I was delighted with that news because the job paid money. My mother didn't believe in giving an allowance to her four sons for any reason. Her version of *allowance* was "I allow you to live here; I allow you to eat here; I allow you to sleep here—now go to work!"

After breakfast I actually ran to the car for the eight-mile trip to the cotton fields. Not one to let minor details slide, I asked Mom, "How much does this job pay?"

"It pays based on your performance and perseverance!"

"I still want to know how much it pays," I asked respectfully. Mother was hardcore on smart-mouthed kids.

"It pays one dollar per hundred pounds picked—not pulled—picked! You can't pull the cotton boll; you can only pick the cotton out of the boll."

"How long does it take to pick one hundred pounds?" I asked. In the backseat I was mentally calculating the fortune I was going to make that day. Silly boy!

"That depends on how hard you work!"

We drove in silence the rest of the way to Mr. Jodick's cotton farm. When we arrived, I was as fired up as an Olympic sprinter, racing for the gold. I jumped out of the car, and Mr. Jodick handed me a sixteen-foot cotton sack. When you're eight years old, a sixteen-foot cotton sack reaches from here to eternity.

Then came the real shock.

Mr. Jodick took me to the row of cotton I was going to pick. The cotton was over my head, and each row was a thousand feet long. From my point of view that cotton row ended at the horizon. Now it began to dawn on me that I would not be as rich as Rockefeller by dark.

"How do you get to the end of this row?" I asked the deeply sun-tanned Mr. Jodick.

"Heads down; hiney up!" he answered. That's a very short Polish phrase that means, "Start working, and start sweating. Don't stop until the job is finished." Persevere! I was soon to learn that perseverance begins with perspiration.

I worked in that cotton patch until cotton season was over. I earned twenty-three dollars and became an instant scrooge. You couldn't get a dime out of my hand with a quart of 3 IN 1 oil.

I must confess that on one occasion I stole my older brother's cotton. Bill went to the weigh-in wagon for a drink of water. Bad mistake! I seized the moment by emptying his cotton sack into mine as I thought, *The Lord giveth, and the Lord taketh away!*

We had a Bible verse for everything at my house. For instance, when I went to school and played marbles "for keeps," Mother called it gambling and pronounced the decree that I could not play marbles again.

I asked, "Do you have a Bible verse for that?"

Without hesitation or blinking an eye she fired back "Yes! Marble not!"

I also confess this was the summer I discovered that water weighed eight pounds per gallon. My eight-year-old creative mind put together this fact: cotton absorbs water quickly. I tried to pour water on my cotton as often as I could so that I could accelerate my income. I got caught the first week. Any eight-year-old who carries a gallon jug of water into the fields at 8:00 A.M. and is out of water by 9:00 A.M. creates suspicion.

At the end of the cotton season my mother took me and my twenty-three-dollar fortune to JC Penney department store in a metropolis called Baytown. There I spent most of my fortune on school clothes and shoes for the coming year.

Throughout my childhood Mother's words of *persevere* and *press on* were burned into my brain. We were never permitted to quit any project once we began it. You could decide not to start, but once you started, quitting was out of the question.

I learned early on that perseverance begins with perspiration.

2

PERSEVERANCE IS SUSTAINED BY PURPOSE

In 1966, when I was twenty-six years old, I was invited to San Antonio to become the pastor of a new church without a building, without a budget, and without a songbook. It was attended by six overly optimistic adults. I had just completed my master's degree at the University of North Texas in Denton and was contemplating beginning my doctorate. You didn't need a master's degree to know that this was an *opportunity* disguised as years of hard work. I had watched my father build three different churches and knew it was a grueling process that must be fueled by divine purpose.

After a time of prayer and fasting, I agreed to become the pastor of this handful of hopeful people. For three weeks we worshiped in a home as we began to answer the basic questions of what our vision statement would be and how we would accomplish it. Obviously, we needed to build or rent a building. We discovered immediately no bank would loan us money.

Their reasoning was that I was twenty-six years of age and had no experience as a pastor. Although I had been preaching for eight years all over the nation in large evangelistic crusades, becoming a pastor was a new venture for me. Second, this was a new church without an established membership and without the financial backing of a denomination. Third, no one in that core of six people had the financial means to sign a legal document that would get us a loan from a bank for any meaningful amount.

After several months, I discovered that Joe Lee Todd, with whom I had attended Reagan High School in Houston, Texas, was the executive vice president of Security Church Finance, a national bond company that existed for the purpose of issuing bonds to churches and other businesses that met their financial criteria. I contacted him and asked Security Church Finance to issue a bond program for our new church, which we had named Trinity Church. After a few days of looking at our midyear financial statements, they graciously underwrote a bond for sixty thousand dollars.

With that sixty thousand dollars, we bought two acres of land on Nacogdoches Road and poured the foundation of the church. We were out of money, but quitting was out of the question. Some succeed because they are destined to, but most succeed because they are determined to. Our purpose was to bring God's truth to the city of San Antonio. It was perseverance time.

By perseverance the snail reached the ark.

—CHARLES H. SPURGEON

Our building plan was simple. We would take offerings each Sunday, pay the utility bills, and buy as many building materials as we could afford with what was left over. I personally organized a construction crew that I led every night of the week, Monday through Friday, for eighteen months.

We started by framing the sanctuary and education wing. Then we covered the roof with CDX plywood. We didn't have the money for shingles or for asbestos siding. Winter came, and it was the most severe winter in San Antonio for thirty years. When the congregation stood to sing "Amazing Grace" on Sunday morning, their icy breath hung in the air as if they were smoking cigars.

We eventually put composition shingles on the roof, and then came the asbestos siding. At last, we couldn't see outside, and those passing by in cars couldn't see inside. No one could lay brick, so we were forced to hire bricklayers for the exterior walls. Then I organized a sheet rock crew to sheet rock the interior of the building.

I discovered that hanging a four-foot-by-eight-foot piece of sheet rock overhead on a rolling scaffold was no easy chore. One piece at a time, one day at a time, one week at a time, one month at a time, we stayed focused to finish the building. We were driven by a divine purpose to build God's house with absolute excellence.

We taped and floated the sheet rock, carpeted the floor, and gave every dime we had to buy new pews. When the last pew was put in place and the workers went home, I turned out the lights, sat on the front pew, and cried like a baby.

I would like to tell you of the vicious attacks we endured, not from the ungodly, but from ministers of the gospel who conducted themselves like the Mafia. For the kingdom's sake, I'll let that rest until Judgment Day when all must give an account of every word by which they are "justified or condemned." As Scripture says, "There are many devices in a man's heart; nevertheless the counsel of the LORD, that shall stand" (Prov. 19:21).

It took us eighteen months to finish building that church and educational complex. On dedication day, the church was packed to the back doors, and all I would have had to do to go to heaven was take off my shoes. God is faithful!

That humble beginning thirty-seven years ago was accomplished through blood, sweat, tears, and perseverance driven by divine purpose.

Do you know your divine purpose?

If not, you will live in a state of perpetual dissatisfaction until you clearly understand God's reason for putting you on this earth.

Saul was a zealous Pharisee who ruthlessly persecuted the early church and tried to destroy it. But God's purpose for Saul's life was for him to preach the gospel of Jesus Christ to the Gentiles (Gal. 1:16).

God's purpose and Saul's passion collided on the road to Damascus. God slapped Saul from his horse, blinded him, and asked, "Saul, Saul, why persecutest thou me?" That encounter changed Paul's life forever. Saul, the Pharisee, became Paul, the founder of the New Testament church. His divine purpose had been revealed to him.

I've met many very successful people who have reached their goals, but they have no peace, no joy, no sense of accomplishment.

Why? Because life without knowing your divine purpose leads to disillusionment and emptiness.

Take time today to examine your life. If you are not controlled by the purpose of God, you are controlled by the world, the flesh, and perhaps Satan himself. Determine to find God's purpose for your life.

The assassination attempt

On December 23, 1971, five years after I became the pastor of Trinity Church, a madman invaded the church with a loaded gun during our Wednesday night Bible study. He walked up the outside aisle next to the wall, roaring like a wild animal, swearing and cursing at the top of his voice. At first people thought this was an illustration of the sermon—until the air was filled with vulgarities and they saw the gun. What happened next was a study in psychology and spiritual maturity.

Some members of the "church triumphant" dove under the seats, screaming in terror. One man who was a weightlifter and went to the gym every day began to crawl down the middle aisle on his hands and knees for the front doors in total panic. Several gray-haired grandmas stood, pointed their fingers at the shooter, and rebuked him in Jesus' name. God bless those chosen few who knew what to do and had the courage to look down a gun barrel and do it. Most of them were women.

As the invader approached the front of the church with his gun extended in his right hand, he commanded me to beg for my life. "I have come to demonstrate that the power of Satan is greater than the power of God," he screamed in demonic rage.

"The Word of God says, 'No weapon that is formed against me shall prosper,'" I responded, quoting Isaiah 54:17.

The gunman was even more infuriated by this response. "Get on your knees," he yelled, "and beg for your life, because on the count of three I'm going to kill you."

"I am in authority here, and I will not bow!" I answered. My divine purpose was to speak God's truth in this place at this time. I was not going to budge.

The shooter lied. He did not start shooting at the count of three. He actually started shooting at the count of two and emptied his gun at me from a distance of eight feet. As he fired, I did not move to the right or to the left.

After this lunatic had fired the final bullet, he ran down the outside aisle of the church. He was crushed into the wall by a university football player who sprinted across the back of the sanctuary to hit him head-on as he cleared the aisle. The gun hit the wall so forcefully the walnut handles popped off. Then several men subdued the gunman.

A man is a hero, not because he is braver than anyone else, but because he is brave for ten minutes longer.

—EMERSON

The police were called, and the shooter was taken the next day to the Rusk Hospital for the criminally insane. After ninety days, a board of psychiatrists judged him to be sane and mentally fit to resume his position in society. The day he was released, he drove home, climbed the highest tree in his backyard, and hung himself.

The day after the shooting, police came to the church and took photos of where the bullets had penetrated the wall behind me on the platform. They put up a two-by-four, eight feet tall at the spot where the shooter had stood, and with a string, measured where his six bullets had entered the wall behind me. I stood on the exact spot I had been during the shooting. Three bullets went to my left and three to my right. I was spared by the angel of God, who parried those bullets right and left. There is absolutely no way you can miss someone from a distance of eight feet with six shots. But God was in control, and His purpose for my life was still to be fulfilled.

The shooting incident was front-page news. Some people quit the church because they felt the teaching on deliverance from demons was too extreme. Some felt unsafe. Some didn't want to endure the embarrassment of telling their friends they attended the church "where the shooting at the pastor" took place. Others stayed and continued to worship on Nacogdoches Road.

The FBI and the bomb
Years later, when I was pastor of Cornerstone Church on Loop 1604, I received a call from the FBI agent in charge of the San Antonio office.

"A bomb has been sent to you by a known bomber and is very deadly," he warned me.

The FBI emphatically ordered us: "Do not open any boxes for the next several days." The television ministry operates by the mail it receives from Salt Covenant Partners in America and around the world. Suddenly, employees in our television ministry were afraid for their lives and with just cause.

The next day I came to work and saw the bomb squad with their dogs, trained to smell explosives. Fire trucks were standing by, as were several ambulances with lights flashing. There were enough police cars to form a parade, all waiting for "the bomb." Employees were ordered out of the building so the dogs could search every square inch for "the bomb." Was the bomb here, ticking, waiting to go off at any second? Needless to say, the work environment was shattered.

Five days later, a bomb blew up in the Dallas post office. Mercifully it was on a conveyor belt high off the floor and blew a large gaping hole through the roof. The FBI called my office immediately. "That bomb was intended for you," the agent said.

A few days later, the local director of the FBI, the FBI specialist on terrorism, and even the assistant attorney general of the United States came to my office. They wanted to explain in detail their legal plan to put the perpetrator in prison.

After listening to their explanation of the charges that would be brought against the bomber and when he might be tried, I interrupted to ask the question I desperately wanted to know. "Why did this man send me a bomb?"

The local FBI director stated, "This bomber sent you, the FBI, and Bill Clinton a bomb on the same day."

I laughed out loud.

They were not amazed.

"What connection did he see between me and Bill Clinton?" I asked.

At that point, the room exploded with laughter. No one could give an answer.

Then the terrorism specialist said, "I know why he sent you a bomb."

The specialist pulled a note out of his shirt pocket as he said, "I wrote the bomber's response down word for word because I knew you would want to know what drove him to do this."

The terrorism specialist read, "When I heard this man preach on television, I knew what he was saying was the absolute truth, and the only way to silence him was to kill him."

God graciously allowed the bomb to blow up in the Dallas post office on a conveyor belt, twenty feet in the air, with the bomb pointed toward the sky where absolutely no one was injured.

The apostle Paul said it well, "So we may boldly say: 'The LORD is my helper; I will not fear. What can man do to me?'" (Heb. 13:6).

Perseverance is sustained by purpose: the divine calling to speak God's truth to our struggling society. To do so we must always remember the perseverance principle.

3

THE PERSEVERANCE PRINCIPLE: IT'S ALWAYS TOO SOON TO QUIT

The most difficult year of my life and ministry was in 1975 during Cornerstone Church's first year when I slept in the garage of our church members, Harold and Jane Hild. This was not a garage apartment. My bedroom was a bare-bones garage.

I put my clothes on a one-inch pipe and hung them in the corners. I put my underclothes and socks in cardboard boxes. There was no air conditioning in the summer and no heat in the winter. I must tell you that a 125-pound Great Dane occupied those glorious quarters with me. Now, I am a dog lover, but I almost slapped that dog through the Pearly Gates one morning about 4:00 A.M. when she licked me in the face. Imagine my face dripping with slobber!

It was a year I shall never forget.

My ministry has continued because of the Perseverance Principle: It's always too soon to quit! There were many nights when I sat on the edge of my rollaway bed, looking into the abyss. The future looked dark, bleak, and harsh. If there were a moment in time when quitting looked like the intelligent thing to do, it was then.

But in the darkness I could hear the voice of my mother: "No son of mine would ever quit." And I could hear the voice of God saying, "But he who endures to the end shall be saved" (Matt. 24:13).

There are four faces of the man of God in the Book of Ezekiel: the lion, the eagle, a man, and the ox. The last face, that of the ox, speaks to us about perseverance. The ox is a plodder. He will plow from sunup until sundown without stopping. Put him in his stall, feed him, and the next day, and the next day, and the next, and the next he will plow and plod until the task is complete. God naturally endued the ox with the Perseverance Principle: It's always too soon to quit!

Perseverance is Job, attending the funeral of his ten children, losing his wealth, his health, and listening to his wife who had a tongue sharp enough to clip a hedge. Remember her encouraging words? She advised him, "Curse [God] and die!" (Job 2:9). Or the words of Job's three dear friends who accused him of sinning, who accused him of folly, who told him God was chastening him and advised him to repent. Yet despite all these dour words, Job persevered. He said, "Though God slay me, I will come forth as pure gold." I will not quit! I will endure! It's too soon to quit!

Unfortunately, our generation lives in the era of instant gratification. We want it now. Recently I passed a large sign on the highway that read, "Antiques manufactured while you wait!"

There comes a time in every life when quitting looks good. When problems seem insurmountable...when giants seem unbeatable...when mountains seem unmovable...when defeat seems inescapable...when retreat seems the only option!

Remember: It's always too soon to quit!

I wish I had a dollar for every time my mother said, "Finish what you start!" She also said, "The very worst men are those who begin and give up!"

Judas Iscariot began as a disciple of Jesus Christ, then betrayed our Lord with a kiss and hanged himself. He began well, but he gave up!

Adolf Hitler began his career in Catholic school wanting to be a priest. He began well, but then he gave in to the demons that birthed the unspeakable hell of the Holocaust.

Joseph Stalin and Karl Marx were both seminary students. They began well and gave up! Stalin murdered thirty million Russians during the birth of Communism.

The Bible does not say, "Those who begin well shall be saved." It says, "They who endure to the end shall be saved" (Matt. 24:13).

Whatever you're going through today, keep trying. Mountains only seem so high from the valley. Unfortunately, the road to success runs uphill, so don't expect to break any speed records. The thing to try when all else fails is "begin again."

By God's amazing grace, in my thirty-seven years as a pastor in San Antonio, I have been permitted to build four different complete educational sanctuary complexes. When young pastors walk through the beautiful five-thousand-seat sanctuary that sits on forty-million-dollars worth of real estate on Loop 1604, they ask the magic question, "What is the secret of this church's success?" They are looking for some secret program, some hidden mystery.

My response is simple: "Give up every idea of quitting...NOW!" It's always too soon to quit! There's a price for running faster, jumping higher, and being better than the competition. Champions force themselves to do what they don't like, to do what must be done in the heat of competition.

My dear friend Dr. W. A. Criswell, pastor of the First Baptist Church in Dallas for fifty years, told a great story of perseverance at Cornerstone Church's dedication service. An evangelist friend of Dr. Criswell's had two beautiful bird dogs in his backyard. One day a little Boston bulldog came snorting and shuffling down the alley. He crawled under the fence, and the evangelist knew there was going to be one big fight.

His first impulse was to take those bird dogs into the basement so they wouldn't hurt the little bulldog. Then he decided to let nature take its course. His two bird dogs and that little bulldog went after it! Fur flew in all directions. There were growls and yelps. The little bulldog, thoroughly beaten, squeezed under the fence and went home.

The next day at the same time, the little bulldog came strutting down the alley, head held high, snorting and pawing the ground. He crawled under the fence and went after those two bird dogs one more time. Fur flew again in all directions. Once again the little dog got the stuffing beat out of him. He squeezed under the fence and went home to lick his ugly wounds.

Would you believe it! Day after day, at the same time, that little bulldog came down the alley snorting and pawing the ground. He crawled under the fence and went to war with those two, bigger, more powerful bird dogs. He was fearless. He was persistent! He would not give up.

After two weeks those bird dogs ran into the basement whining and hiding when they heard that little bulldog snorting down the alley. The little bulldog strutted all over that backyard, head held high, the champion of the canines!

He wasn't the biggest! He wasn't the best! But he was the winner!

Why? He was just too tough to quit! He was the last one standing.

That's perseverance! Staying at it! If you reach the end of your rope, tie a knot in it and hang on!

Many of life's failures are individuals who did not realize how close they were to success when they gave up.

Everyone wants success. Most people spend countless days and years dreaming about success. People talk about it, write about it, visualize it, and go to endless seminars to hear more about it. But until you make up your mind to persevere—to endure to the end—to be the last person standing when the boxing match ends, a successful life will elude you to the last breath you breathe.

Perseverance begins with perspiration; perseverance is sustained by purpose; and perseverance means it's always too soon to quit.

4
PERSEVERANCE PRODUCES CHAMPIONS!

I've never heard a story that inspires me more than that of Wilma Rudolph, the twentieth of twenty-two children. Denis Waitley tells her story in his national bestseller *Seeds of Greatness*.

Wilma did not get what you'd call a head start in life. She was born prematurely, and doctors didn't expect her to survive. These complications resulted in her contracting double pneumonia twice and scarlet fever. A bout with polio left her left leg crooked and her foot twisted inward. The resulting leg braces always seemed like such a nuisance to Wilma. All of this made it difficult for her to compete with her brothers and sisters in the race to the dinner table.

Wilma recalls ever so many bus rides to Nashville, forty-five miles to the south, for the treatments. Once at the hospital she would always ask the doctor, sometimes three or four times during each visit, "When will I get to take these braces off and walk without them?"

Careful not to raise false hopes, he always answered, "We'll see."

On the bus trip home Wilma would visualize herself being a parent, with happy children around her. She would tell her mother of her dreams to make a special contribution in life and to go out and experience the world. Her first vivid thought as a six-year-old was, *I'm going to travel out of this small town and make my place in the world.*

Her mother, who was loving and supportive, would listen patiently and reassure her in those indelible words, "Honey, the most important thing in life is for you to believe it and keep on trying."

By age eleven Wilma began to believe that she would take those braces off some day. The doctor wasn't so sure, but he did suggest that her legs should be exercised a little, so he taught her parents and her siblings how to give Wilma's legs daily exercise.

But Wilma's idea of massage was different from the doctor's. When her parents would leave the house, one of her brothers or sisters would be stationed at the door as a "watcher." Every day she would take the braces off and painfully walk around the house for hours. If anyone would come in, the lookout would help her back on the bed and go through the motions of massaging her legs, to justify the braces being off. This continued for about a year, and, though her confidence was growing, a gnawing feeling of guilt was also growing inside her.

Wilma wondered how to tell her mother of this unauthorized, do-it-yourself rehabilitation program. The family had strong Christian roots as Southern Baptists, and being honest was a virtue Wilma had always practiced.

During her next routine visit to Nashville, Wilma decided judgment day had come. She told the doctor, "I have something I'd like to share with you." She proceeded to take the braces off and walk across the office to where he was sitting. Behind her she could feel her mother's eyes as she walked, knowing that the actions that had brought her to this miraculous moment were strictly against house rules.

"How long have you been doing this?" the doctor questioned, trying to control his surprise.

"For the past year," she said, trying not to look directly at her mother. "I...sometimes...take the braces off and walk around the house."

"Well, since you've been honest in sharing this with me," the doctor replied, "sometimes I'll let you take them off and walk around the house." "Sometimes" was the only permission she needed. She never put those braces on again.

You have to start somewhere.

As Wilma turned twelve, she discovered that girls run and jump and play, just like boys. She had been pretty much housebound, and people always had to come to visit her. Now she began to explore her new, expanded horizon, and she quickly decided that she would conquer anything that had to do with girls' athletics.

Falling down does not make you a failure, but staying down does.

One of her sisters, Yvonne, who was two years older, was trying out for the girls' basketball team. Wilma determined to try out too, thinking it would be fun to be able to play on a team with her sister. The day of tryouts she was crushed to learn that out of thirty girls, she wasn't one of the twelve finalists. She ran home, vowing that she would show them all that she was good enough.

When Wilma arrived home, she noticed the coach's car in the driveway. *Oh, no,* she thought, *he won't even let me break the news to my own parents!* She ran around to the back door and entered the house quietly. Then she pressed against the kitchen door to hear the conversation in the living room.

The coach was busy explaining what time her sister would be home from practice, how many road trips they would take, who would chaperone, and all the details parents need to know when their daughter has made the team. Her father was not a man of many words, but when he spoke, you knew it was the law.

"There's only one stipulation for my approval of Yvonne joining your team," her father said.

"Anything you want," assured the coach.

"My girls always travel in twos," her father said slowly, "and if you want Yvonne, you'll have to take Wilma along as her chaperone."

This wasn't exactly what Wilma had in mind, but this was a start.

However, Wilma soon found out that being placed on a team by your father and being selected by the coach were two entirely different things. She could feel the twelve other girls' resentment, but she also was exhilarated when she saw the new uniforms of black-and-gold satin.

There's something about your first uniform when you play Pop Warner or Little League or become a Girl Scout or join the service that creates a special feeling of identity. You belong when you put on that uniform.

Unfortunately, the team ran out of new uniforms by the time they got to Wilma, so they gave her a green and gold one from the old batch.

Never mind, she thought, as she sat on the end of the bench throughout the season. *I'll get my chance.*

One day Wilma finally got the nerve to confront her coach with her magnificent obsession. The six-foot, eighty-nine-pound straggler came into his office and found the coach just as he always seemed to be, a little gruff and very direct. "Well, what do you want?" he quickly asked.

Wilma forgot her prepared speech and just stood there, shifting her weight from one foot to the other.

"Speak up," he said gruffly. "People who have important things to say get them said! If you don't state what it is, I will never know what your problem is."

Finally Wilma blurted out, "If you will give me ten minutes of your time, and only ten minutes—every day—I will give you in return a world-class athlete."

The coach laughed uncontrollably, not certain he had heard the audacity of her words correctly.

Yet, as Wilma turned to leave, he stopped her. "Wait a minute," he said. "I'll give you the ten minutes you want, but remember I'm going to be busy with real world-class athletes, people who are getting scholarships and going off to college."

Wilma was so excited she wore her gym clothes to school every day underneath her street clothes. When the bell rang, she was the first kid in the gym so she could receive her precious gift of ten minutes of personal instruction. Right away it became obvious that most of the instruction was to be verbal, and that she was making little progress translating the words into real basketball skills. As Wilma sat crying, two boys whom she had known for a long time came up and tried to comfort her.

"I really can't understand why it's so hard for me to do what he tells me. I need help," she said softly.

"We'll go with you for the ten-minute session and then help you practice what the coach is trying to teach you," they volunteered.

The next day they began. Wilma's best girlfriend joined in so that they could play two-on-two, half-court basketball. Day after day they would listen and practice, listen and practice—mastering the game of basketball.

When Wilma and her girlfriend were selected for the team the following year, they both wondered if they could measure up to the real, competitive game. As the inseparable pair discussed their mutual dreams and fears, they decided that the only thing they could do was to *do their very best*. They agreed that if their very best were not good enough, or if they could not cope with the situation, they would be grateful for the experience and walk away from it, having gained something meaningful for the rest of their lives.

The morning after every game during the season they ran excitedly to look in the newspaper to see what had been reported about their performance the previous night. Routine news became: Wilma's friend was number one, and Wilma was number two.

Always go for the gold.

While Wilma was running up and down the courts that year, trying to outdo her girlfriend in their "Avis and Hertz" friendly competition for top billing, someone was watching her. Her high school referee at every game was unknown to her, but he was Ed Temple, the internationally known track coach of the prestigious Tigerbelles of Tennessee State in Nashville. Under his tutoring, some of the Tigerbelles had developed into the fastest women in the country.

One day Temple asked for volunteers from the basketball team, those who would be interested in trying out for a girls' track team. Wilma's reasoning was basic: *Basketball season is over, which means more time for chores at home. Why not volunteer for the track team?*

The first time Wilma ran a race, she found she could beat her girlfriend. Then she beat all the other girls in her high school, and then every high school girl in the state of Tennessee. She and her friend decided to call a truce and settled their longstanding, competitive feud by means of plea-bargaining. She would be No. 1 in track, and her girlfriend would be No. 1 in basketball.

At fourteen, as a high school student, Wilma joined the Tigerbelles' track team and went into serious training at Tennessee State University after school and on weekends. On the campus she met a lovely woman named Mae Faggs, who already had made two U.S. Olympic teams in the past. Mae was the only person, outside of Wilma's immediate family, with whom the teenager would share her dream. She also shared her frustrations of the early years, her ordeal with leg braces, and how it felt having no opportunity to belong. The encouraging, nurturing, and training continued, and so did her victories. By the end of the first summer, Wilma had won the 75- and 100-yard dash and was on the winning 440-yard relay team in the junior division at the national AAU meet in Philadelphia.

One day, nearly two years later, Mae Faggs came up to her and said to her protégée, "Would you like to make our Olympic team?"

Wilma's answer was typical of her youth and reflected the fantasies of her many bus rides back and forth to Nashville: "Do we get to travel?"

"Yes, of course," Mae answered. "The 1956 Olympic Games are going to be in Australia."

"When do we leave?" Wilma implored.

Not immediately, since they first had to qualify for the team at the Olympic trials at American University in Washington, D.C. During the 200-meter dash qualifying heats, Wilma started out leading the pack. Finding herself out in front, ahead of Mae Faggs, she looked around to see where her friend was.

Mae sped by and came in first. Wilma came in second.

"I'm disappointed in you," Mae scolded after the meet. "Qualifying isn't enough; you've got to always go for that gold."

Wilma was eliminated in the semifinals of the 200-meter dash at the 1956 Olympic Games in Melbourne, but went on to win a bronze medal as a member of the team of the women's 400-meter relay team. During the remainder of her stay in Australia, she was part happy, part heartbroken. This kind of a performance wouldn't happen again, she told herself; next time, she would get it right. Wilma was only sixteen, still in high school, and already committing herself to win in 1960!

Back home she resisted any temptation to take advantage of her new celebrity status. Wilma could have thumbed her nose at the neighborhood kids who had been so cruel to her when she had been an invalid in those metal braces. Instead, she let them look at the bronze medal and talked with them about the thrill it had been to win it. Her former tormentors now were her friends; they relished the world-class feeling that comes only once in a lifetime for a little town like Clarksville, Tennessee.

Failure is the path of least persistence.

When we speak of dedication and persistence, there is a tendency to remember only the highlights and gloss over the agonizing realities of what it takes to be world-class. It's important to remember that there were no athletic scholarships for women in those days, and that Wilma was paying her way as she attended Tennessee State University.

At the same time, track workouts were going on every day. What's more, it was mandatory for each young woman to maintain a *B* average or better and carry eighteen units in order to remain a member of the Tigerbelles track club.

To give herself the "winner's edge," Wilma resorted to a type of extracurricular, do-it-yourself program, similar to what she had used years earlier when she was learning to walk without leg braces. When she realized that she was slipping behind the other girls on the team because of her work and study load, she began sneaking down the dormitory fire escape to run on the track from 8:00 to 10:00 P.M. Then she would climb back up the fire escape and into bed in time for "lights out" and "bed check."

At sunrise, the grueling training schedule resumed. Every morning she would run at six and ten A.M., and in the afternoon again at 3 P.M. Week after week, year after year, she maintained the same monotonous, demanding schedule. And this went on for over twelve hundred days!

A living legend

When Wilma walked out on the stadium field for the 1960 summer Olympics in Rome, she was ready. The nearly eighty thousand fans began to cheer wildly, sensing that she was to be one of those special Olympians who captured the hearts of the spectators of the world throughout history (as Jesse Owens and Babe Didrikson did before her, and as Olga Korbut and Bruce Jenner would after her). As she began to warm up for the first event, the cadenced chant began to well up from the stands: "Vilma, Vilma, Vilma." There was never a doubt in her mind, or in theirs: Wilma would be standing on the top platform for the award presentations of that event.

Wilma Rudolph turned in three electrifying performances by breezing to easy victories in the 100-meter and 200-meter dashes and anchoring the U.S. women's team to a first-place finish in the 400-meter relay. Three gold medals—the first woman in history ever to win three gold medals in track and field! And each of the three races was won in world record time.

Wilma had been a little crippled girl who rode the bus to Nashville—isolated from her neighborhood but supported by her parents, family, and a few loyal friends. Now she was Wilma Rudolph, a living legend.[1]

Wilma Rudolph was a portrait of perseverance for the world to admire. Her perseverance produced a champion.

5

PERSEVERANCE IS THE KEY TO PERFECTION

If you're tempted to think that some human beings are so gifted and so intelligent that they only have to extend a little energy to achieve excellence, consider the roll call of masters in the box below, and then walk with me through the life of another master: Thomas Edison.

A ROLL CALL OF MASTERS

Plato wrote the first sentence of his famous *Republic* nine different ways before he was satisfied. Cicero practiced speaking before friends every day for thirty years to perfect his elocution. Noah Webster labored thirty-six years writing his dictionary, crossing the Atlantic twice to gather material.

Milton rose at four in the morning every day in order to have enough hours for his *Paradise Lost*. Sir Walter Scott put in fifteen hours a day at his desk, rising at four in the morning. He averaged writing a book every two months and turned out the Waverly novels at one a month. Virgil spent seven years on his *Georgics* and twelve on the *Aeneid*. Nevertheless, he was so displeased with the latter that he tried to rise from his deathbed to throw the manuscript into the flames.

Beethoven is unsurpassed in his painstaking fidelity to his music. Hardly a bar of his was not written and rewritten at least a dozen times. Michelangelo's *Last Judgment*, one of the twelve master paintings of the ages, was the product of eight years' unremitting toil. Over two thousand studies of it were found among his papers. Whenever Michelangelo, that "divine madman," as Richardson once wrote on the back of one of his drawings, was meditating on some great design, he closed himself up from the world.

"Why do you lead such a solitary life?" asked a friend. "Art," replied the sublime artist, "is a jealous god; it requires the whole and entire man." During his mighty labor in the Sistine Chapel he refused to have any communication with any person, even at his own house.

Consider the perseverance of the honeybee. The bee has been aptly described as "busy." To produce one pound of honey, the bee must visit fifty-six thousand clover heads. Since each head has sixty flower tubes, a total of 3.36 million visits are necessary to give us that pound of honey for the breakfast table. Meanwhile, that worker bee has flown the equivalent of three times around the world.

To produce one tablespoon of honey for our toast, the little bee makes forty-two hundred trips to flowers. He makes about ten trips a day to the fields, taking twenty minutes average for each trip and visiting four hundred flowers. A worker bee will fly as far as eight miles if he cannot find a nectar flow that is nearer.

Therefore, when you feel that persistence is a difficult task, think of the bee and think of Thomas Edison.

Edison did not give up when his first efforts to find an effective filament for the carbon incandescent lamp failed. He did countless experiments with countless kinds of materials. As each failed, he would toss it out the window. The pile reached to the second story of his house. Then he sent men to China, Japan, South America, Asia, Jamaica, Ceylon, and Burma in search of fibers and grasses to be tested in his laboratory.

One weary day on October 21, 1879, after thirteen months of repeated failures, Thomas Edison succeeded in his search for a filament that would stand the stress of electric current. This was how it happened:

Casually picking up a bit of lampblack, he mixed it with tar and rolled it into a thin thread. Suddenly the thought struck him, why not try a carbonized cotton fiber? For five hours he worked on the first filament, but it broke before he could remove the mold. Edison used two spools of thread in similar fruitless efforts. At last a perfect strand emerged, only to be ruined when he tried to place it inside a glass tube. Still Edison refused to admit defeat. He continued without sleep for two more days and nights. Eventually, he managed to insert one of the crude carbonized threads into a vacuum-sealed bulb. "When we turned on the current," he said, "the sight we had so long desired to see finally met our eyes."[3]

Edison's persistence amidst such discouraging odds has given the world the perfection of the electric light! But Edison didn't do this by pure genius; he accomplished it by perseverance, the key to perfection.

Throughout history, great men have known that perseverance is the key to excellence. Have you failed? In your marriage? In your business? In your education? God is the God of second chance. Try again! Don't give an alibi; give another try.

6

PERSEVERANCE IS A PART OF THE CHRISTIAN LIFE

The Bible is a book of perseverance. The portrait of perseverance is seen as Noah works to build the ark for one hundred twenty years with all of humanity laughing at him. His generation had never seen rain. They lived hundreds of miles from water. Noah's bulldog perseverance finished the boat designed by the Architect of the Ages.

Perseverance put the animals on the boat. Perseverance put Noah's wife and children on the boat with blue skies and 72-degree weather. Perseverance is a fire in your bones that will carry you through ridicule, rejection, and reversal.

Perseverance does not need public approval.

Perseverance couldn't care less about being politically correct.

Perseverance says:

◆ In faith, "Mountain, get out of my way!"
◆ "Nothing is impossible to them that believe" (Matt. 17:20).

- ◆ "If God be for you, who can be against you" (Rom. 8:31).
- ◆ "The victory is ours through Christ the Lord" (1 Cor. 15:57).
- ◆ "Faith is the victory that overcomes the world" (1 John 5:4).

There is nothing halfhearted or lukewarm about perseverance. It's bold. It's daring. It's fearless.

Perseverance is Nehemiah rebuilding the walls of Jerusalem when powerful men organized a slander campaign to stop the building project. When slander could not stop him, these men ridiculed him. Finally, when slander and ridicule could not stop Nehemiah, they threatened to kill him.

Nehemiah passed out swords to half his men and bricks to the other half. He made it clear he was ready to fight to the death. The wall was rebuilt to the glory of God through the power of perseverance.

The apostle Paul taught the power of perseverance as he lived his life.

- ◆ After being beaten three times with a Roman cat-of-nine-tails, leaving his back a disfigured mass of scars…
- ◆ After being shipwrecked…
- ◆ After being stoned and left for dead, face down in the dirt, a bloody pulp more dead than alive…
- ◆ After being betrayed by his dearest friends…
- ◆ After living in the hell of relentless scandal…
- ◆ After appearing before the church bound in chains…
- ◆ After walking into one prison after another…
- ◆ Paul put his pen to parchment and wrote: "We are hard pressed on every side, yet not crushed; we are perplexed, but not in despair; persecuted, but not forsaken; struck down, but not destroyed!" (2 Cor. 4:8–9).

The HIT (Hagee International Translation) of 2 Corinthians 4:8–9 reads:

> Hell has thrown the kitchen sink at me, and I'm still fighting the good fight. I'm still enduring! I'm still standing! I will not bend, bow, or burn! I will not look back, let up, slow down, back away, or be quiet. My past is forgiven; my present is redeemed; my future is secure. I no longer need position, prominence, or popularity. I don't have to be right, recognized, regarded, or rewarded.
>
> I now live by faith and walk in divine anointing. My face is set; my gait is fast; my goal is heaven; my road is narrow; my way may be rough and my companions few.

I cannot be bought, compromised, detoured, lured away, turned back, deluded, or delayed. I will not flinch in the face of sacrifice or hesitate in the presence of the adversary. The devil's mad, and I'm glad!

The night before Paul's head was chopped off, this apostle of perseverance again put his pen to parchment in the dim glow of the candle and wrote, "I have fought the good fight. I have finished the race, I have kept the faith. Finally, there is laid up for me the crown of righteousness…and not to me only but also to all who have loved His appearing" (2 Tim. 4:7–8).

Think about that promise. It's available to all of us who persevere. A crown of righteousness.

Have you been knocked down?
Have you been betrayed by a dear friend?
Have you experienced the death of a loved one?
Are you fighting a deadly disease?
Are you in a financial crisis?
Has tragedy struck like lightening out of a clear blue sky?
Get up! Get up! Get up NOW!

The picture of Jacob wrestling with the angel until daybreak shows the power of perseverance in producing spiritual success. Jacob said, "I will not let You go unless You bless me!" (Gen. 32:26).

The angel renamed him "Prince of God" for his effort. The difference between being a "Prince of God" and a common drifter is perseverance!

Solomon in all of his wisdom wrote, "The righteous are bold as a lion" (Prov. 28:1). Jesus Christ, the Son of God, is referred to as "the Lion of the tribe of Judah" (Rev. 5:5). God's people are bold, fearless fighters. We are not on earth to compromise with evil; we are here to conquer evil. The church is not a retirement center for religious fat cats. It's the recruiting center for the victorious army of the living God!

Calvary wasn't a picnic ground; it was ground zero in the universal war zone! It was heaven's high water mark for perseverance! Scripture suggests that we take Jesus' example as we live our daily lives: "Looking unto Jesus, the author and finisher of our faith, who for the joy that was set before him endured the cross" (Heb. 12:2).

How can you tell who is a follower of Christ? Not by the person's speech. People talk the talk but don't walk the walk. They profess Christ but do not possess Christ. If the glowing reports on the fly pages of Christian books were all true, the devil would be in a psycho-ward in hell drinking Maalox, waving a white flag, and sobbing, "Please don't hurt me!"

Perseverance is a part of the Christian life.

7

PERSEVERANCE IS A DECISION

Perseverance produces overcomers! Do you want to be recognized in heaven as an overcomer? Before you answer that question, think about what the Book of Revelation prophesies about overcomers: "He who overcomes shall be clothed in white garments, and I will not blot out his name from the Book of Life, but I will confess his name before My Father and before His angels!" (Rev. 3:5).

And that's not all. The same chapter goes on to say, "He who overcomes, I will make him a pillar in the temple of My God…and I will write on him My new name" (Rev. 3:12).

And that's still not a complete picture of an overcomer. God further promises, "To him who overcomes I will grant to sit with Me on My throne" (Rev. 3:21). Can you imagine a position better than that! Personally I want to be an overcomer, don't you?

An overcomer makes a definite decision, just as Jesus did in the Garden of Gethsemane. He knew all too well the torture that lay ahead. And He naturally began by praying, "Father, if it is Your will, take this cup away from Me." But the Lord did not stop there. He added, "Not My will, but Yours, be done" (Luke 22:42).

Perseverance is Jesus hanging on the cross, bleeding from His hands, His head, His side, His feet. Below boiling skies, blacker than a thousand midnights, our Lord lifts His blood-caked face toward heaven and shouts, "It is finished!"

> What is finished?
> The plan of redemption that began in Genesis 3 is finished!
> Death, hell, and the grave are finished.
> Disease and sickness—finished!
> The guilt of the past—finished!
> The fear of the future—finished!
> The power of poverty to crush your dreams—finished!

The Light of the World has crushed the prince of darkness. Satan is finished. He is defeated and Christ is Lord—and of His kingdom there shall be no end.

Perseverance is a decision! It's a decision that every winner makes, including the gold medalist at the Olympics. What magnificent bodies the runners have. They are the picture of power and strength. The marathon begins, and all run well at first. Then some begin to sweat. After several miles, exhaustion sets in. One gets weary and drops out. Another trips. Another faints. Another gasps for air and drops out.

Who is the winner? The one who endures to the end. The overcomer is the one who receives the crown.

All great living begins when you look into your soul and decide you will not play the role of a coward. You make a definite decision. You will endure. You will persevere—period!

People who have perseverance "do it anyway!" I challenge you to live by these Paradoxical Commandments by Kent Keith.[4]

> You will find that people are unreasonable, illogical, and self-centered, yet you love them anyway!
>
> If you do good, you will be accused of selfish motives. Do good anyway!
>
> Success will win you false friends and true enemies. Succeed anyway!
>
> The good you do today will be forgotten tomorrow. Do good anyway!
>
> The biggest people with the biggest ideas can be shot down by mental midgets with the smallest ideas. Think big anyway!
>
> What you spend years building may be destroyed overnight! Build anyway!
>
> People need help but may attack you for offering your hand. Help them anyway!
>
> Giving the world the best you have may get you kicked in the teeth. Give the world your best anyway!
>
> Be persistent! Never...never...never give up! It's too soon to quit!

CHAPTER FOUR

Secret Three: Your Vision of Yourself and Others

Essentials to True Self-Esteem

THE third secret of the seven secrets of successful living is the secret of true self-esteem. Jesus revealed this secret in Matthew 19:19 when He said, "You shall love your neighbor as yourself."

Notice that this scriptural truth has two parts: Love your neighbor; love yourself. The fact is this: If you do not like yourself, you will not like your neighbor. Realizing your goals and dreams—success—begins with self-esteem. I challenge you to rid yourself of doubts and build self-confidence and a new sense of self-worth. Learn that loving your neighbor and yourself is the secret of happiness in life, in love, and in everything you do.

No matter what has happened in your life, you are not "a complete failure." You are not "a total washout." You are not what other people may say you are. You are what you and God determine you can be.

Begin today to see yourself as God sees you. When that happens, you will be poised instead of timid, enthusiastic instead of bored, successful instead of failing, energetic instead of fatigued, agreeable instead of cantankerous, positive instead of negative, self-forgiving instead of self-condemning, and self-respecting instead of self-disgusting.

Since true self-esteem involves loving both yourself and your neighbor, we will examine love, both from a secular and biblical perspective. Let's begin by looking at love from the world's perspective.

WHAT LOVE IS NOT

1. Love is not emotion.

I have heard young lovers say, "When I get around my girlfriend, I can't breathe."

My response: "It's not love. It's asthma!"

I have heard others say, "When I get around Suzie, I can't see straight."

My response: "It's not love. You need glasses. See an optometrist."

And many other myths about love are just as untrue. For instance, if love is blind, why are so many men attracted to the same beautiful woman? Love is not blind. And love is not what you feel. Love is what you do. Works, not words, are proof of your love.

We are all angels with one wing;
we need each other to fly.

Jesus Christ didn't say, "When I was hungry, you felt sorry for Me. When I was naked, you felt shame for Me. When I was in prison, you were embarrassed for Me. When I was sick, you were sympathetic toward Me."

No, He said nothing of the kind. However, He did reprimand the Jewish people and all of us when He said, "For I was hungry and you gave Me no food; I was thirsty and you gave Me no drink; I was a stranger and you did not take Me in, naked and you did not clothe Me, sick and in prison and you did not visit Me" (Matt. 25:42–43).

The message is very clear. Love is not what you feel. Love is what you do.

2. Love is not sex.

Love is not a hormonal response to a plunging neckline or a short skirt. Love is not "the urge to merge."

There is free love and covenant love, and the youth of the twenty-first century had better learn the difference. Free love takes, while covenant love gives. Free love takes all you can give of your emotions, your time, and your material goods, while covenant love gives you commitment, respect, and support, both emotional and material.

Free love will give you AIDS and an eternal home in the lake of fire. Covenant love gives you a ring and makes your life as the days of heaven on earth.

Contrast these secular myths about love with God's description in the Bible.

What Love Is

Our lives are shaped by the people who love us and by the people who refuse to love us. Every baby reaching out for his or her mother is the portrait of love. Every poet who has dipped his pen in ink has struggled to paint a portrait of love for his generation. Every marriage is an effort to find love. (If a man says marriage hasn't changed him, he is not out of the church yet.)

The apostle Paul dipped his pen in ink and gave the world the ultimate portrait of love. Nothing in literature matches his magnificent description of love—not Shakespeare, not Byron, not Shelley, not Keats, not even Browning with his, "How do I love thee? Let me count the ways."

Love does not keep a ledger of sins and failures of others. Love forgives unconditionally and totally.

In 1 Corinthians 13 the apostle Paul wrote, "Without love I am nothing." The apostle John added to this definition of love when he observed, "We know that we have passed from death to life, because we love the brethren. He who does not love his brother abides in death" (1 John 3:14).

If love is lacking in your life, John said, "You remain in death." You are not a son or daughter of God, no matter what spiritual experience you claim or the number of churches to which you belong. The Bible says, "He who does not love does not know God, for God is love" (1 John 4:8).

Love, in fact, is the signature of the Christian. Jesus said, "By this all will know that you are My disciples, if you have love for one another" (John 13:35). He also commanded His followers, "Love one another; as I have loved you" (John 13:34).

Think about the almost impossible challenge in that statement. "Love one another as I have loved you." How did Christ love us? Unconditionally. Yet we love others because they first loved us. We love others because they come up to our expectations. We love others because they are made of the right stuff and live in the same neighborhood we live in. We love others because they are physically attractive. Girls say, "He's a hunk." Boys say, "She's a fox."

Yet Christianity without love is just another cult. The world does not care what we know until they know that we care. Love does not keep a ledger of past situations and failures. Again Paul thundered, "Without love you are nothing." Of no account—human junk.

True love doesn't have a happy ending; true love doesn't have an ending.

Junk is something that no longer makes any contribution to anything, which reminds me of a car I bought when I was in the ninth grade. When I was twelve years of age, my father made this deal with me: "When you are able to buy a car for cash and pay for the first year's insurance, you can buy a car."

In the ninth grade, in 1954, I bought my first car, which was a 1948 four-door Pontiac sedan with a straight eight engine that was as long as the *Queen Mary*. This beautiful car had a white pearl steering wheel and a sun visor. When I sat down in the deep seat, you could only see the top half of my head over the edge of the windowsill.

I drove that Pontiac through high school and to Bible college. It had four "may-pop" tires, which meant they may pop at any time. It burned so much oil, it looked like a brush fire coming down the road with a bumper on both sides. One time when I was in Bible college I went to the junkyard to buy a used tire. I saw piles and piles of rusted cars, refrigerators, sofas and other furniture, rows of car doors, hubcaps mounted on the wall, and piles of ugly used tires. The discarded items seemed to cover the entire landscape. I said to the junk dealer, "You have a lot of junk here."

The junk dealer looked at me with piercing eyes and said, "Young man, this is not junk. Junk has absolutely no value. What you are looking at here is a field of dreams. This is several acres of potential looking for a place for expression. You are here looking for a used tire because it has value. Therefore, you are looking at unlimited possibilities out there. Potential is everywhere you look." If he hadn't been so serious I would have fallen on the ground laughing. He had to be the Norman Vincent Peale of the junk world.

Are you junk or are you a person who has unlimited possibilities with great potential? Before you answer that question, remember the words of the apostle Paul, "Without love you are nothing." Without love you have no value. You are junk. You can make no contribution to another person.

In his portrait of love Paul went on to say, "Though I speak with the tongues of men and angels and have not love, I am nothing." I have studied Latin, Greek, Hebrew, Spanish, and English, and have mastered none of them. But what if I were eloquent in every language on the earth? What if I knew every dialect? I would have the tendency to say, "I am something!" But God looks from heaven and says through the apostle Paul, "Without love you are nothing."

Then Paul added another asset to his list: "Though I speak with prophecy and have not love, I am nothing." What if I knew the future? What if I could predict tomorrow with 100 percent accuracy? What if I knew what the stock market was going to do tomorrow so I could invest wisely today? What if I knew where the next earthquake was going to be? What if I knew where the next tornado would strike in tornado alley in the United States? What if I knew what was going to happen in the Middle East?

I know what would happen, don't you? Presidents and prime ministers, bank executives and brokerage firm partners, heads of the national weather service and television weather broadcasters would be calling me every morning. Federal Reserve Board chairman Alan Greenspan would want to move into the house next door. Every magazine and newspaper in the world would be covering every word I ever said about financial markets. I would certainly have the tendency to say, "I am something." But Paul said, "Without love, you are nothing, Hagee."

In his definition of love Paul enumerated many accomplishments that are nothing if we have not love, yet he was not finished painting his complete picture of love. He went on to say, "If I understand all mysteries and have not love, I am nothing."

Recently I stood by the bedside of a beautiful child dying with cancer. As I held her limp, emaciated hand I prayed, "Dear God, let us solve the mystery of cancer."

Brilliant scientists are working day and night all over the earth trying to solve this single mystery. Governments and humanitarian foundations are spending billions to find the elusive answer. But what if I could call the American Cancer Society and say, "I've solved the mystery of cancer?"

I would certainly win the Nobel Prize for medicine. My picture would be on the cover of every newsmagazine in the world. I would be front-page news on every newspaper. Television reporters would be stacked in my front yard like cordwood, screaming for an interview. In this climate of universal adoration, I would be prone to say, "I am something."

But God says, "Without love, even if you solved all the mysteries on the earth, you are nothing."

And Paul continued, "If I have all knowledge, without love I am nothing" (1 Cor. 13:2).

It has been my privilege to graduate from two very different universities and observe internationally recognized scholars who have dedicated their entire lives exclusively to one field of knowledge. In many instances, some have dedicated their lives to one specific division of one field of knowledge. After years of intense scholarship, they are still learning about that one element of knowledge, trying to make a positive contribution to humanity.

But what if I had all knowledge in every field, knowledge so vast that I knew more about chemistry than legendary scientist Linus Pauling, more about mathematics and the theory of relativity than Albert Einstein, more about international relations than Henry Kissinger? If I knew all that, you can be sure I would have the tendency to gloat and say, "I am something!"

God Almighty, who has all knowledge in heaven and earth, answers from heaven, "Without love, even though you have all knowledge, Hagee, you are nothing."

Paul built on his portrait of love by saying, "And though I have all faith so that I can remove mountains and have not love, I am nothing" (1 Cor. 13:2).

The world has seen a handful of people with faith so powerful they could pray for the dead, and the dead returned to life. Jesus Christ of Nazareth did this. Smith Wigglesworth of England did this. It would be a natural thing for a person who had such great faith to say, "I am something!"

But God responds this way: "If you raise people from the dead or if you have a miracle ministry that packs stadiums and every disease on the planet disappears in your presence, without the love of God, you are nothing."

Paul concluded this first part of 1 Corinthians 13, which deals with us as human beings in this secular world, in this way: "And though I bestow all my goods to feed the poor...but have not love, it profits me nothing" (1 Cor. 13:3).

This will be a better world when the power of love replaces the love of power.

The rich young ruler came to Jesus and said, "Good master, what must I do to gain eternal life?" Jesus responded, "Go and sell all you have and give it to the poor" (Matt. 19:16, 21). The biblical text paints the portrait of a man who walked away with shoulders stooped and head drooping because he was so exceedingly sorrowful. Why? Because he loved his possessions—the here-and-now success of this world—so much he was willing to compromise his eternal life.

Most people are willing to give some of their possessions to the church, but Jesus asked this man to give everything he had. Think about that. Most people who attend America's churches refuse to tithe when God clearly states all who do not "live under a financial curse" (Mal. 3:9). But Paul said if you give all that you have on this earth to feed the poor while the television cameras are rolling to record your great act of charity, "Without the love of God, you are nothing."

The apostle Paul gave fourteen definitions of love in 1 Corinthians 13. The first seven deal with you, and the last seven deal with your relationship with other people.

Let's look at the seven secrets of true love.

I

LOVE IS PATIENT

Patient love endures. Patient love never gets tired of waiting. Patient love doesn't give up on an alcoholic son or a drug-addicted daughter. Patient love endures a loveless marriage. Patient love locks its jaw and hangs on with undying hope for a better tomorrow.

The portrait of patient love is burned into my brain. It's the portrait of my mother holding my brother who was stricken with grand mal epileptic seizures.

My family has historically lived in divine health. (My mother is, of this writing, ninety years of age and in perfect health. Her vigor and stamina are supernatural. She has a mind as sharp as a razor and as strong as a steel trap.) Therefore, it was an absolute shock to my father and mother when the school nurse called her in the fall of 1948 saying their son, my brother Bill, had collapsed at school.

She and Dad went to the junior high school to take Bill to the doctor as quickly as possible. When we received the news he had epilepsy and had experienced a grand mal seizure, we were stunned. Bill was academically gifted, his vocal ability as a soloist ran off the chart, he was big and athletic—but in one day all his plans for the future changed dramatically.

There was no medicine back then to control the violent seizures. The doctor told my parents not to let Bill play football, ride a bicycle, or climb a tree. If he had a seizure while doing so he might be seriously injured.

Mom's patient love took center stage. If you've ever seen a grand mal seizure, you know it's hideous. Bill's seizures seemed to be triggered by stress.

When Bill would get up to sing and look out over the audience—*wham!* Here came a seizure. Mom would go to him, lovingly wipe the saliva pouring out of his mouth with her handkerchief. She would patiently wait for the convulsive muscle spasm to stop without embarrassment, without caring what anyone thought. Her only concern was for her son.

She would help him off the platform, or the stage in the Christmas pageant, or out of the church where he was trying to give his testimony.

Mom made a vow to fast and pray every supper until God healed her son. In these kinds of situations it's normal for people to keep their vow to assault heaven for the first few weeks. Not my mom. She patiently brought her son's condition before her heavenly Father each and every day.

Yet the more our family prayed the worse the situation became. The seizures seemed to come more frequently.

Six months later...still no improvement! Mom's patient love fixed supper for her family and retired to her bedroom to pray for her son. Day in, day out, Thanksgiving Day, Christmas Day, New Year's Day.

One year later...no improvement. Mom's prayers were pounding the gates of heaven, patiently and relentlessly.

Two years later...no improvement! Mom and Dad took Bill to a very "big name" healing evangelist. Nothing.

Three years later, on an ordinary prayer meeting night, Mother once again asked Bill to come forward for prayer. Mom touched his forehead, and Bill fell to the floor like he had been shot.

"God has healed my son!" she announced triumphantly.

From that day in 1951 until today Bill has been as healthy as a horse. He served in the U.S. military for thirty years with distinction and is now retired with his wife, Elisabeth, in Kentucky.

What made this possible? Mom's patient love, which refused to accept his illness as permanent. When everyone else gave up, she dug in and fought the good fight.

How patient are you?

Do you stand in front of the microwave oven screaming, "Hurry up?" Do you grow impatient brewing instant coffee? I know how you feel. I'm not saying I prefer fast-food restaurants, but the other day I caught myself ordering into the mailbox and driving around the house.

Unfortunately we can't understand a God who is all so powerful and yet patient. When God does not do what we want, we get fidgety and fretful. We must learn this divine principle of the nature of God: God's delays are not God's denials!

We want what we want when we want it, and if God doesn't give it, we scream, "You don't love me" or "Where are You, God, when I need You?" or "Why is God so silent when I need to hear His voice so desperately?" Why? Because greatness is slow to anger, and part of the greatness of God is His eternal patience.

Look at His patience in the plan of salvation. God sent Moses to Israel, and he was rejected. God sent the prophets, and they were stoned.

God sent kings, and they became corrupt. King Saul went to the witch of Endor, seeking direction for Israel, instead of having faith in the almighty God. King David seduced Bathsheba and conceived an illegitimate child. He then entered into a conspiracy to murder Uriah, the husband of Bathsheba. King Solomon allowed his wives to lead him into deep idolatry. But the patience of God did not surrender to the corruption of these kings.

God then sent His only begotten Son, not on a white horse, not pushing and shoving humanity like a supreme sultan, not strutting with a swagger stick like a supreme commander. God sent His Son as a baby in Bethlehem's manger. That Son came touching untouchable lepers. He hugged and kissed the castoffs of society. He wrapped a towel around His waist and washed the dirty feet of His disciples in the upper room during His final hours of life.

God's Son, our Holy Lord and Savior, let Herod's men of war slap Him and spit upon Him and mock Him and crown Him with thorns. They led Him to Golgotha where they nailed Him to a cruel Roman cross outside of Jerusalem. Why did God allow this to happen? Because God's love is patient.

I've learned that true love is patient and steady.

As a teenager, I worked as a longshoreman on the waterfront in Houston, Texas. You could put tons of merchandise on one side of those cargo ships, and they would not lose their balance. On the other hand, canoes flip over very easily; the slightest thing out of balance and you're in the water.

Are you a canoe or a cargo ship? Do you flip your lid at the slightest provocation? Or are you like a cargo ship that's steady in all seasons? Love is patient.

How patient are you with yourself and others?

2

LOVE IS KIND

Kindness is love in action! Kindness is the ability to love people more than they deserve.

On one occasion a woman came into my office for marriage counseling, and in the process of our conversation she said, "My husband doesn't deserve kindness."

I responded, "Give it to him on credit; you do everything else on credit."

Do you want to do something great for God? Then be kind to His children. The result can be as dramatic as Oscar Hammerstein's kindness to Mary Martin.

One evening, just before the great Broadway musical star Mary Martin was to go on stage in *South Pacific*, a note was handed to her. It was from Oscar Hammerstein, one of the writers of the musical, who at that moment was on his deathbed. The short note simply said, "Dear Mary, A bell's not a bell till you ring it. A song's not a song till you sing it. Love in your heart is not put there to stay. Love isn't love till you give it away."

After her stunning performance that night many people rushed backstage, crying, "Mary, what happened to you out there tonight? We never saw anything like that performance before." Blinking back the tears, Mary read them the note from Hammerstein. Then she said, "Tonight I gave my love away!"

Oscar Hammerstein was dying, but he still thought of Mary Martin and her performance. And everyone who attended the performance was blessed by his kindness.

Cornerstone Church is truly a cathedral of kindness. Recently a single mother in our church dropped dead at the age of forty-three from physical exhaustion.

Her husband, a rascal and miserable wretch, abandoned her without cause and left her stranded with three beautiful children. One daughter was in college making straight *As*, desiring to go to law school. The second daughter was in high school making excellent grades, and her only son was the light of her life.

This gallant woman didn't whine and get bitter; she went to work to provide for her children. When one job didn't make ends meet, she would get a second job. She literally worked herself to death trying to support her children. I have deep compassion for the single mothers in America.

When the report reached my desk that this mother had died, I took the need of the family directly to the church body. The house note was behind. The utilities and other bills were behind. What of the children's future, their education, their ability to stay together?

We took a love offering for this precious family of three stranded children. The offering was in excess of fifty thousand dollars. A guardian was appointed by the church. All bills were instantly paid, and the children are living together in their debt-free home with all dreams and hopes for a beautiful life still intact.

In a day three lives were salvaged from desolation. They will live together just like their mom would have wanted because of the kindness of the body of Christ.

How kind are you to yourself and others?

3
LOVE ENVIETH NOT

Think of someone you're absolutely sure loves you. Then go buy yourself a new Mercedes with steam-heated doorknobs, Posturepedic seats, and a luxury package. Drive up in front of that person's house and watch the envious reaction. A wildcat would not be more threatening. Nothing will depreciate that friend's car faster than you buying a new one. (Most of us might not be so envious if our neighbors weren't so extravagant!)

A person generally criticizes the individual whom he secretly envies. The man who belittles you is probably trying to cut you down to his size. When you feel yourself turning green with envy, you're ripe for trouble. True love envieth not! True love is not jealous! True love is not possessive!

In my forty-five years of ministry I have heard this statement many times from frustrated husbands. "My wife is so jealous; she gets mad every time anyone looks at me."

This is the reaction of an emotionally insecure person. Dr. James Dobson says, "If you love something, set it free. If it comes back to you, it's yours. If it doesn't, it never was." There's another version, "If you love something, set it free. If it doesn't come back to you, track it down and beat it to death." That's not love.

Love releases; envy possesses. When you possess someone, you smother that person. He or she fights to get free. You try harder to control the person, who struggles harder to get free. It becomes a fight for emotional survival.

A rebellious teenager who was tired of his father's stuffy rules packed his designer jeans and polo shirts in his shoulder-mounted carryall. Then he looked around the home he had been raised in for the final time.

One night earlier he and his father had their final disagreement; the paternal cord was broken. They had reached a financial agreement that was to be the last money he would receive from a father who loved him dearly. He released the boy to travel the road to perdition.

As the boy walked toward the front porch, his older brother, of whom he was never fond, casually waved goodbye.

The rebel started his Harley Davidson motorcycle, fired up the powerful engines, released the kickstand, and popped the front wheel in the air as he peeled rubber out of the front driveway. He was on his way to "Big D" to live like big, bad J. R. Ewing of South Fork.

His pockets full of money, his head full of big ideas, he arrived in Dallas for a walk on the wild side. He spent his money on prostitutes, in casinos, in bars snorting cocaine, and swimming in a whiskey river that destroyed him.

In less than three months he was gaunt and dead broke. He sought employment from every quarter and could find nothing. At home his loving father was praying that the rebel he had lovingly released would return home.

One afternoon, the father saw the freight train chug up the hill next to the family farm. He watched in amusement as a hobo jumped off and started walking toward his beautiful white ranch-style home on top of the hill.

Then the father focused his eyes on the hobo; he put his right hand up to his forehead to be sure he was seeing perfectly. He was. The hobo was his son.

He ran to his son and embraced him with tears of joy flowing down his face. The boy he had lovingly released had come home broken and contrite.

This story has been plagiarized.

It's the story of the prodigal son.

Is there a prodigal son or daughter in your life demanding to be set free? Lovingly release your child into the hands of God who will crush that arrogance into contrition. If the child is yours, he or she will come back. God will put a hook in that young person's jaw and drag him or her back.

Does your love release your loved one? Does your love release yourself?

4
LOVE HAS GOOD MANNERS

The apostle Paul wrote, "Love…does not behave rudely" (1 Cor. 13:5). Love is never rude. Love does not behave itself indecently.

Our society revels in its crudeness! The "gentleman" is being replaced by something that resembles a macho orangutan. The "lady" has become hip, vulgar, and promiscuous.

What's wrong with being mannerly? It's still in order to pull the chair out for a lady before she sits down—not as she sits down. It's still proper to open the car door for your wife even if you've been married for twenty-five years. It is still OK to carry on a conversation without lacing it with four-letter words. It's still proper to send a thank you card to friends and family. How mannerly are you?

Manners are taught; they are not caught like a virus. The children in your home will carry your manners into their marriages and into society.

A father was watching his young son eat at the dinner table in a very sloppy manner. The father thought this would be an ideal time to teach his son some manners.

"Son, you eat like a pig!"

The son looked at his father blankly. The father, knowing the boy had been raised all his life in the city, thought he had never seen a pig. His manners seminar continued.

"Son, you do know what a pig is, don't you?"

"Certainly," his son responded. "A pig is a hog's little boy."

I have traveled all over the world. It has been my observation that the further from America you get the more mannerly the children become.

If you love your children or grandchildren, you will teach them to be mannerly by example. Manners can be love's clearest voice.

5
LOVE IS LOYAL

In his portrait of love, the apostle Paul wrote, "Love…does not seek its own" (1 Cor. 13:5). Love does not insist on having its own way. True love does not pursue a selfish advantage.

During the Holocaust, a Polish Jewish mother with three children dashed into the woods before the approaching Nazi army. For days the mother and her children survived on roots and grass in the forest.

One morning the starving trio was discovered by a farmer and his son, who demanded they come out of the brush. In an instant the farmer saw they were starving and told his son to give the mother a loaf of bread. The mother eagerly took the loaf of bread and like a famished animal quickly broke it into three pieces. Then she gave all three pieces to her three children.

The farmer's son looked at his father and said, "She kept none of the bread for herself because she's not hungry."

The Polish farmer responded, "She kept none for herself because she is a mother. She is more loyal to her children than she is to herself. Her loyalty is greater than her fear of death."

This type of loyalty is often found in the Bible.

The story of Ruth and Naomi in the Old Testament is the high water mark of loyalty in the Word of God. Ruth, a Gentile woman, stood beside her mother-in-law, Naomi, at the border of Judah as they were about to enter Bethlehem, the house of bread and praise. If Ruth stepped over that border, she was moving into a Jewish society without any hope of ever marrying since Jews couldn't marry Gentiles.

Yet at this moment Ruth gave a unique expression of loyalty to her mother-in-law, knowing that she had absolutely nothing to look for in the future. Listen to her words.

> Entreat me not to leave you, or to turn back from following after you, for wherever you go, I will go; and wherever you lodge, I will lodge; your people shall be my people, and your God, my God. Where you die, I will die, and there will I be buried. The LORD do so to me, and more also, if anything but death parts you and me.
>
> —RUTH 1:16–17

That's loyalty! With the bad press mothers-in-law receive in our society, that's real loyalty! Ruth was committing herself to spend the rest of her life with her mother-in-law. How many men—or women—would do that today?

Is your love loyal? If it's true love, the answer is *yes!*

6
LOVE IS PERFUME

As Mrs. Thompson stood in front of her fifth grade class on the very first day of school, she told the children an untruth. Like most teachers, she looked at her students and said that she loved them all the same. However, that was impossible, because there in the front row, slumped in his seat, was a little boy named Teddy Stoddard.

The teacher had watched Teddy the year before and noticed that he did not play well with the other children, that his clothes were messy, that he constantly needed a bath. In addition, Teddy could be unpleasant. In the next days and weeks and months Mrs. Thompson found out that this was true. She would actually take delight in marking his papers with a broad red pen, making bold *X*s, and then putting a big fat "*F*" at the top.

At the school where Mrs. Thompson taught, she was required to review each child's past record, and she put Teddy's off until last. However, when she reviewed his file, she was in for a surprise.

Teddy's first grade teacher wrote, "Teddy is a bright child with a ready laugh. He does his work neatly and has good manners. He is a joy to be around."

His second grade teacher wrote, "Teddy is an excellent student, well liked by his classmates, but he is troubled because his mother has a terminal illness, and life at home must be a struggle."

His third grade teacher wrote, "His mother's death has been hard on him. He tries to do his best, but his father doesn't show much interest, and his home life will soon affect him if some steps aren't taken."

Teddy's fourth grade teacher wrote, "Teddy is withdrawn and doesn't show much interest in school. He doesn't have many friends, and he sometimes sleeps in class."

By now, Mrs. Thompson realized the problem, and she was ashamed of herself. She felt even worse when most of her students brought her Christmas presents, wrapped in beautiful ribbons and bright paper. One present stood out as so, so different. Teddy's present was clumsily wrapped in the heavy, brown paper that he had obviously gotten from a grocery bag. Mrs. Thompson took pains to open it in the middle of the other presents.

Some of the children started to laugh when she found a rhinestone bracelet with some of the stones missing and a bottle that was one-quarter full of perfume. But she stifled the children's laughter when she exclaimed how pretty the bracelet was, putting it on, and then dabbing some of the perfume on her wrist.

That day Teddy Stoddard stayed after school just long enough to say, "Mrs. Thompson, today you smelled just like my mom used to." After the children left, she cried for at least an hour.

On that very day, Mrs. Thompson quit teaching reading, writing, and arithmetic. Instead, she began to teach children. And she paid particular attention to Teddy. As she worked with him, his mind seemed to come alive again. The more she encouraged him, the faster he responded. By the end of the year, Teddy had become one of the smartest children in the class, and Teddy was one of her "teacher's pets," despite her white lie that she would love all the children the same.

A year later, this teacher found a note from Teddy under her door, telling her that she was still the best teacher he ever had in his whole life.

Six years went by before she got another note from Teddy. He wrote that he had finished high school, third in his class, and she was still the best teacher he ever had.

Four years after that, she got a third letter, saying that while things had been tough at times, he'd stayed in school and would soon graduate from college with the highest honors. He assured Mrs. Thompson that she was still the best teacher he had ever had in his whole life.

Then four more years passed, and yet a fourth letter came. This time Teddy said that after he got his bachelor's degree, he decided to go a little further. The letter explained that she was still the best and favorite teacher he ever had. But now his name was a little longer. The letter was signed Theodore F. Stoddard, M.D.

The story does not end there. You see, there was yet another letter that spring. Teddy said he had met this girl and was going to be married. He explained that his father had died a couple of years ago, and he was wondering if Mrs. Thompson might agree to attend the wedding and sit in the place that was usually reserved for the mother of the groom.

Of course, Mrs. Thompson did. And guess what? She wore that bracelet, the one with several rhinestones missing. Moreover, she made sure she was wearing the perfume that Teddy remembered his mother wearing on their last Christmas together.

After the wedding, Teddy and his best and favorite teacher hugged each other. Then Dr. Theodore Stoddard whispered in Mrs. Thompson's ear, "Thank you, Mrs. Thompson, for believing in me. Thank you so much for making me feel important and showing me that I could make a difference."

With tears in her eyes Mrs. Thompson whispered back. "Teddy, you have it all wrong," she said. "You were the one who taught me that I could make a difference. I didn't know how to teach until I met you."

Love is perfume. Warm someone's heart today with random acts of love. Your love can be the hands of God, reshaping the self-esteem of someone crushed by cruel circumstances beyond his or her control.

7
LOVE YOURSELF

Paul wrote, "Love thinks no evil," and "Love hopes all things." Yet when we have poor self-esteem we are thinking evil of ourselves and refusing to hope the best for ourselves.

What is self-esteem? Webster says *self-esteem* is "self-respect." Fundamentally, self-esteem is how you see yourself.

Whom do you see when you look in the mirror? Do you like the person you see? How you feel about yourself will determine how you answer every one of the following questions:

- Do you like God?

- Do you enjoy thinking about your future?

- Do you like your wife?

- Do you like your husband?

- If you were single right now and met this person for the first time, knowing what you know about him or her, would you marry your husband or wife again?

- Do you like anybody?

- Would you rather be somebody else?

How you feel about yourself will determine your spiritual, emotional, intellectual, and financial future.

One of the best-kept secrets of success is this: We must feel love inside ourselves before we can give it to others. If your heart is full of self-doubt and feelings of inferiority, you have nothing to give your spouse, your children, or those with whom you work.

So I ask this question again. Who are you? When you look in the mirror, what do you see? Do you see beauty? Or do you see someone who you feel is ugly and unattractive? Do you see misery? Do you see grief? Do you see hope?

The only thing in the world you can change is yourself, and that makes all the difference in the world. Everyone thinks of changing the world, but no one thinks of changing the only thing they can change: themselves.

Who are you? Ask people that question, and most of them will answer, "I'm a doctor" or "I'm a plumber" or "I'm an accountant" or "I'm in the military" or "I'm a salesman." The responses go on forever.

I didn't ask you what you do. I asked you, "Who are you?" People can't answer that simple question because they don't know who they are. They have lost contact with themselves, and they are now only related to what they do, not who they are.

Why? Because our world is out of control. The pace has become insane. We are overworked and overwhelmed with five hundred television channels and the Internet. We are working two jobs, trying to keep body and soul together. We have two kids and two cars, and all are conspiring to steal ourselves from ourselves.

Americans are on a merry-go-round, spinning too fast to hold on and too fast to jump off. Children who are being forced to fulfill the dreams of frustrated parents are racing from school to dance lessons, to soccer teams, to football practice, to basketball practice, to the debate team, to music lessons, to Kung Fu karate lessons. In the madness of this rat race, these children lose contact with themselves just as their parents have. We are a fragmented society because of the madness of this pace.

Remember: If you win the rat race, it only means you're the number one rat.

Here's a litmus test to determine if you are accepting a lifestyle that forces you to ignore who you are. Are you constantly tired, stressed out, emotionally flat, or even depressed, worried, or unhappy? Are you just going through the motions of life?

Does your life consist of things you profess to hate, yet you continue to do them anyway? This is a betrayal of who you are. You complain about being overweight, yet you do nothing to change what you will not confront. You are assassinating your self-esteem. Remember this for the rest of your life: You cannot change what you will not confront. That's true with your marriage, your weight problem, your children, or your financial dilemma.

Let me tell you a fascinating story about Ed McClure, who had the courage to confront his problem. I was introduced to Ed ten years ago by my attorney, who presented Ed as one of the most brilliant minds in the hotel industry in America.

Sensational descriptions of his professional accomplishments and his picture were front-page news stories in the *Business Journal* of San Antonio. Ed would buy hotels that were not performing, overhaul them from the front door to the top floor, and transform them into cash cows.

Ed McClure was to the hotel industry as Stephen Spielberg is to the movie industry—in a class all by himself. When my son Christopher decided to make a career change, I took him over to Ed for the training that would produce a hotel magnate in years to come.

This is a beautiful story, with one ugly feature. Ed was about five-feet-ten-inches tall and weighed well over four hundred pounds. He drove everywhere he went because he could not fit in an airplane seat. I feared for Ed's life because his heart couldn't possibly survive much longer.

One day I boldly recommended to Ed that he go to Florida and see my friend Dr. Don Colbert, whom I consider to be one of the foremost nutritionists in America. Ed, like many people with a severe weight problem, had tried every diet on Planet Earth. Nothing worked!

Adding to the frustration was that Ed was a master chef who knew the food industry like I know John 3:16.

I assured Ed that Dr. Colbert could help. He went to Florida, and what happened was a miracle. Dr. Colbert identified every physical and spiritual area of Ed's life that needed healing.

Following Dr. Colbert's plan, Ed lost two hundred pounds in twelve months. When I see him in public I have to look twice. It's Ed McClure. His self-esteem is sky high.

Ed is so motivated that he's now preparing a cookbook of exciting and tasty foods that will cut your weight quickly, safely, and painlessly. Soon you will be seeing television programs featuring Ed McClure and his *Eat Yourself Thin* cookbook. He will be leaving the hotel industry to share with America's overweight legions how to recapture their self-esteem by shedding excess pounds through intelligent and informed food choices. Ed is also beginning to conduct three-day seminars for people like himself who have been assassinating their self-esteem because they can't conquer their weight problem.

Ed had a problem that was killing his self-esteem, and it was destroying his life. He faced the problem, and he's now becoming a health evangelist to America's heavyweights.

Are you assassinating your self-esteem? You don't like your job, but you fail to recognize that you will not be promoted until you become overqualified for the position you now hold. Get excited about your job! There's a word for people who are not excited about their jobs; that word is *unemployed*.

Every job, wherever you find it, will have toil, stress, tension, sweat, and boredom. Work is the therapy of the soul. God Himself worked six days in the creation of the heaven and earth.

In the Ten Commandments He said that we should follow His example: "Six days shalt thou work." That commandment means some of you must slow down and others of you must speed up. If you are not willing to work, you abandon the very nature of God Himself.

Are you betraying yourself by not confronting the areas that might need change? You complain about your lack of education, yet you don't go back to school. You have a litany of excuses. One of them is, "I am too old." That's absolute nonsense. It's never too late to be what you might become. Every university I have ever attended has had senior citizens as old as their early seventies seeking to restructure their lives so they can run the final laps with as much vigor as the first laps.

Your marriage is as dead as Julius Caesar, but you refuse counseling or any positive act that might improve it. This is self-betrayal.

Perhaps you were sexually abused as a child, but you don't do one blessed thing to get that emotional scar healed. Instead, you've made a career of whining over your past. You give your pseudo-intellectual mantra of excuses saying, "I'm depressed." "I was abused." "No one loves me." Stop it! You are worshiping the problem and not seeking a solution. This is self-betrayal.

If you have given up control of your life to a tornado of activity and are living a life that is defined from the outside in rather than from the inside out, you are "play-acting" like an actor on a stage. The biblical word for *play-acting* is *hypocrisy*. (And we know what Jesus thought of hypocrites.) Your intense activity schedule is the portrait of a hypocrite.

The Portrait of a Hypocrite

A hypocrite never intends to be what he pretends to be. Unfortunately, people who lack self-esteem wear masks, pretending to be what they think others will accept.

There's the religious mask. The Napoleonic mask. The intellectual mask. The diplomacy mask. All of these masks are worn to hide who you really are. Years ago on television, the Lone Ranger wore a mask, and every telecast ended with the question: "Who was that masked man?"

Let's examine these masks to see the man or woman behind them.

Here's the man wearing a religious mask. He pretends to be more spiritual than he is. He sings, "When We All Get to Heaven," and he's as mean as a two-headed snake. He pretends to pray but doesn't. He pretends to give, but his annual church contribution wouldn't buy a box of pencils. He pretends to love other people but assassinates them with his toxic tongue. He's a twenty-first-century Pharisee. Jesus Christ said, "Except your righteousness exceeds that of the Pharisees, you will in no way enter into the kingdom of God" (Matt. 5:20).

I have been in the ministry for forty-five years, and I can tell you that people who act spiritual aren't. Jesus was so common in His appearance, so common in His speech, so common in His demeanor that Judas had to kiss Him in the Garden of Gethsemane so the Roman soldiers would know whom to arrest.

Jesus was not wearing a diamond-studded Rolex and didn't arrive in the Garden of Gethsemane in a stretch limo, drinking Perrier water, with Peter shouting, "Heeeeeeeeeere's Jesus!"

He didn't have a pinky ring or a diamond-studded cross around His neck. He was the Son of God, who was so common only His disciples could really identify Him. Jesus didn't wear a religious mask. Neither should we.

Now consider the Napoleonic mask. Some of you may be married to Napoleon. He's an insecure, emotional basket case, who bullies everyone with his mouth. He can never afford to be wrong. He dominates and controls other people with his anger. He has an air of assumed superiority. He has the mind-set, "I thought I was wrong once, but I was mistaken." He is the living essence of the country-western song, "It's Hard to Be Humble When You're Perfect in Every Way."

To those of you wearing the Napoleonic mask, listen up! You have a toxic-turbo tongue because you're terrified someone will look behind your mask and see the trembling, frightened, and insecure Caspar Milquetoast that will wet his pants if Goliath shows up. Knock it off! You are assassinating the hopes and dreams of the people you love by pretending to be what you are not.

Consider the intellectual mask. Intellectual people waste no time telling you how educated they are. Please! You can get a college degree without getting an education. And not all educated people are intelligent. That includes many of the Ph.D.s you know. Some of the most genuinely stupid people I have ever met are hiding behind the ivy-covered walls of a university.

The apostle Paul wrote in Colossians 2:8, "Beware lest any man spoil you through philosophy and vain deceit."

People who wear intellectual masks are like the backwoods resident who went to the city on a shopping trip and bought a jigsaw puzzle. Finally, after working on it every night for two weeks, the puzzle was finished.

The hayseed saw his friend Jed passing by and shouted, "Look, Jed! Look what I have done."

Jed responded, "That's surely something, Bud. How long did it take you to put that puzzle together?"

Bud proudly responded, "Only two weeks."

"Never done a puzzle myself, is two weeks fast?" Jed asked.

"Mighty right, it's fast, Jed. Look at what it says on the side of the box. It says right here, 'From two to four years.'"

America is saturated with intellectual idolatry, and all idolatry is sin. First Samuel 15:23 says, "For rebellion is as the sin of witchcraft, and stubbornness is as iniquity and idolatry."

This verse makes it very clear that rebellion and stubbornness produce witchcraft and idolatry. Who is a stubborn person? A person who will not change his mind in the presence of truth. He will not change his mind when he hears or reads the Word of God because his opinion and his thoughts are his idols. This is intellectual idolatry, which makes you the lord of your life and reduces God to an inferior. Intellectual idolatry is rampant in the church of Jesus Christ.

Finally there's the diplomacy mask. A diplomat is a person who can say something so cleverly no one knows exactly what he said. A diplomat expresses emotions he or she never really feels. Often people say, "I love you," because they are too cowardly to say, "We have a problem, and we need to work it out now." Instead, a diplomat passes out compliments to camouflage criticism. People say things like, "You're great," and then turn the corner and say, "What a jerk that person is."

You may call this tact or poise or making a good impression. God calls it lying.

What do people who lack self-esteem say behind their masks? This is the unheard conversation that you may be having in your mind right now.

"Pastor Hagee, I wear a mask. I wear several masks. None of them are the real me! I'm frightened to show you the real me because you might not like me.

"I'm the great pretender, but don't be fooled. I give the impression that I am secure, that all is sunny within and without, and that I'm confident, cool, and in total command. Please don't believe me, Pastor. Please help me come out of hiding. Underneath this mask, the real me is in total confusion. I'm fearful. I'm lonely. I'm insecure. I'm uncertain. There's unconfessed sin in my life. I've lost control of my life!

"I panic at the thought that my weaknesses might be discovered. That's why I pretend to be religious, intelligent, and diplomatic. Please help me come out from behind these prison walls. Help me become a real person who knows the joy of laughter and the peace of God."

Every church in America has masked men and women sitting on every pew. Every school and every place of employment is packed with people wearing masks. Every family has people hiding behind a mask.

Behind those masks are adulterers, wife beaters, thieves, and liars who live by deceit and deception. There are criminals who have yet to be caught who sing "Amazing Grace" in church. Porno addicts who hide their voyeuristic desires behind the mask of spiritual accomplishment.

I challenge every reader to come out from behind the mask you're wearing and live in the sunshine of God's love, to love your neighbor as yourself and begin to see yourself as God sees you.

Unfortunately two dominant fears sometimes continue to destroy our love of our neighbor and ourselves.

Two Dominant Fears

Rejection

The first fear is the fear of rejection, the fear of being made a fool or failing in the presence of others. This fear of rejection can be traced to early criticisms we receive from our parents or our teachers—and most definitely from our peers. When you were on the school playground some of you were called "fatso" or "beaver teeth" or "buzzard beak" or "bean pole" or "dumbbell ears" or "four eyes" or "motor mouth." Those words stick in your brain and turn you into an emotional cripple.

The spirit of rejection can also crush your child. Even before your child is born, the nurturing moods of the mother during pregnancy are critical. Saying to someone, "I don't want this child" is a verbal curse that will affect your child's emotional development.

A child can get too many *things*, but a child can never get too much *love*. Raise your children with love so that when they grow up they can give love; otherwise, their marriage and their children will be poisoned by your rejection today. Unless you learn to love yourself, you will pass every hang-up you have to your children, and they will pass it to theirs. You will have generational curses in your family that will not be broken until they're broken by the hand of God.

The Bible says, "The LORD is longsuffering and abundant in mercy, forgiving iniquity and transgression; but He by no means clears the guilty, visiting the iniquity of the fathers on the children to the third and fourth generation" (Num. 14:18).

I encourage you parents to go out of your way to affirm your children every day. Shut the television off and talk to them. Hug them at every possible opportunity. All of my five children are grown, and most are married, and I still kiss them every time I see them. They don't get too big for that.

On one occasion, my son Christopher, who was twelve at the time, got out of the house early in the morning to catch the school bus before I kissed him. Several minutes later, when I was driving to work, he was standing on the corner with his friends, waiting for the school bus.

I stopped the car and got out. Christopher knew instantly what I was going to do. He did not want to be embarrassed in front of his friends, so he started running down the street, looking over his shoulder at me and screaming, "No, no, no!"

As I was chasing him down the street, a woman walked out on her front porch. She saw this man chasing this boy who was screaming, "No, no, no!" She put her hands on her hips, and I knew she thought I was a sexual predator.

I yelled at Chris, "Boy, you stop right now!"

He did.

I kissed him.

The lady was stunned, and his friends fell on the ground laughing. Tough. I kissed him then, and will kiss him and every child and grandchild I have every day until the day I die. Love can overcome any rejection.

Change

Our second fear is the fear of change. We hate change, yet change is everywhere. Our physical bodies are changing. If you don't think your body is changing, look at an old photo of yourself. It will take your breath away.

At the age of twenty, everything is great. You look good. At forty, your hair, teeth, and stomach come out. A man, who is bald in the front, is a thinker. A man, who is bald in the back, is a lover. A man, who is bald in the front and the back, just thinks he's a lover.

At fifty, it's patch, patch, patch.

At sixty, all the names in your little black book are the names of your doctors.

At seventy, you get winded playing checkers. You sit in a rocking chair but can't get it going. Everything hurts, and what doesn't hurt doesn't work.

Sometimes change is not a pleasant thing. Yet we cannot stop change. Change is everywhere.

This year we were blessed in my home by the birth of two new grandchildren. Hallelujah! What a blessed change. After threatening to destroy my married children's television sets, grandchildren are finally arriving.

Here are some questions my daughters asked as they were experiencing this change. "I'm two months pregnant," one said. "When will my baby move?" I answered, "With any luck, right after he finishes college."

A second question my daughters asked: "My childbirth instructor says that it's not pain I'm feeling during labor, but pressure. Is she right?" I responded, "Yes, the same way a tornado might be called an air current."

And then the final question: "When is the best time to get an epidural?" I responded, "Right after you find out you're pregnant."

My son-in-law had his own question. "Is there any reason I have to be in the delivery room while my wife is in labor?" I responded, "Not unless the word alimony means something to you."

Change is everywhere! Some people change jobs. They change wives and husbands and friends and churches without ever entertaining the thought that they might be the one who needs to change.

God is constantly trying to perpetuate change. Every twenty-four hours, there's a new day. Every thirty days, a new moon. When you come to Christ, you become a new creature in Christ Jesus. When you die, you're going to the New Jerusalem with a new body that has a new name that will live in a new mansion.

Change is inevitable. And change might be beneficial to you.

If I gave you a pen and paper and said, "Write down the things in your life you would like to change," what would they be?

The Bible says, "And the LORD said, 'Write the vision and make it plain'" (Hab. 2:2). This is a clear directive from heaven to know what you want to become and take definite steps to achieve that goal. It's a vision statement. Take a moment now to write the things you would like to change on a piece of paper.

God is a God of new beginnings. Don't fear change. Live, love, laugh, and be happy. Your divine destiny is in the hands of God, and your tomorrows are far better than you can possibly dream.

I challenge every reader to come out from behind the mask you're wearing and live in the sunshine of God's love: to love your neighbor as yourself and begin to see yourself as God sees you. Next time someone asks the question, "Who are you?" you might answer in your mind or out loud, "I'm a child of God. That makes me special."

CHAPTER FIVE

Secret Four: Mastery of Your Supreme and Most Subtle Enemy

Yourself

HAVING been in the ministry forty-five years, I have observed the heartbreaking emotional and spiritual wreckage of lives that were simply destroyed because of the lack of self-mastery. Ministers who could shake the world with the genius of their thoughts could not, in the final analysis, control themselves. Presidents who had the ability to shape the destiny of the world fell into disgrace because of their lack of self-mastery. There cannot be mastery of life on any frontier until individuals grow in the art of mastering themselves.

Every American holiday is a scene of death and destruction on our highways. Why? A driver filled with rage stomps on the accelerator, out of control of himself, and hits another car filled with people. Or fear causes a driver to jam on the brakes too hurriedly. Or a driver's devil-may-care attitude throws discretion to the wind, and he gambles with a traffic light while navigating tons of steel traveling at a hundred miles an hour. All of these errors can be attributed to the lack of self-mastery.

I have married hundreds of couples, and I'm sure no one walked down the aisle contemplating divorce, yet the majority of marriages in society and in the church end in divorce. Why? Because the discipline that could have restrained the sharp words or the selfish attitude or the cruel act was totally absent. A successful marriage and a secure home require individuals to face up to their responsibilities to master themselves.

In this chapter on self-mastery I have chosen seven critical areas that decades of ministry and counseling have proven essential to the mastery of self and the living of a successful life.

I

THE MASTERY OF WORRY

Many of you reading this book have a Ph.D. in worry. Yet worry can't change the past, and you can be sure it will ruin the present. Worry will get you to only one place ahead of time: the cemetery.

Worry pursues every class of people—the rich and the poor, the intelligent and the illiterate. The young worry, the old worry, people in debt worry, and people with excess money worry (although their worries may be very different from most of ours!).

Singles worry about their romantic life or lack of it. The following ad was placed in the *Atlanta Journal* and is reported to have received numerous calls:

> SINGLE BLACK FEMALE seeks male companionship, ethnicity unimportant. I'm a very good-looking girl who LOVES to play. I love long walks in the woods, riding in your pickup truck, hunting, camping, and fishing trips, cozy winter nights lying by the fire. Candlelight dinners will have me eating out of your hand. Rub me the right way and watch me respond. I'll be at the front door when you get home from work, wearing only what nature gave me. Kiss me, and I'm yours. Call (404) 875-6420 and ask for Daisy.

Over fifteen thousand men found themselves talking to the Atlanta Humane Society about an eight-week-old black Labrador retriever.

We worry about things we have and things we don't have. We worry about things we've said and things we've failed to say. We worry about what we've done and things we've failed to do. We worry about our body's bulges, baldness, and bunions. Some worry because they are not married, and others worry because they are married.

Worry means there's something over which you cannot have your own way. In reality worry is your personal irritation with God because something is going on in your life—or you fear something may happen in the future—that He's permitted, and you can't control.

Worry is your personal irritation with God.

Ever notice how worry always comes at a bad time—a time of crisis? Just when you need a clear mind and creativity to make a great decision, here comes worry like a dark cloud to hide the sun.

There are three dominant reasons to avoid worry.

Reasons to avoid worry

Why do we need to be warned against worry? *We need to be warned against worry because worry is sin!* Worry is faith in fear, not faith in Jesus Christ.

Worry is faith in fear.

Fear is the rejection of faith! The Bible says, "God has not given us a spirit of fear" (2 Tim. 1:7). Fear is proof that Satan has control of your mind. Fear is evidence that you do not trust God to see you through the problem you are in.

We sometimes think it's a great compliment for someone to call us "a person of great faith." Yet it really isn't a compliment since we serve a God who has never failed. It doesn't take great faith to believe in someone who never fails. However, it does require great faith to believe in someone who fails every so often. God has never failed you and never will; therefore, you shouldn't worry.

You also need to be warned against worry because worry is a killer.

America's finest physicians say worry is the mother of cancer, heart disease, high blood pressure, and ulcers. It's not what you're eating. It's what's eating you.

Worry fills your face with wrinkles and apprehension. It paralyzes the mind so that it cannot produce.

Worry robs the body of rest at night and sends you to work shattered, shaky, second rate, and on the naked edge.

Worry has sent millions of Bible-believing Christians to the cemetery long before their time. Christians who claim to follow the Prince of Peace live in an emotional hell. Worry has no place in the life of a believer.

We also need to be warned against worry because worry is so utterly useless. Jesus said, "Which of you by worrying can add one cubit unto his stature?" (Matt. 6:27). Worry has never lifted a single burden. Worry has never solved a single problem or dried a single tear. Worry has never provided one answer for anyone, not ever.

Have you ever lain in bed on a cold winter night, shivering even though there's a blanket six feet away? You didn't want to get up and go get it. It was easier to lie there and worry the rest of the night. The solution is to do something about it. (Tell your wife to get up and get the blanket if you're too lazy to do it yourself!) Don't worry about things that you have the power to change.

Don't worry about tomorrow: It's in the hands of God. The past is history, and the future is a mystery. There is only today. That's why it's called *the present*.

Antidotes to worry

How do we get rid of worry? It's not by getting into an ideal situation, as some of us think, because there is no such thing. There is no ideal marriage or ideal family. No ideal church or ideal business. No ideal university or ideal professor.

Every place you go you will find people, and people are full of faults, failures, fears, and frustrations. There is no ideal time in your life other than today. The young say, "When I get older, I won't worry then." That's wrong. By the time a man finds greener pastures, he's too old to climb the fence surrounding them.

Old age has its own set of worries. (Believe me, I know. I'm not so young myself.) Senior citizens enter the metallic age. They have gold in their teeth, silver in their hair, and lead in their pants.

Women say, "Marriage will make me feel happy!" Wrong! You carry happiness into marriage; you don't find happiness in marriage.

You carry happiness into marriage; you don't find happiness in marriage.

How do you rid yourself of worry? Several key verses in Philippians 4 are an antidote to worry. The apostle Paul said it this way: "Whatever things are true, whatever things are noble, whatever things are just, whatever things are pure, whatever things are lovely, whatever things are of good report, if there is any virtue and if there is anything praiseworthy—meditate on these things" (Phil. 4:8). Control your thoughts, says Paul, and you control your world.

Just two verses earlier in this chapter of Philippians, Paul counseled, "In everything by prayer and supplication, with thanksgiving, let your request be made known to God; and the peace of God, which surpasses all understanding, will guard your hearts and minds through Christ Jesus" (Phil. 4:6–7).

Notice the phrase the *peace of God*. There's a difference between the peace *of* God and peace *with* God.

You cannot be at war with God and have peace with God. Isaiah said, "The wicked are like the troubled sea" (Isa. 57:20). Peace is the gift of God, and He only gives it to those who have reconciled themselves through Jesus Christ to Himself.

In this chapter of Philippians the apostle Paul made one of the most profound statements about worry ever written by human hand: "In nothing be anxious" (Phil. 4:6).

This is one of my favorite verses. I have found it a comforting pillow upon which to rest my head when I was weary beyond words. I have found it a strong staff upon which to lean when my feet were in slippery places. I have found it to be a fortress in the day of battle.

Let me give you an example.

One night as I lay in my dormitory bed while attending Bible college, I awoke in the middle of the night and saw a large man standing in my room. I could hear the sound of my heart beating furiously in my chest.

I looked over at my roommate, who was snoring so loudly he sounded like a Hoover vacuum cleaner. Why didn't he wake up? Two of us could overpower the man who was staring at me. He was moving ever so slightly, as if rocking from one side to another.

Why didn't the man speak?

Why did he just stand there rocking right and left without attacking?

Who was he?

What could he possibly want? It sure wasn't money. If he were looking for money in my room, I would have been delighted to turn on the light and help him look. But there he stood rocking right and left without moving forward.

Then the answer came!

I was not defenseless. I had a deer hunting knife on the nightstand next to my bed. Slowly, I reached for it, wondering if he could see me.

At last I had the razor sharp knife in my hand. I slipped it under the covers and took it out of its leather casing. The man was still rocking back and forth.

I gripped the blade tightly under the covers. I was very good at throwing a well-balanced hunting knife.

With my left hand I pulled back the covers, sprang out of the bed to a standing position, and threw the knife like a guided missile at the man rocking slowly back and forth.

I heard the knife strike its target. I knew I hadn't missed. Turning on the lamp on the nightstand beside my bed I discovered I had killed my roommate's new black raincoat, which was hanging on the door.

The steady flow of air coming from the air conditioning and heating duct in the floor was causing the raincoat to rock back and forth on the hanger. In the darkness it looked very real.

My roommate was still snoring.

I sheepishly went to the door and retrieved my deer knife. It had pierced the raincoat, nailing it to the door.

I returned to my bed, put the knife away, and turned off the light. My snoring roommate hadn't even rolled over. He could sleep through an earthquake.

As I lay in bed waiting for my heartbeat to return to normal, wondering how I would explain the surgical cut in my roommate's new raincoat, the foolishness of worry penetrated my brain.

I had lain in bed several minutes, watching as a raincoat on a hanger moved back and forth, believing with every fiber of my being that my life was in danger. I looked at my snoring roommate and thought, *How blessed is the man who is too busy to worry in the daytime and too sleepy to worry at night.* Worry is interest paid on trouble that never happens.

How reassuring are the words, *In nothing be anxious.* How full of comfort. These words are as tender as the caress of a mother. They are stronger than the everlasting hills.

Whatever you're going through right now, recognize that God is on His throne, and everything's going to be all right. Don't be anxious about your health because Jesus Christ is still the great physician. Don't be anxious about your finances because your Father in heaven is *Jehovah Jireh*, the Lord who supplies all your needs. Moses said it well, "It is He who gives you power to get wealth" (Deut. 8:18).

Don't worry about your children's future. King David said, "I have not seen the righteous forsaken, nor his descendants begging for bread" (Ps. 37:25). The same God who cared for you will care for your children.

Don't worry about your feeling of insecurity because "He who is in you is greater than he who is in the world" (1 John 4:4). When you accepted Christ, you joined a nation of kings and priests unto God, and the royal blood of heaven flows in your veins. When you walk out of your house, angels go before you and behind you. When you roll over in bed, demons tremble with fear.

Don't worry about your marriage. If you and your spouse will obey the Word of God, your marriage can go through the fires of hell, and nothing can touch you. But marriages that rebel against the Word of God for guidance cannot be kept together with money, sex, or ten thousand counselors. I've found that people who carry a Bible that's falling apart have a life that's not.

People who carry a Bible that's falling apart have a life that's not.

WHY WORRY?

Why worry? "When you pass through the waters, I will be with you; and through the rivers, they shall not overflow you.

When you walk through the fire, you shall not be burned, nor shall the flame scorch you" (Isa. 43:2).

Why worry? God Almighty, the creator of heaven and earth, is your Father. He is all-powerful, all knowing, and all sufficient. He has invited you to "call to Me, and I will answer you, and show you great and mighty things, which you do not know" (Jer. 33:3).

Why worry? He will give His angels charge over you to protect you in all of your way (Ps. 91:11).

Why worry? You are covered by His precious blood.

Why worry? You are anointed with Holy Ghost power. You have the favor of God. You have the power of attorney to use His name: "Whatever you ask the Father in My name," He said, "He will give you" (John 16:23).

You and you alone are responsible for the thoughts you think and for the emotional attitudes that rule your life. That's self-control. That's self-mastery.

Climb on the wings of faith into the presence of the living God. Lift your hands and praise the Lord in faith. Worry will vanish and faith will explode. Your heart and mind will be ruled by the peace of the living God. Remember the words of the apostle Paul, "Be anxious for nothing."

We need to master worry, and we need to master fear, which often causes us to worry.

2

THE MASTERY OF FEAR

Five Hebrew words translate into the English word *fear*. In fact, fear is mentioned in the Bible about six hundred times. It's no small subject.

Jesus Christ commanded, "Fear not." From Genesis to Revelation, from Abraham to John on the Isle of Patmos, we hear that command given over and over: "Fear not."

This command was given to Abraham when he was told to take Isaac to Mount Moriah. This command was given to the people of Israel as they stood at the Red Sea. This command was given to Moses, to David, to Daniel, to Jerusalem, and to the disciples. This command was given to the mother of Jesus when Gabriel told her she was expecting the Christ child. This command was given to Peter as he was sinking in a stormy sea. This command was given to the apostle Paul as the ship on which he was sailing was about to sink in a raging fourteen-day storm.

You will either conquer fear,
or fear will conquer you.

In order to master our tendency to fear, we need to understand the difference between the emotion of fear and the spirit of fear. God gives the emotion of fear to all of us to help us respond to life-threatening situations. The spirit of fear comes from Satan; he gives you the spirit of fear to harm you.

The emotion of fear

Animals experience the emotion of fear. Startle a rabbit in a thicket, and what happens? You never saw such a leap of faith! Any deer who can't jump ten feet out of the brush when its afternoon nap is disturbed by gunfire and come down with its legs pounding will not live through deer season.

The fact is that healthy fear keeps you alive. Years ago when I was conducting revival services in Spearman, Texas, the pastor told me not to get out of the car as we drove up in front of the parsonage where I was staying. I asked him why, and he responded, "We have lots of rattle-snakes in Spearman, and you need to have this flashlight to walk to the house." I turned on the flashlight and two rattlesnakes were within six feet of the car door. Healthy fear forced me to make an adjustment to their presence.

I have five wonderful children whom I call the "Fabulous Five": Tish, Christopher, Tina, Matthew, and Sandy, my baby. When they were young, I taught them to fear certain things. "Do not play with matches and gasoline," I told them. "Do not play with guns." "Do not touch a can with a skull and crossbones on it." Not all fear is evil.

Some pseudo-intellectuals say, "If you don't draw us by love, you can't drive us by fear." I don't believe this is true.

Let me ask you this question: Why do you pay the IRS? Is it because you love to send checks to the government? No. It's because you fear the very real possibility of living the remainder of your life in Leavenworth if you do not.

Why do you take out fire insurance? Because you love your insurance agent? I don't think so. You take out fire insurance because one fire can wipe out a lifetime of investment.

Why do you lock your doors at night? Because of a natural fear of murderers, rapists, and thieves. Locking your door gives you the time to get your .357 Magnum and open fire.

God also planted the emotion of fear in our moral nature to make us uneasy with our sin. David writes, "My flesh trembles for fear of You [God], and I am afraid of Your judgments" (Ps. 119:120). The psalmist gave the same warning: "Be wise, O kings…serve the LORD with fear, and rejoice with trembling. Kiss the Son, lest He be angry, and you perish in the way" (Ps. 2:10–11). And Solomon wrote, "The fear of the LORD is the beginning of knowledge" (Prov. 1:7).

Why should we fear God? Because we'll catch hell if we don't. God is not a doting grandfather, sitting benignly in the heavens. He is almighty, all-powerful, and the judge of all the earth, and someday we will bow before Him. It's not a matter of if we will bow before Him; it's only a matter of *when* we will bow.

God's not in heaven saying,
"Let's make a deal!" He's in heaven saying,
"This is the deal!"

The emotion of fear is God-given and contributes to our well-being. Not so, the spirit of fear.

The spirit of fear

The spirit of fear is the product of the prince of darkness. Disease has killed its thousands, but the spirit of fear has killed its tens of thousands. Your greatest crisis will come from the *fear* of trouble, not the *presence* of trouble.

Psychiatrists describe the spirit of fear as phobias, and they have identified seventy-five different phobias that produce abnormal, irrational, and mind-crippling fear. This spirit of fear will break your spirit, destroy your defenses, and disarm you in the day of battle. The spirit of fear will bring terror to your deathbed.

Regardless of your profession of faith, if you live with the spirit of fear, you are a practicing atheist. Paul told the early Christians: "For God has not given us a spirit of fear, but of power and of love and of a sound mind" (2 Tim. 1:7).

If you live with the spirit of fear, you are a practicing atheist.

Where was the spirit of fear born? In the Garden of Eden. At first Adam walked with God in the garden. Adam talked with God as a child talks with his earthly father. But after Adam sinned, he heard the voice of God calling, "Adam, where art thou?" and Adam hid in fear. Adam was never afraid of God until he sinned and took the forbidden fruit.

The spirit of fear continues in men because sin continues to rule their lives. Sin creates fear, and sin sustains fear. Like a virus, fear invades the soul, looking for filth upon which it may feed. Sin gives fear a license to rule your life.

The spirit of fear can have four harmful consequences.

First, fear can attack your mind!

I read the story of a hobo who slipped into an empty banana car to steal a ride to the next city. He lay down on a pile of straw and dropped off to sleep, but he was awakened by something crawling on his face and hands. He brushed it away, but the crawling kept on. At last he sprang to his feet, more annoyed than afraid.

The hobo struck a match and saw one massive tarantula. The match went out, and the darkness engulfed him. He sprang for the door, only to find it locked. He pounded the door until his fists were bloody. There was no response.

When the hobo was released the next morning, he was a complete maniac. Not because of physical pain. Not because a single tarantula had harmed him. He was driven mad by the spirit of fear.

The strongest men in the Bible suffered from fear. David was the champion who killed Goliath, yet the Bible says that when David was in battle he "waxed faint" (2 Sam. 21:15). Elijah sat under the juniper tree, hiding from Jezebel and shaking from fear. He was so afraid he cried out to God, "Lord, take my life. It is enough" (1 Kings 19:4). Peter was terrified of an eighteen-year-old girl the night Jesus was crucified. He swore, "I know not the man" (Luke 22:60).

Second, fear can be contagious! A man in a Midwestern town started running down the street, screaming, "The dam has broken!" Men in the barbershop heard him and instantly joined in the panic, running into the street screaming, "The dam has broken."

Women shopping in the supermarket heard the mob and joined them. The police and firemen joined the mob. Soon the street was filled with people screaming, "The dam has broken!"

One old man ran as far as he could run and then sat down on the curb for a moment and thought, *I've lived here all my life. What dam?* The truth was there was no dam. There was no danger. There was only contagious fear.

After a few minutes, the red-faced citizens came shuffling back into town, embarrassed by their collective response to fear.

Fear spreads on the wings of doubt and destroys like the plague. Let one church member say, "Miracles don't happen anymore," and the spirit of doubt will snuff out faith in an instant.

Yet Scripture tells us that "without faith it is impossible to please God" (Heb. 11:6). Faith is the victory that has overcome the world from biblical times into the present. Faith drove Abraham to look for a city whose builder and maker was God. Faith drove Moses into Pharaoh's court, shouting, "Set my people free." Faith drove David to face Goliath while forty thousand cautious cowards watched. Faith and fear cannot exist in the same mind. When fear knocks at your door, send faith to answer, and no one will be there.

Third, fear can become a self-fulfilling prophecy. Job said, "The thing I greatly feared has come upon me" (Job 3:25). The man who constantly fears for his health, who lives with his fingers on his pulse and with his tongue poked out before the mirror, will die years before God intended.

I heard a shocking story about a man named Nick who was a strong, healthy rail yardman. He got along well with his fellow workers and was consistently reliable on the job. Yet throughout his years working in the yards, Nick had a deep fear that he would be locked in an isolated, refrigerated boxcar. One summer day the train crews were told they could quit an hour early. Right after the other workmen left the site, Nick was accidentally locked in a refrigerated boxcar, which was in the yard for repairs.

He panicked!

He shouted and banged on the walls until his voice went hoarse and his fists were bloody. Nick believed the temperature in the car was zero degrees. He thought, *If I don't get out of here I'll freeze to death.*

Shivering uncontrollably, he scrawled a message to his wife. "So cold, body's getting numb. If I could just go to sleep...These may be my last words."

The next morning the crew slid open the boxcar's heavy doors and found Nick's body. An autopsy revealed that every physical sign indicated he had frozen to death. But the car's refrigeration unit was broken. The temperature inside was never lower than 61 degrees. Nick's fear became a self-fulfilling prophecy.

Fourth, the spirit of fear can rob you of your spiritual inheritance. Moses sent twelve spies into the Promised Land, and ten came back saying, "We were like grasshoppers in our own sight" (Num. 13:33). Joshua and Caleb said, "The land we passed through to spy out is an exceedingly good land. If the LORD delights in us, then He will bring us into this land and give it to us" (Num. 14:7–8).

Unfortunately the Israelites believed the majority report. And God let every man and woman in Israel from the age of twenty years up die in the wilderness. Fear destroyed their spiritual inheritance. Are you letting it destroy yours?

Fear comes through unbelief. John the Revelator wrote, "The cowardly, unbelieving...shall have their part in the lake which burns with fire and brimstone" (Rev. 21:8). Unbelief makes God a liar. If God is not true, if He is not to be believed, He is unfit to be God. Unbelief is treason against God. Millions of Christians who sit in churches every Sunday singing "Faith Is the Victory" are numbered in heaven with the "fearful and unbelieving."

Let's consider the six deadly fears we must conquer to live life successfully and combat these fears with biblical truth.

THE SIX DEADLY FEARS

The fear of the unknown

The fear of the unknown drives the insecure to read horoscopes, to play with Ouija boards, and to consult palm readers in an attempt to discover the future. Yet God's Word tells us future events in the Book of Revelation.

Bible prophecy tells us when the world will end, how it will end, where it will end, and what will cause it to end. (If you doubt this, read my book *From Daniel to Doomsday*.[1])

Put down your horoscopes and your Ouija boards. Disconnect your psychic hotline. Instead, start reading the Word of God, and the unknown explodes with absolute clarity.

The fear of death

America is saturated with voices telling us how to live, how to look young, stay slim and trim, think positively, make more money, and have more friends. All of these are reasonable goals, but they are limited in scope because they only deal with life on earth.

From the moment you are born, your life is in the process of ending. There is an undeniable and unchangeable truth on the earth: One out of one dies. The Bible says, "It is appointed for men to die once" (Heb. 9:27).

Only those who are prepared to die
are truly prepared to live.

Death takes no holidays. Death is no respecter of persons: It comes to the rich and powerful as well as the poor. It snatches the intellectual with his Ph.D. just as it takes the ignorant. Its bony fingers pull the young and beautiful into the yawning mouth of the grave, just as it does those ravaged by old age. Life is not permanent; it is transitory.

James described our fragile state: "It is even a vapor that appears for a little time and then vanishes away" (James 4:14). King David said, "Every man at his best state is but vapor" (Ps. 39:5). The psalmist wrote again that our life is like "grass which grows up: in the morning it flourishes and grows up; in the evening it is cut down and withers" (Ps. 90:5–6). Solomon stated the parameters of life very clearly: "To everything there is a season, a time for every purpose under heaven: a time to be born, and a time to die…" (Eccles. 3:1–2).

What is death? Ask three doctors that question, and you'll get four opinions. The Bible tells us precisely what death is. Physical death is the separation of the spirit and soul from the body: "…the body without the spirit is dead" (James 2:26). But there is a tragic and horrible death; it's spiritual death. This death is separation from God for all eternity, making hell your eternal home!

To Hindus and Buddhists, death means reincarnation. To Islamic terrorists, death while killing infidels (Christians and Jews) sends a person to Paradise where seventy virgins await to give them sexual pleasure. To atheists, death is to die like a dog, which means complete annihilation.

When I'm called to the hospital to stand beside the bed of a beloved parishioner who is dying, I hear these remarks from friends and family members: "I don't want to think about it." "I'm too young to die." "I'm too mean to die." "I'm not going to die." People make these irrational statements in a feeble effort to escape the reality of their own deaths.

Jesus had a difficult time with this type of denial from His disciples. He told them repeatedly that He would be betrayed and crucified, but they refused to listen. Peter even rebuked Jesus. "Far be it from You, Lord; this shall not happen to you!" (Matt. 16:21–22). Jesus told Peter the truth, but he did not want to hear it. Do you?

Do you deny the place death has in your life? If so, consider these words of King David: "Yea though I walk through the valley of the shadow of death, I will fear no evil; for You are with me" (Ps. 23:4). David called death a "shadow." The shadow of a lion cannot hurt me. The shadow of a snake cannot bite me. The shadow of a sword cannot cut me. A shadow is harmless. Jesus Christ has conquered death, hell, and the grave. Death is now called "the valley of the shadow." Death has no power over you and cannot hurt you.

Jesus Christ was crucified and placed in the borrowed tomb of Joseph of Arimathaea. The Lord explored the world of death. He arose on the third day and joyously announced, "Because I live, you will live also" (John 14:19).

Jesus appeared to John on the Isle of Patmos and said to him, "Do not be afraid; I am the First and the Last. I am He who lives, and was dead, and behold, I am alive forevermore, Amen. And I have the keys of Hades and of Death" (Rev. 1:17–18).

Are you ready to die?

Are you ready to die? I repeat, only those who are prepared to die are prepared to live. If you were to die in the next sixty seconds, where would you be? In heaven with God the Father or in the place called *hell* with the prince of darkness and his demonic legions? Those are the only two options.

If you have the slightest doubt about where you will be when you die, I want you to pray this prayer:

> Lord Jesus, I ask You to forgive me of all my sin. Cleanse me by Your precious blood of all unrighteousness. Come into my heart, and live today as Lord and Savior. From this day forward, I will follow You. I will be Your servant. I will read and obey Your Word. And now because of Christ's shed blood at the cross, I am saved. I am a child of God. All of my past is forgiven. Angels are writing my name in the Lamb's Book of Life. Heaven is now my eternal home.

Congratulations! You have just received eternal life. I encourage you to tell all your family and friends as soon as possible. You no longer have to fear death. Consider the story of Steve Sawyer, a hemophiliac teen who received a contaminated blood transfusion.

Soon after the transfusion, Steve was diagnosed with the AIDS virus and cirrhosis of the liver. In college Steve accepted Christ as Savior through Campus Crusade for Christ and spent his final years traveling throughout the United States, speaking to more than 100,000 students worldwide and helping to lead more than 10,000 students to faith in Jesus. "I know I've been given heaven," Steve once said, "so what am I going to do about it?"

A little over a year before he died, Steve said, "I have spent all this time on earth trying to do what Christ wants me to do and trying to be as much like Him as I possibly can—failing miserably more often than I would like to admit, but still trying. To be able to finally get there and look Him in the face and say, 'I may have screwed up, but it doesn't matter because of what You've done for me. Here I am; now I can finally see why it is I've been doing all this.'"

On Saturday, March 13, 1999, Steve departed this earth to be with the Lord. His mother says that just before Steve died, he sat up in bed and said, "Wow!"[2]

That's what it means to be a Christian.

The fear of man

Many of us are driven by the fear of other people's opinion. We are controlled by the criticism of people we know. We live in torment because of slanderous false accusations. Yet the Bible says, "The Lord is my helper and I will not fear what man shall do unto me" (Heb. 13:6).

If you are a woman in the workplace, do not fear your overbearing boss. You render him powerless with the divine confidence that comes from God. Solomon wrote, "The fear of man brings a snare, but whoever trusts in the LORD shall be safe" (Prov. 29:25).

Do not fear any man or group of men for any reason. King David said, "Though an army may encamp against me, my heart shall not fear; though war may rise against me, in this I will be confident" (Ps. 27:3). Stop living life with your fingers crossed. Instead walk in the divine confidence of the fearless life.

The fear of failure

The worst kind of failure is the failure to try. Yet the man who gets up one more time than he's knocked down cannot fail. In an earlier chapter, I mentioned many of the well-known entrepreneurs like Thomas Edison who kept on keeping on, despite failure. All of us need to remember them when we fear failure.

According to the Bible, God has no failure planned for you. Jeremiah 29:11 says, "'I know the plans I have for you,' declares the LORD, 'plans to prosper you and not to harm you, plans to give you hope and a future'" (NIV). If God has no failure planned for you, why are you afraid you will fail?

The fear of betrayal

Every divorce is born in betrayal.

Every case of child abuse is an act of betrayal.

Every act of gossip is an act of betrayal.

Judas betrayed Jesus. Absalom betrayed David. Demas betrayed Paul (2 Tim. 4:10). Sooner or later, someone you love will betray you. Your reaction is to either get bitter or get better.

How did Jesus react to Judas? Jesus did not succumb to self-pity. He did not retreat or turn away. When Judas approached Him in the

Garden of Gethsemane, Jesus said to Judas, "Friend, why have you come?" (Matt. 26:50). God's love exposes itself at the cost of embarrassment. His love does not fear shame or betrayal.

We fear the unknown; we fear death; we fear man; we fear failure; we fear betrayal; and we fear lack.

The fear of lack

Have you ever noticed that when a TV weatherman announces that a hurricane is coming, people race to the supermarkets and shop until the shelves are bare? Why? The fear of lack! Yet Paul wrote in Romans 8:32, "He who did not spare His own Son, but delivered Him up for us all, how shall He not with Him freely give us all things?"

Wall Street may go bust. The United States Treasury may eventually collapse, but the kingdom of God will never go broke! Stop living in the fear that the God who controls everything will let you die with nothing.

If we overcome these six deadly fears, we will, in fact, master the spirit of fear.

3
THE MASTERY OF ANGER

Have you ever been really angry? I mean red-faced, eye-popping, foaming-at-the-mouth angry? Good—you're normal!

Anger is a powerful divinely planted emotion that can be used for constructive or destructive purposes.

What makes you angry? Here are some responses I received from Cornerstone Church members in a church survey.

- I'm angry because "my spouse has filed for divorce without cause."

- I'm angry because "my father sexually abused me as a child."

- I'm angry because "I was passed over for a promotion on my job because of my race or because I was a woman in the workplace."

- I'm angry because of "an unexplained tragedy in my life, the death of a child, a life-threatening sickness, or financial ruin."

- I'm angry because "my life is out of control."

We often use the phrase *getting mad* to describe our anger. It's a fitting phrase. As a general rule when we lose our temper, we lose our sanity.

The question I want to ask you is this: When you get really angry, do you sin? Is all anger sin? Is anger ever helpful?

Paul wrote in Ephesians 4:26, "Be angry, and do not sin." Jesus said in Matthew 5:22, "Whoever is angry with his brother without a cause shall be in danger of the judgment." Note the phrase *without a cause*.

Anger can be OK if the cause is godly. So the question becomes, what is the motivation of the anger? When Jesus invaded the temple, He was the portrait of righteous wrath.

The truth is that all anger is not sin!

Jesus entered the temple—the house of God, the house of prayer—at a time when His church had been converted into a marketplace where people were robbed in the name of God. God's Word said that those who came to celebrate the feast were to present their sacrificial lambs to the priest for examination. OK—except that the priests would find flaws in the animals that did not exist. They would place the so-called flawed animal in a pen and then sell the worshiper another animal at an extravagant price. Later that same day, the priest would sell that "flawed animal" to another person.

Righteous Jews were as ashamed of what was happening in the temple as Jesus was. The outer court was a dirty, smelly, noisy marketplace. Imagine the deafening den of sellers hocking their wares over the noisy bleating of sheep. Then add the cackling of caged birds and the bargaining of moneychangers. And don't forget the bellowing of oxen and the loud voices of the religious racketeers. Into this madness came Jesus of Nazareth, the Son of God, the Prince of Peace. He was not coming to worship but to fight against the false values that had been brought into His church.

His eyes were blazing with rage as He invaded the house of God. He seized the whip of twisted cords. He swept the moneybags on the nearest table to the floor, scattering the coins. He turned over one table, then another, and another until all were smashed.

The Avenger of God stormed through the temple, driving out the cattle and releasing the doves, the sheep, and the goats. He scattered the terrified Pharisees with this war cry: "It is written, 'My house shall be called a house of prayer,' but you have made it a den of thieves" (Matt. 21:13).

What is the message of this scene? Did Jesus slip out of character? Did He lose His temper? Did Jesus sin? No. This scene has two messages for us.

First, anger is love's clearest voice when the cause is righteous. False values were evident in the house of God, and the loving, compassionate Jesus showed His outrage. That's a message for twenty-first-century Christians. There is a time to get off our blessed assurances and allow righteous anger to motivate us into divine action.

Unfortunately, America is being saturated with false values. We are becoming a nation of pagans. Morality is mocked, and America is rotting at the core with sexual disease. We have become a society of drive-by shootings, drugs, divorce, delinquency, and death by abortion. The tragedy of our day is that the situation is desperate, but the church is not. We watch the prince of darkness devour our children, destroy our marriages, and devastate our finances and health without protest.

The tragedy of our day is that the situation is desperate but the church is not.

Instead our response should be an outpouring of the righteous rage expressed in the words of King David: "Let God arise. Let His enemies be scattered" (Ps. 68:1). We are not here to be a carpet for the adversary. We are the ambassadors of Jesus Christ on this earth, just as Florence Nightingale was years ago.

Hospitals were horrible until Florence Nightingale got angry. She was not a gentle, timid angel of mercy. She was a stubborn and high-tempered woman. She hounded and badgered government officials to provide decent treatment for the wounded and dying until the bureaucracy trembled at the mention of her name. With the call of God on her unconquerable soul, she changed the condition of hospitals into houses of hope.

Some things are worth getting mad about. How can we love people and stand passively by as they are wounded or exploited by greedy men?

If I told you that someone was going to kill your son or your daughter, would you get angry? I hope so. But we are allowing drug lords in our cities to kill our sons and daughters every day, and we shrug our shoulders as if we are helpless. America is being buried in an avalanche of pornography sponsored by organized crime that turns on sexual deviates who rape our daughters and sodomize our sons. Pornography has no place in our homes or in our hearts. Get it out!

Mothers Against Drunk Drivers have the acronym M.A.D.D. They are driven by righteous anger to rid the streets of drunk drivers. God bless them all.

The second message of this scene in the temple is that anger is not a sinful emotion. Just as there are no bad pianos, only bad piano players, there are no bad emotions, only bad people. All emotions are God given. Every baby is born with the emotion of anger. Fail to feed him, and see how angry he can get. However, when that baby becomes forty-five years of age, he should have learned to harness his anger when dinner is not promptly served.

Two kinds of anger can be destructive: uncontrolled anger and misdirected anger.

Uncontrolled anger

Uncontrolled anger is sin. Recently I was playing golf and saw an allegedly intelligent man wrap his new golf club around a tree because his drive went in the woods. Was it the golf club's fault? Obviously not. Could this violent outburst redirect that drive onto the green? Obviously not!

I've seen grown men kick their cars in uncontrolled rage because the car wouldn't start. They slam the door, hit the hood, and call the car names you will not find in the movie script of *Terms of Endearment*. Forget that the car is out of gas or that the man hasn't changed the plugs in sixty thousand miles or that the battery came out of Noah's ark.

Beethoven is thought to have caused his own deafness by falling into a fit of uncontrolled anger. Physicians are now telling us that uncontrolled anger releases into the body chemical poisons that cause diseases like cancer and heart disease. Angry people have strokes at a greater rate than those who live with the peace of God in their hearts. Anger gives birth to ulcers. When you let yourself live in a state of uncontrolled rage, you are committing sin. You are, in fact, killing yourself.

Read through the Bible and notice the parade of men who destroyed themselves by their uncontrolled anger. Moses' inability to control his anger first appeared when he murdered the Egyptian who was beating a Hebrew slave. Then this anger reappeared when Moses came down from Mount Sinai and saw his congregation worshiping a golden calf. In uncontrolled rage he threw down God's Ten Commandments and smashed them to pieces. In each of these instances Moses' anger was as righteous as Jesus' anger in the temple. However, Moses responded with anger that was out of control.

This type of uncontrolled anger appeared a third time in Numbers 20, when God told Moses to "speak to the rock" so the water the Israelites so badly needed would come from it. Moses was so angry with his rebellious congregation that he struck the rock in rage. His frustration with other people's conduct affected his relationship with God.

Is that true of you?

If so, remember God's answer to Moses' final act of uncontrolled anger. God forbade Moses to enter the Promised Land with the children of Israel. Three times in Deuteronomy Moses prayed for God to change His mind, and God said that His judgment would stand. Moses' uncontrolled anger killed his dream. His anger kept him from his divine destiny!

Anger is just one letter short of danger.

Have your dreams been destroyed by your uncontrolled anger? Has your marriage been crucified by hateful words, spoken in anger? Have your relationships with your children been crushed by words of absolute anger? Have your relationships with other believers been corrupted because of your uncontrollable anger?

Uncontrolled anger drove Cain to murder his brother Abel in cold blood. Uncontrolled anger separated the elder brother from his loving father. When his brother, the prodigal son, returned from wasting his life and his father's money in a faraway land, the forgiving father killed the fatted calf in celebration. This made the elder brother so angry that he would not join the festivities. He felt he was being treated unjustly since he had remained faithful to his father yet never received such a celebration. His anger separated him from his father and his brother. How about you? Does anger separate you from your loved ones?

Misdirected anger

We probably suffer more from misdirected anger than uncontrolled anger. On one occasion when I was in Mexico on vacation, I went to a bullfight. I watched the picadors torment the bull with their lances until the bull, in misdirected anger, would blindly charge the red cape held by the matador. The bull ignored the real source of his problem: the prissy matador in bright green pants shouting, *"Toro, toro, toro."* I became so frustrated, I cheered for the bull. "Swing your horns to the right," I yelled. "That's the source of your problem."

I almost started a riot. As soon as I shouted, the bull swung to the right and threw the matador ten feet in the air, and hundreds of angry Mexicans were staring in my direction. The bull had finally attacked the real problem.

Anyone who angers you conquers you.

What are you mad about? Are you attacking the problem or symptoms of the problem? Are you blindly charging a red cape or solving the problem?

One day when Abraham Lincoln stood on the docks of New Orleans, he watched a black woman sold into slavery, leaving her husband and son behind. Lincoln dug his fingernails into his hands until they bled as he thought, *That's wrong. And if I ever get the chance, I'll stop slavery.*

An internal rage exploded. Not uncontrolled or misdirected anger, but a quiet resolve that carried Lincoln through political defeat after political defeat until he became president of the United States. Unlike Moses, Lincoln accomplished his dream: He signed the Emancipation Proclamation, which ended slavery in America forever.

When is it wrong to be angry?

When we are angry without a cause!

It is wrong when we are bitter or resentful and speak hateful things of others. Proverbs 15:18 says, "A wrathful man stirs up strife." Solomon wrote in Proverbs 21:19, "Better to dwell in the wilderness, than with an angry and contentious woman."

How do we master our uncontrolled and misdirected anger?

Controlled anger

Let me suggest four ways to control anger:

1. Become Spirit-filled.

We cannot always control our emotions with our own will power, but once the Holy Spirit controls us, our emotions will fall in line. The apostle Paul wrote in Galatians 5:22: "The fruit of the Spirit is love, joy, peace, long-suffering, kindness, goodness, faithfulness, gentleness, self-control," which is the opposite of being angry and losing self-control.

The fruits of the Spirit are only possible when you walk in the Spirit. This is a daily process of dying to self and drinking in the living water of the Word of God. Are you Spirit-filled or self-filled? Are you driven by the Holy Spirit or controlled by an evil spirit?

2. Learn to overlook a transgression.

Proverbs 19:11 says, "The discretion of a man makes him slow to anger, and his glory is to overlook a transgression."

"A happy marriage requires a deaf husband and a blind wife."

Christ is our example of how to respond to injustice. After cleansing the temple as the Avenger of God, He was personally attacked by the Roman government when He was arrested and falsely accused. Roman soldiers slapped Him in the face, spit on Him, ridiculed Him, and crowned Him with a crown of thorns. His response? "But Jesus still answered nothing" (Mark 15:5). As the mob screamed for Jesus' blood He stood before Pilate in absolute silence, even though He had all power in heaven and earth.

That's controlled anger. Proverbs 16:32 says, "He who is slow to anger is better than the mighty, and he who rules his spirit than he who takes a city."

Did someone hurt your feelings ten years ago, and you're still not over it? Overlook the other person's transgression, and your life will be content.

3. Don't become friends with angry people.

Proverb 22:24–25 says, "Make no friendship with an angry man...lest you learn his ways and set a snare for your soul."

Young lady, if the young man you're dating is driven by uncontrolled anger, dump him today. Young man, if the young lady you're dating has uncontrolled anger, love at first sight is cured by a second look. Keep looking!

Father, do you have a child who goes from one temper tantrum to another? Solomon offers this advice: "Foolishness is bound in the heart of a child; but the rod of correction shall drive it far from him." When I was a child and lost my temper, my father would always help me find it with a strap in his hand. I learned to control my anger.

4. Learn to laugh.

The Bible says, "The joy of the LORD is your strength" (Neh. 8:10). Laughter can be the antidote for uncontrolled and misdirected anger; laughter can even be a healing balm for disease.

Several years ago, just before I went to the platform to deliver the commencement address at Oral Roberts University, a beautiful and gracious middle-aged woman from Virginia walked up to me and gave this delightful testimony.

Her father, who was a prosperous Virginia farmer, was dying with cancer. The large tumors in his stomach were visible to all those around him. She gave her father one of my tapes entitled, "Being Happy in an Unhappy World," and he began to listen and laugh. The more he listened, the more he laughed. As friends would come by to say their final farewells, they would listen to the tape and laugh.

Instead of dying, this man started eating. When he went to the doctor for an examination, the doctor said, "Your cancer is in complete remission."

This man laughed his way to life. Medical science says that laughter releases an enzyme in your physical body that heals. Have you forgotten how to laugh?

You need to choose between the anger that is killing you and the joy of the Lord, which will heal you emotionally or physically. Anger destroys your body, your soul, your spirit, your marriage, your health, your children, and your peace of mind. Make the choice between laughter and anger. Choose laughter!

We need to master our tendency to worry; we need to master our unwarranted fears; and we need to master our uncontrolled and misdirected anger.

4
THE MASTERY OF DEPRESSION

Often when I am searching for a sermon series, I survey my congregation and ask them to list the major problems in their spiritual lives. On the survey, depression is the number one emotional problem in a congregation of eighteen thousand people.

Who gets depressed? Almost everyone at some time. Let me define depression as "a negative state of mind that causes a change in your mood or a change in your behavior—and in severe cases, a change in your physical body."

Depression is the opposite of being happy. Depression covers everything from the blues to minor mood swings to severe depression, which your psychiatrist would call psychosis. (In this chapter I am not talking about clinical depression.) Look at the heroes of faith who were depressed.

Job was depressed and cursed the day he was born by saying, "May the day perish on which I was born" (Job 3:3). You don't have to be Sigmund Freud to see depression in Job's statement.

Elijah shouted toward heaven, "LORD, take my life...I am the only one left [living for you]" (1 Kings 19:4, 10). Pity-party prayers lead to depression.

In the Psalms King David often expressed his depression with statements like "Why are you cast down, O my soul?" (Ps. 42:5). David was depressed over decisions that had backfired. For instance, while he was busy with the affairs of state and marshalling his army, he had little time for his son Absalom. The everyday decision to spend his time as he did throughout his son's childhood backfired on him when Absalom betrayed David and brought his kingdom into civil war.

The disciples were depressed. They had Jesus Christ for a pastor, who was God on earth, but still had very real emotional and spiritual problems. (That's a comforting thought to every pastor on the planet.) Jesus said to them, "Let not your heart be troubled" (John 14:1).

Charles Haddon Spurgeon suffered from depression after a tragedy occurred in his church. The prince of preachers was victimized by a certified halfwit who leaped to his feet in Spurgeon's church and screamed, "Fire!" A stampede ensued, and several church members were trampled to death. The heart of Charles Spurgeon was broken, and he sank into deep depression. He was taken to the home of the senior deacon where constant prayer bathed his soul until he recovered.[3]

Abraham Lincoln suffered from severe depression. Winston Churchill suffered from terrible depression and said, "It follows me like a black dog."

I repeat: Everyone gets depressed at some time. Here are five major causes of depression. Check to see if one of these causes might be causing you to feel blue.

Five major causes of depression

The first cause of depression is extreme disappointment. Ever notice how no one gets depressed when everything is going right? Who needs God with money in the bank, no debt, and good health? Then comes a broken marriage and bankruptcy. Or perhaps a crisis with your children or tragedy that strikes like lightning out of a clear blue sky. Depression comes charging like a ravenous lion out of a thicket. Suddenly you need God and need Him desperately.

The second cause of depression is a lack of self-esteem, which we talked about in chapter four. I often advise the members of my church, "Every day as you wake up, you must confess: 'I am special! I am loved! I am unique and a child of God. I was born an original and refuse to become a cheap copy. I am created a little lower than the angels with the royal blood of heaven flowing in my veins. I am on my way to heaven, and nothing on this earth can defeat me.'"

The third cause of depression is unfair comparisons. Comparing yourself with someone else who always scores more favorably than you is unscriptural, ungodly, and unholy. Let me shock you! There will always be someone in your profession better than you. There will be a better doctor, a better lawyer, a better salesman, a better teacher, or a better mother. Lady, there will always be someone prettier than you. Mister, there will always be someone more handsome or intelligent than you. You are what your genetic code says you are going to be, and that was determined the moment you were conceived.

The fourth cause of depression is unrealistic goal setting. You can be anything in life you want to be, but you can't be everything. The apostle Paul said, "This one thing I do" (Phil. 3:13). Find out what you do best in life, and do it with all your heart, soul, mind, and body. Stop trying to be the jack-of-all-trades and the master of none. Do one thing better than anyone else, and your prosperity and success are absolutely guaranteed.

Tiger Woods is the greatest golfer in the world. John Grisham is one of the greatest authors in the world. Pavarotti is one of the best tenors in the world. None of them are trying to be pro-football players. They are doing what they do best. Find your field and stay in it!

The fifth cause of depression is biological malfunction, a chemical imbalance that medical science can regulate. I encourage every person who feels depressed to get a good medical examination. On one occasion a church member came into my office and said to me, "I have a demon."

I talked to her for about an hour, and, after listening to her story, I responded, "You do not have a demon. You're in a state of depression." I requested that she call her physician and get a complete medical examination. She went reluctantly.

Two weeks later she came into my office as happy as a lark and thought I was a genius. She went to a physician who balanced her hormones, and life was beautiful. If you are depressed for a long period of time, you must consult a Christian counselor or psychiatrist.

Not taking care of your physical body is to be possessed with the spirit of stupid. Some people ruin their health as they strive to make a fortune and then spend that fortune trying to regain their health. Your body is the temple of God. Take care of it. It's the only one you have.

I suggest six steps to help defeat the depression you might be feeling at this time.

SIX STEPS IN DEFEATING DEPRESSION

1. Attack your problem with the power of the gospel.

Many problems are rooted in sin. I believe in counseling, but not eternal counseling. I believe in looking for solutions, but not perpetual sympathy. Too many people want their sins explained, not forgiven. They want to be right, not reconciled.

I cringe when I hear this phrase, *I can't.*

"I can't" love my husband or wife.

"I can't" discipline my children.

"I can't" stop taking drugs.

"I can't" give up my live-in lover.

That's an absolute lie. Change the words *I can't* to *I won't,* and you have at least faced the truth.

In Philippians 4:13, Paul wrote, "I can do all things through Christ who strengthens me." A Christian who is depressed continuously is depressed because he is choosing to be depressed, unless there is a chemical imbalance in the person's makeup. This Christian rejects God's principles by refusing the Spirit-filled life, which is evidenced by love, joy, and peace.

Quit jabbering about being Spirit-filled when you are moping around the house feeling sorry for yourself. Stop talking about your relationship with Christ when you harbor resentment toward another brother. You are a Bible-thumping grouch and need to discover what real conversion truly means.

2. Spend time each day meditating on God's Word.

Who controls your mind—the Holy Spirit or Hollywood? Your mind is like a fantastic computer: "Trash in…trash out."

When you watch forty hours of sex and violence on television, that's trash in. All that can come out is trash. And the Holy Spirit can't live in a trash dump.

Romans 12:2 warns against this. "Do not be conformed to this world," the apostle Paul wrote, "but be transformed by the renewing of your mind." David wrote in Psalm 1:2: "But his delight is in the law of the LORD, and in His law he meditates day and night." If you want the happiness of God, you must have the holiness of God.

God's Word is a penicillin shot for depression. When you are depressed, remember the following scriptures:

> Why are you cast down, O my soul?
> And why are you disquieted within me?
> Hope in God, for I shall yet praise Him,
> The help of my countenance and my God.
>
> —PSALM 43:5

> Peace I leave with you, My peace I give to you; not as the world gives do I give to you. Let not your heart be troubled; neither let it be afraid.
>
> —JOHN 14:27

> These things I have spoken to you, that in Me you may have peace. In the world you will have tribulation; but be of good cheer; I have overcome the world.
>
> —JOHN 16:33

3. Get rid of grudges daily.

The Bible says, "If you are angry, don't sin by nursing your grudge. Don't let the sun go down with you still angry, get over it quickly" (Eph. 4:26, HIT PARAPHRASE).

Hopefully you have identified any uncontrolled and misdirected anger and are ready to deal with it. Certainly forgiveness is a part of this process, and we will talk about forgiveness in another section of this chapter.

Family harmony is particularly essential to your spiritual and mental health. Unfortunately, unresolved family conflicts can last forever. The Middle East is on the verge of World War III because of a family feud that started six thousand years ago between Isaac and Ishmael. The message is very clear: Get tight with your family. Don't allow grudges to keep you apart.

4. Decide to be enthusiastic!

Stop making a career of your problems. And don't avoid activities that seem difficult. You won't grow. Go where the expectations and the demands to perform are high. Get excited about your life.

Humility is a virtue; timidity is an illness.

Years ago I read the story of a college football player who had great ability but was simply not motivated. As a fullback he had the power, speed, and open-field agility that left tacklers scattered all over the field behind him, facedown in frustration. His coach tried to get him to use this ability, but nothing worked.

One day a telegram came to the coach as he stood on the practice field. The father of the unmotivated fullback had died. The coach kindly informed the player of his father's passing, and the boy left immediately to travel out of state so he could attend his father's funeral.

The player returned just in time for the homecoming game against their archrival. "Can I play today, Coach?" he asked.

"Son, you have more athletic ability than anyone on this team, but you've been such an unmotivated goof-off all year it would be wrong to replace someone who has given his best."

The game began, and the archrival marched down the field at will. At halftime the score was 27-0.

"Coach, can I please play now?" the young fullback asked again.

"Go ahead! You can't make things any worse," responded the dejected coach.

The formerly unmotivated player raced onto the field like his shoes were on fire. He carried the ball like an enraged bull, ripping through the opposing team at will. Play after play, first down after first down, touchdown after touchdown—until his team won 28 to 27 in the closing seconds of play.

The exuberant fans stormed the field and soon tore down the goal-post. Finally the team managed to get off the field into the dressing room. The stunned coach walked over to the previously unmotivated fullback who had just single-handedly smashed their archrival.

"Son, I knew you had the potential to be a great player," he said. "Can you tell me why you waited until today to play such an enthusiastic game?"

The player paused for a moment as tears began to form in his eyes. "Coach, you know that my father died this week. What you don't know is that my father was blind all his life. He never saw me play one game. Today he saw me play for the first time, and I wanted to do my best."

Every one of us has the potential to be enthusiastic. The word *enthusiasm* comes from the Greek words *en* (in) and *theos* (God). In God. Some people see this word as meaning "to be inspired by God, to be possessed by God." I believe God builds enthusiasm into a human being. It's impossible to believe the Bible and be a pessimist.

If you lose your enthusiasm, you turn your back on your divine inheritance. Enthusiasm draws people and success toward you; depression drives people and success from you.

Now I extend a challenge to you. Go to your job tomorrow with an enthusiasm never seen in you before. If you are a mother, be enthusiastic with your children. Send them out of your home each morning with enough confidence to wrestle Hulk Hogan.

If you are a father, be enthusiastic with your family. Let them know in word and deed that they are the absolute top priority in your life. Be a loving leader, a good provider, and a protector of those you love.

If you are in Christ, you are bound to be enthusiastic.

"But," you may say, "my life is hard. I don't feel good, I haven't been treated well."

Listen to me! Life is a blend of laughter and tears, a combination of rain and sunshine. Make this affirmation, "I will not allow this heart-ache to deter me from living in delight today. Today, with God's help, I take control of my life. Lord, give me peace, give me love, give me joy, and give me excitement for today."

5. Spend time each week with committed Christians.

Proverbs 13:20 says, "He who walks with wise men will be wise, but the companion of fools will be destroyed." The truth is, you become like your friends and family, whether you intend to or not.

Many years ago a man named Max Jukes lived in New York. He did not believe in Christ or in Christian training. He fathered 13 children. He refused to take his children to church, even when they asked to go. He has 1,026 descendants. Of these, 300 were sent to prison for an average term of thirteen years; 190 were public prostitutes; 509 were admitted alcoholics and drug addicts. His family, thus far, has cost the state in excess of $420,000. Surely the agnostic influence of their ancestor filtered down through his many descendants who made no contribution to society.

Jonathan Edwards lived in the same state at the same time as Jukes. He too fathered 13 children. He loved the Lord and saw that his children were in church every Sunday. This beloved preacher also served the Lord to the best of his ability. Edwards had 929 descendants, and of these 430 were ministers; 86 became university professors; 13 became university presidents; 75 authored books; 7 were elected to the United States Congress; and 3 were governors. One descendant was vice president of his nation. Jonathan Edwards' descendants never cost the state one cent. This great preacher not only influenced his era for Christ; his Christian beliefs and values filtered down through his many descendants, who contributed immeasurably to the life of plenty in this land.[4]

Beliefs and values are contagious. Spend time each week with committed Christians.

6. Do something nice for one special person every week.

Sometimes depression can be caused by an over-concentration on ourselves and our problems. Instead we need to spend some time thinking of others. The Bible says, "Give, and it will be given to you" (Luke 6:38). A loving act—your time, flowers, a card, or homemade cookies—will enrich someone else's life and make you a happier person.

For a number of years in our marriage Diana and I have practiced what we call O.W.E.—"one way everyday." Each day we find one special way to say, "I love you." It's simply amazing what one simple loving act can do to make that day unique and special.

Remember you're as happy as you choose to be.

5
THE MASTERY OF RESENTMENT

Resentment is an emotional prison built brick by brick, hurt by hurt, and tear by tear. The mind that is poisoned by resentment lives constantly in a dark world ruled by suspicion and distrust. Those tormented souls living in the sewer of resentment are eternal victims in the unending melodrama of woe and doom and gloom.

Resentment is the inability to adjust emotionally to unexpected displeasure, a hateful remark, or an act of betrayal. It is impossible to live life without being offended by someone about something at sometime. The Bible makes this clear. It says, "It is impossible that no offenses should come" (Luke 17:1).

You see resentful people everywhere—in hospitals, in rest homes, in jails, in stores, in offices, and in homes. Resentful people sit next to you in your church. They sing next to you in the choir. They work next to you at work. They lie next to you in the bed. They eat next to you at your supper table. Many cannot function on their jobs or in their marriages because of the wounds and hurts—real or imagined—that have occurred in their lives. Their ministry potential is destroyed by a resentful disposition that corrupts everything and everyone they touch.

Resentment is always more pronounced when the offense happens within a family. The American Civil War, where brother fought against brother and fathers fought against their sons, brought resentment and division in America that lingers to this day.

People demonstrate three universal signs when the spirit of resentment snares them.

Three universal signs of resentment
The first cardinal sign of resentment is hostility. This person's speech is a poisoned stream of criticism of others, and his or her hostile acts of aggression never cease. If this hostility is directed inwardly, it can produce thoughts of suicide. Hostile people vacillate between depression and anger.

The second cardinal sign of resentment is anxiety. You are anxious about everything. You worry about problems you've never had and will never have. You worry when everything's going great, wondering when your life's going to go south. Every day you find something to be mad about or resentful toward. You call yourself a Christian and profess to follow the Prince of Peace, but you live in perpetual torment.

The third sign of resentment is a guilt complex. You might ask, "What's the difference between a guilt complex and the true guilt that drives one to repentance?

A guilt complex is driven by the spirit of condemnation, which comes from Satan. You live under a dark cloud of oppression. You pray but never feel joy or peace. You are seldom hopeful and are generally pessimistic. You feel a constant state of defeat and oppression.

However, when the Holy Spirit convicts you of sin, you feel true guilt and are driven to repentance. Once you repent, the guilt vanishes, and you feel wonderful, free, and full of hope for the future. The divine release is supernatural.

You will never be set free from the spirit of condemnation by reading self-help books. Yet you can be free instantly through the power of Jesus' name and the blood of His cross. The apostle Paul wrote, "There is therefore now no condemnation to those who are in Christ Jesus" (Rom. 8:1).

I have found that four things will help release you from resentment.

Four releases for resentment

First, admit you are resentful. You cannot change what you will not confront. Don't make excuses for your irrational behavior. Look at the face in the mirror and say out loud, "There are going to be some changes made." Take action today. There is no such thing as indecision: Either you decide—or you decide not to decide; but in either case you have made a decision.

Second, go to the person who has offended you and be reconciled. The cure for resentment is reconciliation. If you have allowed resentment to separate you from a member of your family, a brother or sister in the body of Christ, or a dear friend in the workplace, go to the person who has offended you and be reconciled. If you will not forgive another of their offense toward you, God cannot forgive your offense toward Him (Matt. 6:12).

Third, stop your pity party! Stop blaming your mother or father for the person you've become. Choices have consequences, and you are today what you decided yesterday to become. You are as happy or miserable as you choose to be. Stop playing the blame game that I mentioned in chapter two. Stop whining, "Nobody understands me" or "Nobody really cares about me."

Fourth, recognize the immutable sovereignty of God. Hear this loud and clear: Nothing happens to you without God's permission. You may not understand what's happening, but be assured that God has not been taken by surprise.

People often become resentful when tragedy strikes their lives, and they blame it on God, saying, "This is the will of God." Their inability to understand God's will and man's free-moral agency brings confusion and deception that make their resentment justified.

You don't really believe that a compassionate God would deliberately strike down your little girl with a deadly disease, do you?

You don't really believe that a loving God would send a heart attack to your husband and "will" that he die at the age of thirty-six, leaving you with three children to rear alone, do you?

You don't really believe that a caring God would cause a plane to crash and "will" that two hundred people die in that tragedy, do you?

In your heart of hearts, you know that God is love, but the confusion comes in deciphering what is the will of God. People say, "Isn't everything that happens God's will?" Absolutely not! God is omniscient, and nothing can happen that lies outside His knowledge. God is omnipotent, and nothing can happen outside His permissive will. But everything that happens is not God's intentional will because of the free moral agency of man. Man, as a free moral agent, has a God-given right to choose, and those choices bring consequences.

You will have the opportunity on a regular basis to become very resentful. If you allow resentment to fester in your soul, it will destroy your heart, your soul, your mind, and your body. If you recognize resentment in your speech or in your thoughts, confess it and move beyond it.

Christians have been called to master our tendency to worry, to master our unwarranted fears, to master our uncontrolled and misdirected anger, to master our tendency to be depressed, and to master our resentment.

6

THE MASTERY OF A LACK OF FORGIVENESS

You will never master yourself until you learn how to truly forgive other people. Forgiveness means a full pardon from the pain and penalty of the past. It's the canceling of a debt. It's a fresh start, another chance, a new beginning. Forgiveness is not softhearted foolishness. It's a major step toward self-mastery.

Do you have the courage to forgive? I can give you three reasons why forgiveness is not an option for you.

Three reasons for forgiveness

First, forgiveness is essential for your healing. Jesus was called the Great Physician. He saw the relationship between forgiveness of sin and healing. He often said, "Thy sins be forgiven thee....Be healed" (Matt. 9:2; Mark 2:5).

One night the phone rang at my home. It was late, and I heard the crying on the other end of the line before I heard a voice speak. Then I recognized the voice of a dear friend and parishioner. He told me that his wife of fifteen years had just asked him for a divorce. There had been no quarreling, not even a dispute. There was no warning. Not a hint, and then, like lightning out of heaven, his wife announced, "I want a divorce."

His wife had just informed him that she had been having an affair with a man in her office for months. She could no longer pretend that she loved her husband. Instead she said of this new man, "I love him, and he loves me. Of course, I'll want the children. We'll be married as soon as possible and move to another state."

By this woman's confession, my friend had been a loyal husband. He had provided handsomely for their family. Now three beautiful children who were the love of his life were about to be scattered like straw in a whirlwind.

His wife filed for a divorce on the grounds of "irreconcilable differences," which in many cases is legal terminology for adultery. The court gave her the children and a handsome child-support settlement.

Then the father returned to a house full of memories. The places where his children's pictures hung on the walls were visible. There were empty closets where his children's clothes had been. There was a rag doll under the bed, a toy pistol in the yard, a forgotten football in the garage—all haunting testimonials of his three children's absence. The house was filled with the thunderous sound of silence.

The emotions of the father vacillated from deep depression to words of rage. One day his world had been secure, happy, and filled with the beauty of life. The next, it was filled with rejection, bitterness, haunting memories, and heartbreaking loneliness.

He said to me, "Pastor Hagee, all I've worked for, all I've dreamed about for fifteen years, has been destroyed in a day. My life is ruined! I don't deserve this, Pastor! If I could take the calendar and rip the date of the divorce from my life, I'd be in heaven."

My friend's emotional nightmare affected his job performance. His friends were withdrawing from him because his speech was an endless litany of remorse and pain. After weeks he came to my office, and we both knew what he wanted to talk about. He sobbed his way through the gory details of his tragedy one more time.

Finally, he opened the door for healing and freedom with the question, "Pastor, what can I do to end this misery?"

"For your emotional, mental, and spiritual survival you must do something you've never even slightly considered," I answered.

He looked at me and snarled, "What's that?"

I looked him straight in the eye. "You must forgive your wife today—totally and completely."

He was obviously enraged by the thought. "I don't feel like forgiving her or that scum bucket she ran off with." (In truth, "scum bucket" is a cleaned up version of what he actually said.)

For one hour this man sobbed his way to complete forgiveness. Then finally he was free. He was ready for a new beginning. He had reached a point in self-mastery in which he was ready to live his life. Why? He had the courage to forgive.

Second, forgiveness can save your eternal soul. If you will not forgive another, God cannot forgive you. And if you remain in a state of unforgiveness, you cannot enter the gates of heaven. Is the grudge you're bearing toward another person sending you into eternity without God?

Bishop Hazen Werner tells the story of a father whose son was among the first to be sent to the Pacific in World War II. When his son was getting on the train at the end of his last leave, the father wanted to say so many things to him but didn't. The train pulled out of the railroad station, the boy was gone, and his father knew he might not see him again. That day the father thought, *If my son is killed, I hope every Japanese will die.*

When this man's son was killed in combat, the father's words came back to haunt him: *If my son is killed, I hope every Japanese will die.* He fell on his knees, asking God for forgiveness.

A year later, the father took the insurance money he had received from the government for the death of his son and placed this money in an offering for missions to Japan.

The father knew that what Japan needed—and what we all need—is forgiveness, not more punishment.

Forgiveness is not an emotion. It is, first, an act of your will. Then God's peace, which you need to survive in every storm, will come later. If you don't forgive another, you will live in hell every day the rest of your life.

Forgiveness is not optional.

Third, forgiveness is not optional. Jesus said, "For if you forgive men their trespasses, your heavenly Father will also forgive you. But if you do not forgive men their trespasses, neither will your Father forgive your trespasses" (Matt. 6:14–15). Luke 6:37 says, "Forgive, and you will be forgiven."

The apostle Paul wrote, "And be kind to one another, tenderhearted, forgiving one another, even as God in Christ forgave you" (Eph. 4:32). If God is perfect, and He forgave you, why can't you, with all your faults and failures, forgive others? Don't say, "I can't." The truth is you won't.

There are sixty-two references to forgiveness in the New Testament, and twenty-two of those sixty-two times involve forgiving others. Without that, there is no forgiveness for ourselves, not ever. If you will not forgive another, God cannot forgive you.

When is the last time someone really hurt you? Take a walk through the corridors of your memory. Someone, somewhere in your past rejected you in such a way that you still remember it. Do you fantasize about smashing your fist into the faces of some of the people from your past? Do you mentally scheme about how to embarrass them publicly? You will never be free until you learn to forgive them.

Were you abused as a child? Did you cry in the night and no one came?

Did your tears fall on your pillow unnoticed by anyone? Maybe you were sexually molested. There's an inner rage known only to God and others who have been sexually molested. There is freedom through forgiveness.

Did you suffer through your parents' divorce as a child? Were you placed in an orphanage, unwanted and rejected? Did you stand alone on visitation day waiting for someone to come, and no one ever came? Are you bitter and resentful? There is freedom in forgiveness.

The list is endless, but the point is this: The only way you're ever going to have self-determination and emotional freedom is through forgiveness. Why? Because until you forgive the person who hurt you, freedom is not possible. Think about it! The person you detest the most has become your master. This person is not hurting; you are. For your sake, forgive and be free.

To forgive another without demanding a change in his or her conduct is to make the grace of God an accomplice to evil.

However, to forgive another without demanding a change in his or her conduct is to make the grace of God an accomplice to evil. The forgiveness that Christ teaches in the Bible demands a change.

Forgiveness expects a change

The Pharisees caught a woman in the act of adultery, which makes me wonder where the Pharisees were when they caught her. Perhaps they were standing in line, just waiting to accuse her. When they brought the woman to Jesus, He forgave the woman, saying, "Go and sin no more" (John 8:11). He expected a change in her conduct.

How does this translate into the twenty-first century? When a husband asks his wife, "Will you forgive me of adultery?," her answer is, "Yes, I'll forgive you if you'll change. But if this is going to be a pattern of conduct, hit the road and don't even think about coming back."

When a homosexual son confesses his sin to his father and asks for forgiveness, the biblical answer is, "Yes, you are forgiven, but you must change. We will not accept homosexuality as an alternative lifestyle."

I repeat: Granting forgiveness without demanding a change becomes a license to sin. That kind of forgiveness is not found in Scripture. Jesus did not teach it. Paul did not teach it. Today we teach it because it covers up the stench of our godless, undisciplined lives.

"OK," you might be saying, "you've convinced me that I should forgive. But that's easier said than done!"

How do I forgive someone?

First, forgive immediately. The Bible says, "Therefore if you bring your gift to the altar, and there remember that your brother has something against you, leave your gift there before the altar, and go your way. First be reconciled to your brother, and then come and offer your gift" (Matt. 5:23–24).

The message is very clear: Forgive immediately. On the day of Pentecost, Peter told his audience to forgive so that "your sins may be blotted out" (Acts 3:19). Not scratched out with "I'll pray about it" written in the margin. Stop the façade. God is not listening to your prayer while you have angst in your heart against a brother.

Religious people are forever trying to earn God's forgiveness. They know their lives are saturated with sin so they do ridiculous things trying to earn forgiveness. They join the church. They give money to the poor. They physically punish themselves.

I was in Mexico visiting a Catholic cathedral and saw a man crawling on his bloody knees toward the altar. Why? He was trying to get forgiveness. He was so sincere but so wrong. Christ forgave him at the cross. You are forgiven because God loves you. You are not forgiven because you do good things. You are forgiven because the blood of Jesus Christ has removed every crimson stain from your soul. Paul wrote, "We have redemption through His blood" (Eph. 1:7).

God is in a hurry to forgive. He dumps the ink well over your record and crumbles the page and burns it never to be remembered anymore. You don't have to beg God for forgiveness. He's eager to forgive you. He's eager to give you a new beginning. Extend God's grace to those who have harmed you.

Second, be reconciled. You take the initiative and go to your mother, father, wife, or husband and make the matter right. Remember, nothing is ever settled until it's settled right.

Third, forgive yourself. Often the most difficult act of forgiveness is the forgiveness of ourselves. You can forgive another's foolish mistake, but not your own. If God has forgiven you, forgive yourself.

"How often shall I forgive?" Peter asked Jesus. At that time in history, there was a teaching that if a man forgave three times, he was a righteous man. After three times you could pick up stones and stone to death the one who sinned against you. Peter was looking for a place to stop forgiving and start stoning.

Jesus enlarged the boundaries of forgiveness. He said, "Forgive seventy times seven" (Matt. 18:22). Technically that's 490 times, but actually the message is, "Forgive until it becomes a habit."

Are you willing to forgive? You will never master yourself until you are willing to forgive another.

We Christians have been called to master our tendency to worry, to master our unwarranted fears, to master our uncontrolled and misdirected anger, to master our tendency to be depressed, to master our resentment, and to master our lack of forgiveness. There is one more area of mastery to discover.

7

THE MASTERY OF A LACK OF REPENTANCE

The last word of Jesus Christ to the church was not the Great Commission. The Great Commission is indeed to be our focus until the end of the age, but the Lord's last word to the church was "repent." "Repent…or else." (See Revelation 2:5–16.)

That was Jesus' command to five of the seven churches in Asia, and I'm sure that ratio still holds. Five out of seven churches, and five out of seven Christians, need, first of all, to repent.

There is a Bible truth most Christians simply do not grasp. That truth is this: God does not punish people for sinning; He punishes them because they refuse to *repent* of their sin.

Let me use Adam and Eve as an illustration. Satan seduced Eve to tempt Adam to eat the forbidden fruit. Adam and Eve hid themselves and used fig leaves to cover themselves. In the cool of the evening God came searching for them. "Where art thou?" He asked. When God asks questions, He's not looking for answers. He knew where they were. He knew they had sinned, and now He was going to give them an opportunity to repent.

God questioned Eve about her part in the forbidden fruit drama. Eve blamed it on the serpent. God quizzed Adam about his part in taking the forbidden fruit. Adam, like most husbands, blamed it on his wife. Neither of them repented, but both of them justified their actions because they blamed their actions on someone else.

All they had to do to stay in the Garden of Eden was to repent. But no—they chose to rationalize their sin away rather than admit it. Satan's substitute for repentance is man's rationalization of evil.

Satan's substitute for repentance is man's rationalization of evil.

Let's go back in time to the decade of the fifties when psychiatry and various forms of therapy began to achieve credibility in America. If you accepted Freudian psychiatry, when you did something wrong, you no longer had to hold yourself responsible. Who was to blame? Your parents! "It's all their fault; emotionally they crippled me; they scarred me; they were overly demanding or compulsive or permissive or abusive. They made me what I am. If I do something wrong, don't hold me accountable. It's my parents' fault!"

The sixties—with our nation in turmoil from the assassinations of John F. Kennedy, Robert Kennedy, and Martin Luther King, and with rioting sweeping across our major cities—gave rise to a new way of thinking: If you did something wrong, you had a new place to cast blame. "It's not your fault; it's society's fault." Therefore, you could burn down cities because of the racism in society; you could burn your draft card or burn the flag or take over your university because of America's military industrial complex. The bottom line was the rationalization: "Don't blame me. It's society's fault."

Then came the seventies, the "Me Decade." That decade came up with an even better and more sophisticated concept: Nobody's at fault! The seventies gave us no-fault insurance and no-fault divorce. The seventies featured the sexual revolution and the breakdown of the traditional family. If you acted in an immoral manner, you didn't have to take responsibility for your actions. All you had to do was use one of those clichés that became the battle cry of that decade: "I've got my own life to live." "Don't try to lay a guilt trip on me." "I'm OK; you're OK." "I can do whatever I want; don't hold me accountable; nobody's to blame."

With the coming of the eighties traditional values returned to our culture through the Reagan revolution and the "moral majority." The concept of individual responsibility and personal accountability, which is so basic to our Judeo-Christian heritage, returned to its proper place as the accepted norm of American society. But the Reagan era is over now. Not only did our beloved former president have Alzheimer's, our nation collectively has Alzheimer's about what's right and what's wrong.

Today we have a new concept concerning responsibility and accountability, a perspective more radical and more dangerous than any of these earlier ones. Now the thinking seems to be: If something goes wrong, it's not your parent's fault, and it's not anyone's fault, and it's not society's fault. If you do something to hurt another person, it's that person's fault! The victim is held responsible.

One of the most brutal attacks in memory was that which took place in 1989 in Central Park to a young woman who was viciously beaten and raped while jogging through the park at night. She has now gone public with a book and has appeared on several television talk shows. I am not surprised that many people called in and questioned what she was doing out late at night, jogging in Central Park. Their implication? She was asking for trouble. That's the attitude some people have these days whenever a rape takes place. It was the victim's fault.

Was your house robbed? You should have had the burglar alarm on. Did someone steal your car? You shouldn't have parked it on that side street. Did someone walk up and grab your purse? You shouldn't have been carrying it. Rape, robbery, murder—we hear it all the time these days. Forget the criminals; it's the victim's fault.

I repeat: "Satan's substitute for repentance is the rationalization of evil." Yet the basic foundation of our Judeo-Christian faith is that you are responsible for what you do. Justifying or rationalizing what you do is demonic deception. It will destroy your soul and put you in an eternal hell.

The word *repent* is not a word designed in heaven to make you feel bad about who you are or what you've done. The word repent has a very significant meaning. *Re* means "to return." *Re-pent* means "to go back to a place." *Pent* is a word meaning "the highest position," such as a penthouse or pinnacle. So the word *repent* means "to go back to the place of highest position."

What was the place of highest position for man? It was his status in the Garden of Eden where God and man walked and talked together in the cool of the evening as friends. That was before sin destroyed the relationship, and God and man were separated. Repentance is not designed to make you feel bad about yourself. God offers repentance so you can return to the Garden of Eden and walk and talk with Him as a personal friend.

Repentance is not to shame you, embarrass you, or make you feel inferior or inadequate. Repentance is designed to get you into the presence of God. There is no other road. Repentance is the passport to renewing your relationship with God!

In summary, the man or woman who would climb the stairway to the stars must master worry, fear, uncontrolled anger, depression, resentment, forgiveness, and repentance. By passion, by conviction, and by unswerving determination, you will conquer your supreme and most subtle enemy—yourself!

CHAPTER SIX

Secret Five: Level One Communication

The Conversation of the Soul

THIS chapter is lovingly dedicated to people who are married, those who want to be married, and those who are sorry they are married. There are three phases to marriage: lust, rust, and dust. You know which phase you're in without asking Dr. Phil.

I know marriages are made in heaven, but so are thunder and lightning. If love is a dream, marriage is the alarm clock. Mister, you know that argument you won with your wife last night? Well, it's not over!

Communication in marriage is an art, and sometimes this art can become so twisted the real meaning is lost.

Husbands, how many of you have ever told your wife something as clearly as you can speak, and she got it wrong—all wrong!

Wives, how many of you have told your husbands something as clearly as you can speak, and he got it wrong—all wrong!

Parents, how many of you have told your children something as clearly as you can speak, and they got it wrong—all wrong!

Problems and differences in a family are not dangerous; they are normal. But not being able to communicate those differences is very dangerous. The man or woman who cannot or will not communicate is alone. You can be in a house with a spouse and five children and be alone. You can be in a crowded room and be alone. You can go to a church gathering of thousands and be alone. If you can't communicate with the people around you, you are a prisoner on an island of your own creation.

WHAT IS COMMUNICATION?

Communication is an exchange of feelings or information. It takes two people to communicate—one sending, the other receiving. The single most important ingredient in a long-term marriage is the ability for both partners to communicate. Communication is to love what blood is to the body. When communication stops flowing, you're dead.

Communication is to love what blood is to the body.

Communication is not out-yelling your wife. Communication is not out-talking your husband. Nor is communication out-screaming your children.

Unfortunately, husbands and wives, fathers and mothers, who are riddled with doubts and fears are dogmatic. They are never wrong because they are too emotionally weak and insecure to allow anyone to disagree with them. If you demand that your spouse agree with you in all things, you are denying your spouse's emotional and intellectual life. He or she will have a mental breakdown or will get a divorce to save his or her sanity—but trust me, that spouse will not stay married to you.

The truth is, our deep feelings must be expressed or we will explode. I liken it to a child trying to hold a beach ball under water. He presses the ball under the water and struggles to keep it there, but the instant he slightly loses his balance, the ball explodes out of the water and into the air. In the same way, emotions that are suppressed can only be contained so long. The instant you lose your emotional balance ever so slightly, you will explode.

Every person in a marriage and family relationship must remember that he or she is not a stone statue frozen permanently in one position.

We human beings are constantly in the process of change. In other words, if you knew me yesterday, please do not think that you are meeting the same person today. I may have changed overnight.

Have you ever heard this statement from people who were getting a divorce: "We just grew apart"? How did they grow apart? The answer is they quit communicating. Notice, I didn't say they quit talking. I said they quit communicating.

I'd like to give you seven secrets of communication. These principles have served me throughout the years in my family life and my ministry. They are based on both biblical truths and many decades of living.

I
KNOW THE FIVE LEVELS OF COMMUNICATION

Psychologists have determined that communication between human beings is expressed on five levels. Communication begins with level five, which is the least effective level of communication, and moves toward level one, which is a symphony of the soul between two human beings who love each other.

Level one is your goal. Unfortunately level five is where most married couples live in a high-tech generation that has us united around a television set with the all-powerful remote control in our hands.

Let's look at each of these levels of communication so we can understand the areas that are weak.

Level five communication: Cliché conversation

On this level, we talk in pretense and sham. Our emotional masks stay on. We never reveal what we really think or feel on this shallow level.

Cliché conversation goes like this: "How are you, Sweetheart?"

"I'm fine."

The truth is you may have a 104-degree fever and be on the brink of convulsions, but you mechanically answer, "Fine." Why? You're just talking; you're not communicating the deepest feelings of your heart.

Cliché communication sounds like, "How is your family?" The response is, "Fine."

Yet your wife hasn't spoken to you in five days. You have two kids in jail, and the IRS is repossessing your house. You've seen more joy in a lobster tank than in your home, but you respond, "Fine." It's mechanical; it's meaningless; it's cliché conversation.

I've heard people ask, "How have you been?" If you answer the person's question by giving every gory detail of your depressing life, the other person probably thinks, *Hey, I don't want to hear your life story. I was just making conversation.*

Unfortunately most family members and Americans use level five communication.

Level four communication: Reporting facts about other people

On the fourth level of communication, we report the activities of others. The Bible calls this *gossip* and *tale bearing*. Some people search for dirt concerning other people like it was gold. They spread more filth over a telephone than you can find in a commercial vacuum cleaner. The more interesting the gossip, the more likely it is to be untrue.

Communication is an exercise of the mind, but gossiping is merely an exercise of the tongue that leaves a cancer on the soul. I know a lot of Christians don't gossip; they "share." For instance, sometimes a member of a small Bible study or home group will mention a situation that needs prayer but shouldn't be revealed to others. That's gossip.

---

*Communication is an
exercise of the mind, but gossiping is
merely an exercise of the tongue that leaves a
cancer on the soul.*

In a certain town, gossip mongers reported that a local pastor had gone to a place where his wife was attending a meeting against his will. They reported that the pastor had dragged his wife from the place and forced her to go home. Upon learning of the gossip racing through the town, the minister inserted an ad in the local newspaper as follows:

1. In the first place, I never attempted to influence my wife in her views of her choice of a meeting.
2. In the second place, my wife did not attend the meeting in question.
3. In the third place, I did not attend the meeting.
4. In the fourth place, neither my wife nor myself had any inclination to go to the meeting.
5. And finally, I do not now have and never have had a wife.

So it goes with those who report facts about other people. If you allow yourself to become a party to listening to them, you are a coconspirator in the act of assassinating another's character. You are just as guilty as the gossips themselves.

There are four rules by which to measure the merit of every conversation.

1. Is it true?
2. Is it necessary?
3. What's my motive in telling this? Remember that the Bible says, "Do all to the glory of God" (1 Cor. 10:31).
4. Will everyone involved benefit from my telling it?

If you can't answer *yes* to those four questions, be quiet.

In level four communication, there is no personal or self-revealing statement. Conversation on level four is empty, shallow, and meaningless. Unfortunately, that's all many of you have in your marriages.

Why? Because you are afraid of telling your partner who you are and what you really feel about anything. You don't talk about your dreams and desires. You are afraid to reveal your needs and concerns or your sexual frustrations. You don't want to talk about money management and reversing the debt cycle in which you find yourself. You live in a penitentiary of silence that will destroy your marriage as certainly as cancer will destroy your body.

I encourage you today to speak the unspeakable and think the unthinkable and give total expression to both. It will save your marriage and your sanity.

I encourage you today to speak the unspeakable and think the unthinkable and give total expression to both. It will save your marriage and your sanity.

Level three communication: Sharing of ideas

On this level, I will share some of the things I feel. I will share some of my ideas and some of my decisions. I will give you just a peek at the real me. However, as I communicate, I will watch your every move carefully.

If you raise your eyebrows or narrow your eyes, if you yawn or look at your watch, if you keep reading the newspaper or keep watching the television, I will not continue communicating at this level.

If I do continue talking about the same subject, I will go back to level four or five where my speech is totally superficial. Our relationship has become weakened because of your failure to respond to me. Our love is less. Our silence is the death certificate of our marriage.

Some of your marriages are as dead as Julius Caesar. Others are gasping their last breath because you refused to honestly communicate your deepest feelings to the one to whom you have given your covenant to share the entirety of your life.

Level two communication: Revealing real feelings and emotions

Level two is gut-level conversation. This is the real me. This is what I feel deep in my soul. This is what I love, what I fear, and what I long for.

Communication in marriage must be prioritized on this level for your marriage to survive. Level two communication has no fear of a blow up or pouting or resentment because of a petty disagreement. If you demand that your partner in life agree with you in all things, you will never get to level two conversation. You are an emotional Hitler, and the people in your home will refuse to live in your private penitentiary.

Level one communication: Peak communication

Level one conversation is the symphony of the soul. It is two human beings in absolute honesty, like two violins playing a masterful concerto in perfect harmony. The Bible says it this way, "If two of you agree…" (Matt. 18:19). The word *agree* is the Greek word for *symphony*.

There is no pretense here. There is no fear, no snide remarks. Level one conversation contains no rejection. There is absolute transparency because I am not trying to hide any detail of my life from you. I am willing to stand before you totally naked. This is conversation of total compassion for the other person, which permits him or her total and absolute freedom.

The survival of your marriage is threatened when you and your spouse only chatter about trivia. When you report facts about other people, your marriage is very unhealthy. When you hide behind a mask in pretense of being what you never can be, real communication will never happen. But when you practice level one and level two conversation, you will function as God intended when He said "the two shall become one" (Mark 10:8).

2

FOUR DEADLY PHRASES TO AVOID IN CONVERSATION WITH YOUR CHILDREN

The first secret of communication is to avoid four deadly phrases in conversation with your children.

As I mentioned before, I call my five children the "Fabulous Five." All have now moved out of the house, and Diana and I are adjusting to the thunderous sound of silence. (Thankfully, grandchildren sometimes break that silence!) When the Fabulous Five were home, our time together was literal heaven on earth.

Our favorite times were around the supper table when I would ask each child about every aspect of his or her day and then inquire about the coming events in his or her life. "How did you do on your test?" "When is your next ball game?" After the child gave me a specific day, I would assure him or her, "I'll be there, front and center." I'm great at asking questions, so the conversation went on and on: "Did you get the speaking part in the school play?" "Why can't you get along with your English teacher?"

After many wonderful years of listening to my children around the supper table, I can say with some authority that there are four statements that should not be part of your conversation with your children. The first is that often-heard declarative sentence "When I was your age..."

"When I was your age..."

My daughter Sandy says, "The older Dad gets, the further it was to school when he was a child and the deeper the snow was in those days. And he walked uphill both ways, not just one." That brings laughter and nods of approval from everyone around the table but me.

Every generation believes the next generation knows nothing about how to manage their affairs and especially how to manage money. When my children would stick out their hands, asking for money with cherubic smiles on their faces as if I were a walking ATM machine, I would smile back and say, "When I was your age, I was dragging a sixteen-foot cotton sack in one-hundred-degree heat for ten hours a day to earn one dollar."

It took all the joy out of the moment. The message was sent to my children that there was a serious generation gap, and I wasn't doing anything to build a bridge over to their side. I wasn't listening to their pleas and really wasn't concerned about their problems. Wrong message! I dropped that phrase and adopted this knee-jerk response when they asked for money to go to the movies or buy new clothes: "How much?"

That's a lot better than, "When I was your age…" Since I was going to give the money anyway, why not give the money with joy rather than make my child feel like I didn't care about him or her?

Dr. Bill Ligon, one of the great pastors in the state of Georgia, told me a story about his teenage son that struck me deep in my soul. Dr. Ligon's son asked if he could have a car. The son was a model youngster in every way. His grades in school were honors level. His participation in the church was enthusiastic.

This model teenage son had located the exact car that he wanted. But because the price was a little more than the father could afford, he told his son no.

Dr. Ligon said to me, "Later the Holy Spirit spoke to me and said, 'It doesn't pay to be a good boy in your house.'"

So the next day Dr. Ligon went to the bank and borrowed the money. He bought the car, drove it home, and parked it in the driveway. Then he placed the keys in his son's hands and said, "It pays to be a good boy."

That's a principle I have followed for all the years my children were in my home. If they followed the rules I set for the house, I blessed them without question to the fullest limit of my ability. If they broke the rules, I punished them quickly and severely—then hugged them until I was sure they knew I loved them without question. This principle has produced five fabulous children, and I urge you to try it.

By the way, Dr. Ligon's son is now an outstanding lawyer who is presently serving as a judge in Georgia.

"You just don't understand…"

When teenagers engage you in a serious conversation about the person they're dating, the movie they're going to see, the money they're spending, the curfew you want them to keep, and your response is less than enthusiastic, they look at you as if you were Ivan the Terrible and whine, "You just don't understand."

The fact is you do understand. You know from personal experience that your child is trying to do something that is detrimental—and perhaps will destroy that beloved young person. God, in His infinite wisdom, gave you a twenty-year head start on this child's experience.

God, in His infinite wisdom, gave you a twenty-year head start on this child's experience.

Let me dip into my sack of stories about the Fabulous Five. This is a painful story, but every word is true. On one occasion, one of my daughters was dating a young man of whom I disapproved. He attended our church, said all the right things at the right time, and presented himself nicely, but my spiritual Geiger counter went crazy every time I was around him. The fuzz on the back of my neck would stand up. I knew as well as my name is John Hagee that something was wrong, seriously wrong.

Diana and I prayed together about this dating relationship, and both of us felt this continued romance would only bring great distress to our daughter. So I did what any responsible parent would do: I told my daughter she could no longer date this young man. She replied with that familiar mantra, "Dad, you just don't understand!"

It took all the restraint I had to keep from leaping out of my easy chair like a rocket launched from Cape Kennedy as I shouted, "You're the one who doesn't understand!"

I didn't. I bit my tongue until it bled and calmly responded, "In time you will see the wisdom of this decision. Your emotional involvement clouds your decision-making process."

The verbal response that came gushing from my daughter's mouth was less than joyful.

Weeks passed, and I thought the matter was settled. How foolish of me! One day I received a handwritten letter from my daughter, stating that she wanted to talk to me when she came home from the university that Friday. I changed the few appointments I had scheduled for Friday evening and went home at 5:30.

I parked the car in the garage, entered the house, and walked directly to my bedroom, better known at the Hagee house as the "meeting place." Diana and my daughter were waiting for me. Both sat in stone-cold silence. There was enough tension in the air to give a migraine headache to a brass doorknob.

I sat down in my white leather chair—with my daughter sitting on the floor directly in front of me, and my wife sitting on the bed—and opened the conversation as I do all conversations, straight to the point. I looked deeply into my daughter's dark brown eyes and asked, "What do you want to talk about?"

"I want to tell you why I think you should accept Harry* as someone I want to date."

She waited for me to respond. I didn't. Then for thirty minutes she skillfully articulated the qualities and virtues of Harry as she perceived them.

I listened to every thought and opinion she had. I admit she presented her case masterfully, and I am certain many fathers would have said something like, "Well, we'll give it another try and see what happens."

I didn't!

"Let me tell you why the answer is still no," I said.

Her face fell, and the tears started flowing instantly. This was absolute agony for me, but deep down in my soul I knew I was absolutely right.

My daughter upped the ante! "Dad, I'm going to date him with or without your approval."

I didn't flinch or hesitate. Without raising my voice I said, "Give me your car keys, your credit cards, and your cell phone. The money in your checking account belongs to me. The clothes you're wearing and the clothes in your closet are yours. You can move out of the house today."

It was a moment when time stood still. I could tell that my daughter was considering every word I'd said, and she knew I was not bluffing. We were staring eyeball-to-eyeball, waiting for the other to blink. Diana was sobbing. Yet I knew my daughter's entire life was hanging in the balance. To allow her to do as she wanted would have been parental cowardice of the highest level.

Within a few minutes, which seemed an eternity, my daughter decided to stay in the house and not defy my spiritual authority. Two days later she discovered serendipitously that Harry had been dating two other girls while swearing his undying loyalty and love for her. Their relationship ended instantly.

The next Friday, just seven days later, my daughter came into my bedroom, sat on my lap in that white easy chair, kissed my face, and softly whispered into my ear, "Thank you, Daddy, for saving my life." Her life and perhaps eternal destiny had turned 180 degrees in one week.

* Harry is an assumed name.

When you face a crisis with your child, ask God to help you stay calm, be totally loving, and give you divine insight so you can respond in a way that will save your child's life. God is a father, and He will not fail to give you clear direction for the life of your child.

God is a father, and He will not fail to give you clear direction for the life of your child.

"Why can't you be more like…"

The Bible is very clear about making comparisons between ourselves and others. Paul told the Corinthians, "For we dare not class ourselves or compare ourselves with those who commend themselves. But they, measuring themselves by themselves, and comparing themselves among themselves, are not wise" (2 Cor. 10:12).

For a parent to tell one child, "Why can't you be more like…," is a critical mistake. It says to your child, "I don't like who you've become, and I don't approve of you."

For a schoolteacher to say, "Why can't you be more like…," is an absolute betrayal of the student. My younger brother Jack and I attended the same middle school in Houston, Texas. I graduated five years before Jack and had been voted the most outstanding student in the graduating class by the faculty, based upon academic and extra-curricular accomplishments. Upon graduation, my picture was hung in the school hall for years to come.

My brother Jack was—and is—a gentle, happy-go-lucky soul who was, unfortunately, assigned the same homeroom teacher I had while attending George Washington Middle School. Jack's academic philosophy at that time in his life was, "You can pass just as far on a C as you can on an A+." It required a cast-iron constitution for Jack to hear the often-repeated slur: "Why can't you be more like your brother John?"

Jack's answer was a good one: "Because John is John, and I prefer to be myself."

Hurray for Jack!

Unfortunately, not every child has Jack's fortitude. One unfavorable comparison can crush the emotional life out of children, sending them into full retreat psychologically. The resulting scars can be deep and permanent.

When your child says, "You like her better, don't you?" gracefully avoid that question. Instead say with conviction, "I think *you* are wonderful. I enjoy being around *you*."

Never say, "I love you both equally!" You're in a trap from which there is no escape. Look your child in the eye and convince him or her you truly believe there's no one on earth quite as special and unique as he or she is. The child is eager to believe it, and every word you say is absolutely true.

"This is God's will…"

When trouble or tragedy strikes the life of your family or your child, never say "This is God's will." God's will is difficult enough for master theologians to understand, so it's beyond the ability of your child to remotely grasp.

To say to your children in an hour of tragedy, "This is God's will," forces your children to think of God as cruel and uncaring. Or when they pray and their prayers aren't answered, don't run to the "it's-God's-will" escape. It's much easier to say, "It's God's will," than for us to examine ourselves and find out why we're missing His will.

When my children Tina and Matthew were four years and three years of age respectively, our church family experienced a great tragedy. Richard and Helen Medina and their three-year-old daughter, Meredith, were killed in a head-on auto crash three days before Christmas. The driver in the other car, who caused the crash, was drunk and survived with minor injuries.

Richard and Helen were leaders in our church. They sang in the choir, taught a Sunday school class, led a cell group Bible study, and played on the church softball teams. They were two of the most loving and gracious people you could find on Planet Earth.

Walking into the church on Christmas Eve and looking at those three gray caskets (one of which was so tiny) broke my heart.

What do you say when life makes no sense? This was not the will of God; a drunkard murdered three precious people by mishandling his God-given power of choice. Choices have consequences!

Several days after the funeral, I picked Matt and Tina up from the church day-care center. I could tell instantly that Tina was extremely upset.

Since Matt was the smallest, I carried him in my arms and led Tina to the front seat of my pickup truck. (In Texas, if you're not driving a truck, you're driving a toy. To this day I drive a red pickup truck.)

As I pulled away from the curb, Tina started asking me a barrage of questions.

"Daddy, where is Meredith?"

"Sweetheart, she's in heaven with Jesus."

"Daddy, where is heaven?"

"Heaven is a wonderful place where Christians go when their life on earth is over."

"Daddy, I want Meredith to come and play with me. If heaven is such a wonderful place, why can't she come back and play with me?"

I saw the tears running down her face and knew I was seriously missing the mark.

"My teacher said, 'This is God's will,'" Tina said quietly.

"Your teacher is wrong." I saw Matt looking at his sister with deep compassion. What was going through his three-year-old mind? I had two earned university degrees and was striking out with my daughter as I tried to explain the hereafter.

In an instant three-year-old Matthew came to my rescue. He put his arm around Tina, hugged her, and said reassuringly, "Don't worry, Tina, we're not Christians. We're Mexicans, and Mexicans never die." (My wife, Diana, is Hispanic.)

Matthew's answer brought total and instant comfort to Christina, although it didn't directly answer her questions about heaven. (He seemed to understand her underlying question, the same one we all have in such circumstances: If this happened to my friend, couldn't it also happen to me?)

I pulled the truck off the road and laughed until I cried. Sometimes God speaks through children.

3

LISTEN FOR GOD'S COMMUNICATION

When God speaks, do you hear? I have often heard people say, "If God spoke to me, I would surely know it." Would you? God is constantly trying to speak to us, but the question is: Are we listening? The Bible says, "He who has ears to hear, let him hear" (Matt. 11:15).

God is constantly trying to speak to us, but the question is: Are we listening?

God spoke so naturally to the young boy Samuel one night that he thought it was the high priest Eli. God had to speak three times before it dawned on either Samuel or Eli that God was trying to speak audibly.

Finally Eli told Samuel, "Go, lie down; and it shall be, if He calls you, that you must say, 'Speak, Lord, for Your servant hears'" (1 Sam. 3:9).

Note that Samuel was to say that he was listening.

The air where you sit right now is supercharged with electronic messages flooding past you from radio and television stations. Yet you can't receive them because you do not have an electronic antenna in your head tuned to that frequency.

In the same way God is constantly sending His will and His revelations over the frequencies of heaven, but His children do not have their spiritual antennas up to receive what God is saying. God talked to Adam and Eve face-to-face. God spoke from the thick darkness to Moses, telling him to go back to Egypt and lead the Israelites out of persecution. God spoke through angels to Abraham, saying, "Your ninety-year-old wife is going to have a baby about this time next year." When Abraham told his wife this, she laughed—I believe from pure hysteria. When you're ninety, having a baby is not number one on your to-do list.

OK, you say, God spoke to those biblical people, but He doesn't speak to me. Let me correct you there. God does speak to you today in several ways.

First, God speaks plainly and powerfully through the Bible. He expresses His will and His wisdom to each of us. God speaks through children at times, for the Word says, "Out of the mouth of babes and sucklings hast thou ordained strength" (Ps. 8:2 KJV).

The Ten Commandments are only a start of God's wisdom. The Old Testament gives us His direction for His people, the Israelites, and for us. And the New Testament reveals the truth of His Son's direction for our lives.

God also communicates to humanity through nature. God created nature, and He controls nature. Nature is God's billboard for the past and God's billboard for tomorrow.

Sodom and Gomorrah, two magnificent cities, were utterly destroyed by the divine artillery of fire and brimstone. God's message for Sodom and Gomorrah? He will never tolerate sodomy as a way of life. Nations may accept it and defend it by law, yet God will never call it but one thing: abomination.

In the Book of Genesis, God commissioned Noah to build an ark, and the citizens laughed, criticizing the man of God and his message. Noah preached for 120 years without one convert, but he continued to build an ark for the salvation of his family. God's message to humanity through the flood: "I am the Judge of all the earth. You will answer to Me someday."

God had the flood timed to the last second. Genesis 7:11 records that it occurred "in the six hundredth year of Noah's life, in the second month, the seventeenth day of the month, on that day all the fountains of the deep were broken up, and the windows of heaven were opened."

When the fountains of the deep were opened, those skeptical citizens began to race toward the ark. This ark was yesterday's mockery. Now this same ark was today's miracle. As the waters rose, they scratched and clawed at the sides of the ark, screaming in terror for Noah to open the door. He could not, for God had closed the door. The opportunity of yesterday was gone for all eternity.

The strong and the powerful ran to the highest hill and saw society floating by in a watery grave that embraced the world. After forty days and forty nights, all of the earth was covered with the silence of death. Through nature, God had once again spoken that He and He alone was the judge of all the earth. He and He alone controls what happens on this planet.

God divided the Red Sea for Moses. He held the sun still for Joshua (Josh. 10:12). He produced a severe drought for Elijah to bring godless Ahab and Jezebel to their knees (1 Kings 17:1).

When Jesus was on the Sea of Galilee with His twelve disciples, fierce winds blew through the Jordan Valley and threatened their lives. The Creator of heaven and earth stood in the tossing boat and shouted, "Peace be still" (Mark 4:39). In the Greek, this phrase reads, "Be muzzled." That speaks of absolute control. What happens in nature is not accidental; it's God's voice on parade.

GOD'S VOICE IN NATURE

Listen to the testimony of God's influence in nature:

"The LORD has His way in the whirlwind and the storm" (Nah. 1:3). That's control.

David wrote, "For He commands and raises the stormy wind" (Ps. 107:25). David continued, "He calms the storm so that its waves are still"-(Ps. 107:29). That's control.

The prophet Isaiah put his pen to parchment and wrote, "Behold, the LORD rides on a swift cloud" (Isa. 19:1). That's control.

Some people might say, "That's in the Bible, Pastor. I've not seen God do these things today." Well, I have.

Immediately following World War II when steel was virtually impossible to get, my mother and father were building a church, and the foundations of their new church had been dug by hand and were wide open to the rain that was forming in black clouds overhead. If water filled the trenches of that foundation, the building program would be in utter chaos.

While hanging her clothes on the clothesline in our backyard, my mother looked into those boiling black clouds and prayed, "Lord God Almighty, Your Word says You ride on the wings of the storm. I am asking You to stop the rain and do not let the foundation of Your house be destroyed."

The church was one mile from our home. When mother finished her prayer, torrential rain gushed from the black clouds.

One hour later, my father arrived home, and it was still raining.

"How much damage has been done to the church foundation?" Mom asked.

"None!" Dad clapped his hands together for pure joy. "I have just driven through the most savage thunderstorm I have seen in all my life. But when I came to within one-half mile of the church property, it was like someone had drawn a line across the highway, saying that the rain could not come another inch."

God heard my mother's prayer and stopped the rain to save that building program from months of delay and dollars the church didn't have. Our God controls nature.

In yet another instance, my grandfather, who was a Pentecostal preacher in the state of Oklahoma, went to the fields of his church members who were farmers and prayed for God to stop an army of bugs that was eating their crops level with the ground. My grandfather and Bible-believing Christians gathered at the edge of those crops and prayed God's protection over them, quoting Malachi 3:11: "And I will rebuke the devourer for your sakes, so that he will not destroy the fruit of your ground." Not one member lost his crop, because God controls nature, and He communicates to us through nature.

What is God going to say through nature in the future?

In the times that lie ahead, God will announce the end of the earth. "I will show wonders in heaven above and signs in the earth beneath: blood and fire and vapor of smoke. The sun shall be turned into darkness, and the moon into blood, before the coming of the great and awesome day of the LORD" (Acts 2:19–20).

John the Revelator describes this moment in Revelation 6:12–14: "I looked when he opened the sixth seal, and behold, there was a great earthquake; and the sun became black as sackcloth of hair, and the moon became like blood. And the stars of heaven fell to the earth, as a fig tree drops its late figs when it is shaken by a mighty wind. Then the sky receded as a scroll when it is rolled up, and every mountain and island was moved out of its place." This is a description of God's awesome power in nature during the end times.

What else is God saying about the future? The Bible says, "For nation will rise against nation, and kingdom against kingdom. And there will be famines, pestilences, and earthquakes in various places" (Matt. 24:7).

Consider the increase of earthquakes in history:[1]

In the fifteenth century there were 115 earthquakes.

In the sixteenth century there were 253 earthquakes.

In the seventeenth century there were 378 earthquakes.

In the eighteenth century there were 640 earthquakes.

In the nineteenth century there were 2,119 earthquakes.

In the twentieth century earthquakes happened with such rapidity and regularity that tremors are considered "life as usual" in California.

The U.S. Corps of Engineers is studying the fault that runs under the Mississippi River from the Gulf of Mexico to the Great Lakes. Engineers believe that this massive fault could create a royal gorge, dividing America in two by a line that will run from the Great Lakes straight down to New Orleans.

This fact is not a surprise to God. John the Revelator says the "big one" is coming! "And there was a great earthquake such a great and mighty earthquake as had not occurred since men were on the earth....Then every island fled away, and the mountains were not found" (Rev. 16:18, 20).

Throughout history God has used earthquakes to communicate to those who are hard of hearing.

God used an earthquake at the Crucifixion to split the veil of the temple from the top to bottom, telling the world that His Son had died on the cross. This same earthquake released people from their graves who walked into Jerusalem and were recognized by those who had attended their funerals.

God used an earthquake at the Resurrection as an angel rolled the stone away, not to let Jesus out, but to let us in. The empty tomb is the only tourist attraction on earth where people line up for blocks to see nothing! It's empty! He's gone!

The empty tomb is the only tourist attraction on earth where people line up for blocks to see nothing! It's empty! He's gone!

God used an earthquake to liberate Paul and Silas from the jail in Philippi. They sang in the midnight hour after being beaten for preaching the Word. They walked out of that Philippian jailhouse, keys in one hand and a convert in the other.

And now we are waiting for the earthquake John the Revelator predicted, which will literally reshape the geography of the world. God is shouting for all to hear: "I am the Lord and there is no one like me, not in the earth or in the heavens above." (See 1 Kings 8:23.)

4
LISTEN TO YOUR CONSCIENCE

Your conscience is a God-given instrument that allows you to determine right from wrong. Conscience is the lamp of God saying, "This is the way, walk in it." Conscience is the compass of the soul.

When your conduct goes one way and your conscience goes another way, conscience will make your bed (even if it's a Posturepedic mattress) a bed of hot coals.

- ◆ What made Adam and Eve hide from God in the garden? Their consciences!

- ◆ What made King David cry out, "Have mercy upon me, O God?" His conscience!

- ◆ What made Pilate's wife write, "Have nothing to do with this just man?" Her conscience!

- ◆ What made Judas Iscariot scream in torment, "I have betrayed innocent blood?" His conscience!

- ◆ What made Peter weep after he denied Christ three times? His conscience!

Yet a person with a quiet conscience can sleep in thunder! A quiet conscience is like a mighty fortress in the day of battle.

Still men battle with this inner voice from God that says, "Stop. Turn around. Repent of your sin." Some try to drug their consciences into silence, but they awaken only to scream louder. Others try to drown their consciences in a river of whiskey, but like bloated corpses, they pop to the top, demanding to be heard.

Thank God for your conscience. Before radar, before sonar, before the compass, God provided every man this built-in navigational direction finder.

Ignore your conscience, and you will destroy your soul. Ignore your conscience, and you will destroy your peace of mind. Ignore your conscience, and the voice of God will depart from you. You will destroy your marriage, your health, and your business. You will destroy your family, your children, and eventually your eternal soul.

Yet your life can be as the days of heaven on earth if you will learn to keep your conscience clean and pure before God.

You may be wondering, *How does my conscience affect my communication?*

Let me give you this illustration. The husband comes home from work. He's tired and very upset. He got a cut in his paycheck and a speeding ticket on the way home. He now has a migraine headache. He steps in the door, and his wife chirps up with, "The IRS called today and wants to investigate our tax returns for the past seven years. The washing machine broke, and your mother-in-law is moving in with us tomorrow."

The husband will yell back, "Shut up!" Before he can get his mouth closed, his conscience screams, *That was uncalled for; apologize to your wife immediately!*

His soulish self, driven by his stubborn will, shouts back, *If you apologize to her, John Wayne, you'll be living on your knees for the next twenty years. Stand your ground, or live with a hook in your nose forever.*

What will you do? If you're spiritual and led of the Spirit, you'll apologize instantly. If you're carnal and driven by the flesh, you'll pout, drink Maalox, and chew Rolaids—all because you're mule-headed.

What does God do? He puts His bit and bridle in your mouth like a trainer breaking a wild horse and brings you to your knees. Your prayers are hindered. Your life is lousy. You hear a voice from heaven saying, "If mama ain't happy, ain't nobody happy!" You muster up your courage and squeak out a feeble, "I'm sorry, dear!"

Who apologizes in your home? The spiritual one. Not the macho meathead over in the corner acting like a lobotomized ape. The weak ones pout, whine, and complain. Strength apologizes, motivated by a conscience that is driven by the Spirit of God.

How does conscience affect communication? Let me give you a second illustration. You hear real good, juicy gossip; I mean it's really good! Your conscience screams: *Keep quiet; say absolutely nothing!*

Your mind shouts back: *Why not tell the truth? The truth never hurts!* (By the way, that statement is an absolute lie.) Your flesh says: *Yes, that's right. Tell it; tell it; tell it!*

What will you do? If you're spiritual, you'll shut your mouth! If you're an immature, spiritual brat, you'll say, "Let's just make this a matter of prayer. But I heard that the minister of music is in love with the organist." (Of course, the organist is the wife of the minister of music, but it makes a good story.)

One woman said to me, "I can keep a secret; it's the people I talk to who can't keep a secret."

"Stop talking to them then," I wanted to say.

How does conscience affect communication? Let me give you a final illustration. You're lying in bed after a hard day. It's 11:00 P.M., and you're tired to the bone. Your conscience says, *It's time to pray. I want to hear from God!* Your mind says, *You need to read the* Wall Street Journal. *You can pray tomorrow!* Your flesh chimes in, *You're tired. It's been a hard day. Eat another bowl of ice cream, and turn on the television!*

What will you do?

If you're spiritual, you'll get out of bed and pray. If you're immature and dominated by your feelings and emotions, you'll eat another bowl of ice cream until you turn into a mountain of fluff. You'll turn on the television and watch the eleven o'clock news and probably the late, late show.

When you come to church the next Sunday, you can't feel the presence of God because the spiritual man has been starved into silence. You've bathed your mind in trash, and you wonder why the Holy Spirit avoids you like the plague.

To master our lives, the spiritual man must master the flesh and the mind. And we need to remember: Nothing that happens has meaning until we give it meaning! It's not what you hear; it's how you apply what you hear.

To master our lives, the spiritual man must master the flesh and the mind.

Let me give you this illustration. You hear that your boss has maligned you and questioned your ability. You were happy as a lark five minutes ago, but now you have chosen to allow this bad news to destroy your peace of mind. You lower your head and walk with your shoulders stooped. You pooch out your bottom lip and look as haggard as possible.

Your flesh says, *I'm hurt. I've been offended!*

Your mind says, *This is a personal attack. I should get angry and resign immediately.*

Your conscience thunders back as the spiritual voice of heaven, *"Blessed are you when they revile you and persecute you, and say all kinds of evil against you falsely....Rejoice and be exceedingly glad, for great is your reward in heaven"* (Matt. 5:11).

Your spiritual man also recalls the words of King David: *"Many are the afflictions of the righteous, but the LORD delivers him out of them all"* (Ps. 34:19).

And finally your spiritual man recalls the words of the apostle Paul: *"Rejoice in the Lord always. Again I will say, rejoice.... For our light afflic-tion, which is but for a moment, is working for us a far more exceeding and eternal weight of glory"* (Phil. 4:4; 2 Cor. 4:17).

What attitude will you choose? Will you choose to whine or to be a warrior? Are you going to be a victor or a victim? Trials must surrender to triumph if you listen to your conscience.

5
Beware of Communication Killers

Five communication killers will destroy every attempt you have to communicate with those you love.

The first communication killer is fear of rejection, which I spoke about in chapter four. People are afraid of being rejected or ridiculed. When your spouse looks at you and says, "You don't look as good as you used to," may I ask the question, who does? If you think you haven't changed, get your wedding gown or tuxedo out of the attic and try to put it on.

The first commandment of communication is this: If I expose my nakedness to you as a person, do not make me feel ashamed. Oh, I may continue to talk to you, but I will never, never, never tell you how I feel about anything again. I'm afraid to tell you who I am, because if I tell you who I am, you may not like me, and that's all I have to offer you.

The second communication killer is lack of honesty. Our society places value upon being authentic. But the truth is that most of us lie. We all wear masks over our real faces and play our roles like actors on a stage. Let's add two new masks to the ones I mentioned in chapter four.

There's the John Wayne mask of the big, strong, invincible iron man. The John Wayne type says, "I don't need mushy conversation. I told you I loved you back in 1952 when we were married, and that's enough."

The result? His wife knows he wears a John Wayne mask, but she quits telling him she loves him. Then he bawls like a baby, saying, "You don't love me like you used to."

The truth is he got what he asked for. I know a man who didn't kiss his wife for ten years, and then shot someone who did.

There's the Messiah mask. Meet God's little helpers, the saviors of the universe, the general managers of Planet Earth and all nearby planets. They spread themselves so thin doing so many things they have nothing left to give their marriage. They're so heavenly minded that they're no earthly good. Be real! Let God be supernatural. You be natural. Stay home and take care of your family.

Be real! Let God be supernatural.
You be natural.

What mask are you wearing? Take it off, and introduce yourself to your wife, your husband, and your children.

People play roles so other people will accept them. This is emotional suicide. Why? Because when that person changes, you're going to have to find another role to please that person. In the shuffle, you're going to lose contact with someone very important to you: Yourself. You will wake up one day saying, "Who am I?"

I would like to say this to all singles who are dating: People wear masks on a date. They have their best foot forward. Anyone can be terrific for three hours on Saturday night. The real person is home in a cage waiting for you to say, "I do!" Be honest with each other. Be real! Remove the mask and give yourself a chance at a wholesome relationship.

A third communication killer is an explosive response. Husband, if you're shouting at the top of your voice at your wife, this is not communication. An explosive response is not limited, however, to men. One husband told his friend, "My wife and I had words last night, but I never got a chance to use mine." Intimidation through temper tantrums is not communication.

There is no nakedness comparable to psychological nakedness. When your wife or husband points out your deficiency, you grasp for something to cover you up. If you are choleric or sanguine in temperament, you'll explode. You are saying to your wife or husband, "You are coming too close to the real me. Stay away, or I will explode."

The fourth communication killer is tears. Women tend to use this weapon (although some men I've known also use it very effectively). The first spat after marriage, the wife turns on the water works, and this teaches the new husband, "Don't go beyond that line or I will drown you." This wife is saying with her tears, "Don't tell me about my shortcomings or I'll cry!" The result? All meaningful communication stops and manipulation begins. And manipulation is the weapon of the control freak.

The fifth communication killer is silence. Some call it pouting. Others call it "the silent treatment." Many Christians master this technique because we realize it isn't spiritual to explode in anger, so we pout for two weeks.

Pouting is uncontrolled anger. It's the leading cause of high blood pressure, ulcers, and other diseases. It's also the leading cause of divorce.

We have developed communication systems that permit men on the earth to talk to men walking on the moon. Yet very often, husbands and fathers can't talk to their wives or children who are sitting across the breakfast table.

When you and I, as husband and wife, can honestly tell each other who we are, what we think, how we feel…when you and I can honestly tell each other what we love, honor, esteem, hate, fear, desire, hope for, believe in, and are committed to…then, and only then, can each of us be a real person in valid communication.

Avoid these five communication killers, and you will be close to level two and level one communication.

6

BE OPEN TO YOUR IMAGINATION

When I gave marriage counseling years ago, I used what I called the "Ezekiel method of communication." This is communication through imagination.

Ezekiel was the preacher in a concentration camp of Jews who were in exile in Babylon. These Jews were slaves and refugees of war. They had lost their homes, their freedom, and their hope. King David wrote, "We sat down, yes, we wept when we remembered Zion" (Ps. 137:1).

Ezekiel wanted to communicate with them, so God told him to go down and "sit where they sit." Who wants glib words of wisdom from a longhaired prophet who has no scars on his body? Most people will not listen to a man who has not experienced what they have.

So Ezekiel became a captive. He went down to live with them. He let the blows of humiliation that fell on their backs fall on his back. He looked at the world through their eyes and felt what they felt. Ezekiel wrote, "I sat where they sat" (Ezek. 3:15).

This changed his viewpoint. When he sat where they sat, he knew what they felt. I encourage husbands and wives to communicate with each other using Ezekiel's principle of communication: Be open to your imagination of the other person's situation.

Be open to your imagination of the other person's situation.

Children can enter other people's worlds through imagination. Put a stick horse between a boy's legs and a hat on his head, and he is the Lone Ranger. Give a little girl a doll, and she becomes a mother.

On one occasion, an insensitive husband had little appreciation for his wife who was taking care of three small children in a crowded house. After their communication difficulties had continued for much too long, this couple came into my office for counseling. I listened to her describe the distress and tension under which she lived, and then I looked at this John Wayne and said, "Why don't you sit where she sits?"

He glared at me from across my desk. "What do you mean?"

"I want you to pick a day, any day, and stay home all day and take care of your three holy terrors. I want you to clean the house and wash the dishes. I want you to cook the meals and mop the floors. Please wash and iron the clothes and change the diapers. I want you to potty train your little fellow. Please answer the phone promptly and courteously. Go get the groceries. And when your wife comes in the door at five-thirty, have supper on the table, look as fresh as a daisy, and have the passion of love shining out of both your eyes."

"You're crazy! That's absolutely impossible!"

I responded, "What? You got tired just talking about it? I didn't ask you to do it for a week or a month. I asked you to do it for one measly day."

That counseling session ended abruptly because this husband refused to "sit where she sat."

Think about it! You can't really know how life is for another person until you see it from his or her perspective.

Doctors are wonderful. My family is full of them. But I think every doctor should be sick just once and be admitted to his hospital under the name of John Doe. Every doctor should experience the joy of some iron-side nurse walking into his room at five-thirty in the morning, sticking him in the behind with a needle six inches long, and asking sarcastically, "Are you resting well?"

Every policeman should be given a ticket in a city that has a reputation of using traffic violations as a source of income. In such towns these policemen hide behind a bush all day long with a radar gun.

Every preacher should have to sit in the pew and listen to some of his dry, meaningless, and long-winded preaching. Believe me—this will drive him to his knees and to long hours of study.

Every church member should have the chance to sit where the preacher sits. To prepare two original, entertaining, life-changing, and theologically deep sermons every week that will change every life in the congregation. To counsel twenty neurotics and study thirty hours. To do five television shows and visit the sick, kiss the babies, marry the living, and bury the dead. To talk on the phone until midnight with an endless line of people who ask you stupidly, "Do you have a minute?", and then ramble eternally about nothing. Throw in three banquets, a crusade here and there, two or three death threats a month, and you have a great job.

A classic prayer says, "Lord, help me never to judge another man until I have walked in his moccasins for two weeks." Ezekiel did exactly that by sitting with the Jews in captivity for seven days.

Have you ever watched people on the streets pass a beggar with a tin cup? Watch closely! The people who give are not the bankers and the silk-stockinged crowd. The people who give are the poor people who have felt the pain of poverty. They have sat where that beggar sits, and they know how he feels.

One of the dumbest things you can say in the hour of another person's crisis is, "I know how you feel!" You can't possibly know unless you have experienced exactly what that person has experienced. You have to sit where this person sits.

Unfortunately sometimes words are too feeble to express the pain of the heart. The hurt is so deep, so intense, that the only communication possible is compassion. A hug. An embrace. Holding a trembling hand when tears become a language of their own. To share a moment of suffering or sorrow in silent compassion is real communication.

No cord or cable can hold as tightly as love's compassion. Jesus Christ loved you so much that He was willing to come to earth to sit where you sit and to feel what you feel. Compassion is a result of your relationship with God.

*No cord or cable can hold as tightly
as love's compassion.*

7
SPEAK THE TRUTH IN LOVE

Paul told the Ephesians, "Speak the truth in love" (Eph. 4:15). The more truth you speak, the more love you should convey.

A very successful businessman came to my office in tears because his wife of fifteen years had just left him. I asked him, "When is the last time you told your wife how much you loved her?"

He responded stiffly, "About ten years ago." When I seemed shocked, he continued. "Why should I have to tell her, 'I love you'? I gave her a new house, a new car, and beautiful clothes, and she ran off with a man who lives in a shack. What can he give her that I haven't given her?"

"Just one thing," I answered. "Love!"

Houses, cars, clothes, and jewels are not gifts but apologies for not giving the greatest gift of all: yourself. Until you give yourself, all other gifts are meaningless.

Give your partner or your family the gifts of the heart—the gift of love, the gift of kindness, the gift of joy and understanding, the gift of sympathy, the gift of tolerance, and, when all else fails, the gift of forgiveness. Sooner or later, both of you will fail.

Truth is a two-edged sword. Be very careful when you approach your wife or your husband with it. In order to speak the truth in love, be sure to plan a good time for communication with your partner. In the Hagee household, I wake up at 6:00 A.M. and explode out of bed with enough energy to hurt myself. Diana doesn't warm up until about 9:00 A.M. We don't talk much in the mornings. When she gets up and gets in high gear, she can move mountains—but it won't happen early.

Lady, when your husband comes home looking like a matador who got gored and trampled by a wild bull, don't tell him the washing machine broke and you scratched the back fender of his new Mercedes. Wait until later—much, much later.

Then you must allow for a reaction time. Remember, you have had the advantage of thinking about what you are going to say. You have pondered his or her reactions and mentally rehearsed your counter. You have prepared your case as cleverly and thoroughly as the famous courtroom attorney Clarence Darrow.

You may have taken your partner by surprise! Don't be amazed if he or she thinks about your conversation for a day or two and comes back with a whole new response. Your partner may recognize that he or she made some commitments that are impossible to live up to.

If your spouse points out an error in what you said, be willing to say, "I'm sorry." When you're wrong, say, "I'm sorry." And when you're right, be quiet. Don't grind salt into the wound. Remember the day will come when you will make a mistake and will need to be forgiven. The apostle Paul wrote, "All have sinned and fall short of the glory of God" (Rom. 3:23).

Finally, pray together and for each other. It has been said often and bears repeating again, "A family that prays together stays together."

Yet how many husbands and wives fail to pray with each other and for each other every day? The Bible clearly says, "Far be it from me that I should sin against the Lord in ceasing to pray for you" (1 Sam. 12:23). Not praying *with* your family and *for* your family is sin!

In summary, communication with your spouse, your children, your friends, your peers, and God is born in the passion to be a part of their lives. Communication is not striving to become an oratorical Vesuvius, spewing your intellect into the four winds of heaven. Communication is giving a part of your heart whether it is to one or to a million. Anything less is treason to a relationship.

CHAPTER SEVEN

Secret Six: The Power of Continuous Prayer

The Precursor to Great and Mighty Accomplishments

WHEN I was a child, my mother and dad would gather the family in the living room, and Mother, who had earned her theological degree, would tell her sons to kneel, saying, "We're going to talk to God!" That's what prayer is: talking to God our Father, who loves us with an everlasting love.

His desire is for us to have the best things in life. He has promised, "No good thing would He withhold from those who walk uprightly" (Ps. 84:11). All that God is, and all that God has, is available to the person who learns the secret of prayer.

My mother's statement about prayer is as follows: "Some prayer; some power. More prayer; more power. Much prayer; much power." The question each of us must ask is this: How much power do I want from God? Your answer is probably very simple: lots. Yet we have as much or as little of God's power right now as we are willing to pray to receive. A prayerless Christian is a powerless Christian.

"Some prayer; some power. More prayer; more power. Much prayer; much power."

Jesus did not teach His disciples how to preach, but He did teach them how to pray. He did not teach them how to raise funds or how to build up their donor base, but He taught them the principles of prayer before He sent them out to evangelize the world.

I have talked with prime ministers and presidents. To talk to one of these people, you must make an appointment months in advance, and your time is always strictly limited. They have great power, but at the same time their power is limited because they are men controlled by other men. But I can talk to Almighty God at any time, for as long as I want, and when I'm finished He doesn't shrug His shoulders and say, "I can't help you, John." He says, "I will make a way where there seems to be no way." (See 1 Corinthians 10:13.) He says, "Call to Me, and I will answer you, and show you great and mighty things, which you do not know" (Jer. 33:3).

Some of you may still not be convinced that you should spend every day in prayer. Let me give you four specific reasons why prayer should be an essential part of your life.

Why pray? Because prayerlessness is sin!

Prayerlessness Is Sin

A prayerless Christian is a weak Christian. A prayerless church is a weak church. A prayerless nation is a defeated nation. A prayerless family is a divided family.

Father, do you pray for your wife? Do you pray for your children? If you do not, 1 Samuel 12:23 says you have sinned against the Lord.

I am the second son of a preacher. As a teenager, I heard ten thousand sermons delivered by some of the best preachers in America. Yet I felt zero desire to be converted. One night when I was coming in late, slipping through the house in my socks so my mother's bird-dog ears would not hear me, I saw a light shining out from under her bedroom door.

As I passed by I heard her sobbing voice, pounding the gates of heaven: "Lord God in heaven, save my son John. If he leaves home without receiving Christ, he'll be lost forever."

I assure you, she was right.

I slipped into my bedroom and lay down on my bed, which was now a bed of hot coals. In the next days and weeks, those tear-stained words, "Lord, save my son John," hammered in my ears day and night. Three months later I surrendered my life to Christ, crushed by the power of my mother's prayer.

I have preached the gospel of Jesus Christ for more than forty-five years. I have preached in football stadiums packed with seventy-five thousand people. I have preached in the beautiful cathedrals of Europe and in the mud huts of the Third World. I have proclaimed the gospel to millions around the globe over radio and television.

Why did all this happen? My mother went to war with the devil for my soul in her prayer room—and the devil lost. She prayed me out of the fires of hell and into the arms of God.

Who is lost in your family? Are you praying without ceasing for their salvation? If not, please be informed, God says you are sinning against Him if you don't pray for them.

Why pray? Because God answers prayer.

GOD ANSWERS PRAYER

Several years ago our congregation joined together in a time of fasting and prayer for the healing of Lizzy Gross, the ten-year-old daughter of our minister of music, John Gross. Lizzy's mother, Lestra, had taken Lizzy to an optometrist when her left eye began to drift to the side. Her mother thought it was simply a lazy eye.

After the optometrist examined Lizzy, he told Lestra to take Lizzy to a neurologist, who ordered an MRI and other tests. After a thorough review of her condition, the finest physicians in San Antonio determined that Lizzie had an incurable, untreatable cancerous tumor in the center of her brain. The physicians gave absolutely no hope of survival.

Our church was grief stricken. We got on our knees and went to war for Lizzy's life. Thousands of people were praying night and day that God would heal this beautiful, blue-eyed, blonde-haired little girl.

In spite of our prayers, Lizzy's condition grew progressively worse. Her doctors had said, "The last sign will be that she will have such severe headaches she will not be able to attend school. When she comes home from school, she'll never go back again."

I remember as if it were yesterday when her father came into my office and said, "The school called and said, 'Come get Lizzy. She has a headache.'"

I put my arms around John Gross, and we prayed together, yet again, for poor Lizzy. I felt a surge of faith like I had never felt in my life before that point in time. After our prayer, I said to John, "Go home and give Lizzy an aspirin like it was an ordinary headache, and let's see what God does."

The next morning, Lizzy woke up without a headache. Her left eye began to come back toward the center. Her eye/hand coordination began to dramatically improve. Her eyelids, which had been droopy, were back to normal.

These were dramatic signs, yet her parents were fearful of becoming overly optimistic because they had been submerged in so much negative pronouncement by the medical community.

The next Sunday, John and Lestra brought Lizzy to my office and said, "Can you see a change in Lizzy?" Instantly, I saw massive improvement. I told John to take Lizzy to the doctor the next day and ask for another MRI. I felt positive God had answered our prayers.

The next day an MRI was taken, and there was no cancerous tumor in her brain! It had simply disappeared. It was so utterly shocking that her physician called me and said, "What did your church do in the spiritual treatment of Lizzy Gross?

"I am one of the best oncologists in this nation, and I did not misdiagnose this girl. A few weeks ago she came in here with a cancer in the center of her brain, and I have a second MRI that says she has no cancerous tumor in her brain. It's gone."

I responded, "We prayed, and God heard our prayer. The God we serve cannot fail. He is still a miracle-working God."

That was thirteen years ago. Since that time, it has been my pleasure to marry Lizzy to the love of her life, and her future is bright and without limit because of the miracle-working power of God's children when they pray and seek His face.

Why pray? Because we are commanded to pray.

WE ARE COMMANDED TO PRAY

Jesus said in Matthew 6, "*When* you pray," not "*If* you pray." The apostle Paul told the Thessalonians, "Pray without ceasing" (1 Thess. 5:17). Many Christians know the power of prayer, the pattern of prayer, the priority of prayer, and the purpose of prayer—yet they do not purpose to pray.

The tragedy of our day is not unanswered prayer but unoffered prayer. You have a choice. Prayer will either make you stop sinning, or sin will make you stop praying. You will either embarrass sin, or sin will embarrass you.

The tragedy of our day is not unanswered prayer but unoffered prayer.

Why pray? Because anointed prayer rises above.

ANOINTED PRAYER RISES ABOVE

The apostle Paul was stoned and left for dead. Yet he didn't ask the church to pray for the rheumatism that was caused by the stones that broke his bones. When he was jailed, Paul didn't say to the church, "Pray for me. I'm in jail. They have whipped me with a Roman cat-o'-nine-tails. The blood is running down my back and onto the floor in puddles. I'm going to be in the news again as a fanatic and be shown on national television in handcuffs."

Paul did say, "Pray that I might speak the Word of God with boldness" (Acts 4:29). Boldness is what got him thrown into jail, and he wanted more of it. If there were ever a time in America's history when Americans need to speak the Word of God with holy boldness, it's right now.

An almighty and all-powerful God is sitting on His throne in heaven with His hand cuffed behind His ear to hear the petitions of His children. He's listening for us to ask Him to do "great and mighty things," to show signs and wonders of the power of God. He's listening for us to pull down the strongholds of the addictions that enslave our children, our husbands, and our wives. He's listening for us to pull down the strongholds of abortion and pornography and divorce. He's looking for us to pull down the demonic forces of witchcraft, which divide the nation. He's looking for us to pray for a national revival that will turn this nation away from the moral sewer in which we find ourselves.

So what do we ask Him for? We get down on our knees and ask God if He'll water the grass while we're gone to Florida.

When you get down to pray, remember that you're talking to almighty God. The blast of His nostrils can split the cedars of Lebanon. He holds the seven seas in the palm of His hand. He weighs the mountains on a scale and the hills in the balance. Ask Him for things so staggering, so big, that God slides to the edge of His holy throne and says to the angels, "Did you hear what that kid asked for?

"Do it, angels! Faith like that excites me! Get down there with the answer. Move those mountains of impossibilities. Heal that incurable disease. Restore that dead marriage. Set her addicted son free. Send a financial harvest that staggers his mind."

As a child I read the story of a mighty king of unlimited wealth, riding through his kingdom on his horse with his knights. On this journey he met three peasants of his kingdom, walking on the trail.

He asked the first, "What do you want?"

The peasant responded, "I want your horse."

The mighty king looked at the peasant and said, "Your request is denied." All the knights laughed. They rode on until they came to the second peasant.

The king asked the second peasant, "What do you want?"

The second peasant said, "I want your house."

The king looked at him and said, "Your request is denied." Once again the knights all laughed raucously.

They rode on until they came to a third peasant, and the king asked him, "What do you want?"

The third peasant said, "I want your horse, your castle, and half your kingdom."

Without hesitation the king said, "It's yours."

His knights were stunned. One asked, "Why, O king, are you giving this man such a vast fortune?"

The king responded, "Because I'm tired of small requests when I have so much power and so much wealth to offer. Men of vision excite me."

What do you need? Nothing is impossible with God. You can ask Him for it right now and He'll give it to you.

Do you need supernatural wisdom to make a difficult decision? "Ask and you shall receive."

Do you need peace that surpasses understanding? Ask! "Nothing is impossible to them that believe."

Do you need to experience the impossible? Open your mouth in faith believing because you're not talking to the president of the United States. You're not talking to a billionaire of limited means. You're talking to the Unlimited Creator of heaven and earth. He has the power to divide the seas, and He will not fail you.

Ask Him for the impossible! Ask Him to defeat the giants in your life because our God is a giant killer. Ask Him to divide the Red Sea before you, which will bury Pharaoh and his army. Watch Him turn your enemies into fish food. Ask Him to send fire from heaven as He did for Elijah. Ask Him to walk with you through the fiery furnace as the fourth man in the fire as He did with three Hebrew children. Ask Him, for He's the God who cannot fail, and He's waiting to show you His mighty power.

> *Ask Him to defeat the giants in your life because our God is a giant killer.*

Seven principles of prayer have guided me throughout my life, and I want you to discover them so these principles will serve you the rest of your life.

I

PRAYER SHOULD BE YOUR FIRST CHOICE, NOT YOUR LAST CHANCE

I am now in my forty-sixth year of ministry, and I can recall countless times when distressed souls have walked into my office, telling the most heartrending stories, and then pleading, "Please, let's do something about this."

When I say, "Let's pray about this together," invariably they look at me in frustration and say, "I really want to do something about this!"

I want to tell you this: You're not doing anything about your problems until you're praying about them.

I have talked to God and seen Him heal marriages that seemed impossible to restore. I have seen Him break the iron yoke of drug addiction over the sons and daughters of His saints. I have seen Him calm the troubled sea of the soul.

I have watched with wonder as He has supernaturally transformed the finances of businessmen. I have seen Him bless with blessings that cannot be contained because He has promised to make you the head and not the tail (Deut. 28:13). He has promised to "increase your territory," just as He did for Jabez in 1 Chronicles 4:10. He has promised to plant you by rivers of living water, that you shall not wither, and whatsoever you do shall prosper (Ps. 1:3).

2
PRAYER IS GETTING YOU PREPARED TO DO GOD'S WILL

God never forces you to do His will, but He often places you in extreme adversity that drives you to your knees and prepares you to do His will.

When Saul, the Pharisee, was strutting down the Damascus road, threatening the New Testament church, God looked over the balconies of heaven at this brilliant, opinionated, Type-A, hard-charging crusader and said, "That's my man!"

God stripped Saul of his religious arrogance and blinded him by a bright light from heaven. Like a helpless child, Paul was led into Damascus to the house of Judas. Scripture tells us, "And he was three days without sight, and neither ate nor drank" (Acts 9:9).

Three days in darkness saturated with soul-searching prayer. Then God told Ananias, "Arise and go to the street called Straight, and inquire at the house of Judas for one called Saul of Tarsus, for behold, he is *praying*" (Acts 9:11, emphasis added).

Saul's prayer was not getting God ready to do Saul's will, which was to put Christians in prison. Saul's prayer, in the sanctuary of blindness and forced helplessness, prepared Saul to do God's will.

Doing God's will is the gateway to gaining the favor of God!

Does God have you in a dark place? Seek His face with a pure heart, and light will break through with the brilliance of the noonday sun. Doing God's will is the gateway to gaining the favor of God!

3

PRAY SCRIPTURE

My mother is the greatest prayer warrior I've ever known. As a child, I heard my mother pray the Scriptures because they are the promises of God, and they will not return void.

When Mother kneels to pray, God looks over the banister of heaven and says, "Hello, Vada!" When Mother prays the Scriptures, mountains are moved, sickness and disease retreat, the unknown becomes known, and every complex adversity is transformed into a parade of miracles!

Let me give you several examples of how to pray Scripture.

What is your problem? Your burden? Your crisis? Find the verses in the Bible that relate to what you're going through and pray those verses. (In the beginning you might need to consult a concordance. You would look up the word *worry*, for instance, and then look for the passages that apply to your difficulty. As you become more familiar with God's Word, praying Scripture will become automatic.) Remember, it's not what you're going *through*; it's what you're going *to* that counts.

Let's take the example of a person going through a dark valley of sorrow, grief, and perhaps depression.

Praying the Scripture would sound like this:

> Heavenly Father, I come to You in the mighty name of Your Son and my Savior Jesus Christ. You know my heart is full of grief, and so, according to Your Word, I've come before Your throne to rejoice.
>
> Father, this is the day the Lord hath made, I will rejoice and be glad in it. I delight myself in You, Lord. You are my shield and buckler, my fortress and my high tower. You are the bright and morning star. You are the Prince of Peace. Happy am I because God is my refuge.
>
> Father, Your Word declares that You rejoice over me with joy and that everlasting joy is upon my head. In the midst of my sorrow, I receive Your joy, I receive Your gladness, I receive Your peace, which the world cannot give and cannot take away. The spirit of rejoicing, joy, and laughter is my heritage.
>
> Father God, my mouth shall praise You in the day of trouble, for You are the strength of my life; of whom shall I be afraid? Though a host should encamp against me, my heart

shall not fear; though war should rise against me, in this will I be confident.

For in the time of trouble You shall hide me in Your pavilion. You shall set me upon a rock. And now my head shall be lifted up above mine enemies; therefore will I offer sacrifices of joy unto the Lord.

Because of the power of Your Word, Satan is a defeated foe. I am not moved by my adverse circumstances. Let God arise and His enemies be scattered. Amen!

The Scripture verses used in this prayer are Psalm 27:1–8; Philippians 4:4; Isaiah 51:11; Psalm 118:24; Psalm 144:15; and Psalm 68:1.

Are you being attacked in your finances or your business? Pray in this fashion:

Satan, I speak to you and the demon spirits who obey you. I bind you in the mighty name of Jesus and confess the Word, "My God shall supply all my needs according to His riches in glory" (Phil. 4:19).

Are you being attacked in your health? Pray in this fashion:

Satan, I speak to you in the mighty name of Jesus and say that your principalities, powers, and demon spirits are bound from operating against me in any way. According to the Word of the Lord, I confess that by His stripes, I am healed (1 Pet. 2:24). I shall live and not die (Ps. 118:17). Jesus is my great physician.

Are you being attacked in your emotions? Are you filled with fear concerning something in your immediate tomorrow? Is there anything in your past over which you are bitter? Is there resentment in your heart over something your parents have done to you? Satan is controlling your mind for your destruction. Pray this prayer:

Satan, I speak to you in the mighty name of Jesus Christ, the Conqueror from Calvary, the Lord of glory who has defeated you. I bind you in every oppressive spirit that is attacking my life. I command the spirit of fear to go. I command the spirit of bitterness to go. I command the spirit of resentment to go.

And now, according to your Word, O Lord, I receive the peace of God, which surpasses understanding. Your Word says, "You will keep him in perfect peace, whose mind is stayed on You" (Isa. 26:3).

We pray Scripture to remind God of His promises in the Bible and also to remind ourselves of those promises, which are valid at this moment in our lives. Obviously we cannot pray Scripture unless we know Scripture. Get into God's Word so you can pray Scripture with power.

4

CONSIDER THE POWER OF TWO

Two in agreement can do more than two million in discord. Matthew 18:19 reads:

> Again I say to you that if two of you agree on earth concerning anything that they ask, it will be done for them by my Father in heaven.

Paul and Silas demonstrated the power of two as they sang in the jail at Philippi. In response, God sent angels to shake the foundations of that jail. Paul and Silas walked out of the jail with the keys in one hand and converts in the other. They knew the power of two.

There are two witnesses in Revelation 11:3: Enoch and Elijah. They have the power to turn water into blood. They have the power to call fire from heaven. They have the power to call plagues and draught to cover the earth. The antichrist and all of the earth will hate them. But they have that supernatural power because they are two in agreement.

Jesus sent His disciples out two by two. He gave them the authority to bind and loose things on this earth, and if they did so this would be honored in heaven through the power of two.

You will need that power when you deal with the strong man referred to in Luke 11:21–22. This Scripture says that there is a strong man [Satan] whose objective is to attack you. That strong man will attack your marriage, your health, your finances, your peace of mind, and your children, seeking to rob, to kill, and to destroy.

God has given you an answer to Satan's power. That answer is to bind him with supernatural prayer when you and another believer come into agreement (Matt. 12:29).

How much power can people in agreement have? The answer: the power of life and death. The following is a true story related to me by believers in London, England.

During the brutal reign of Joseph Stalin, who murdered thirty million Russians and brought godless communism to Russia, Stalin let it be known that he planned to murder the Jews of Russia.

When the believers in England heard this report, they committed themselves to fasting and prayer for the Jews of Russia. Praying in the Spirit, they bound the demonic forces that drove Joseph Stalin. Three weeks later, Joseph Stalin had a brain hemorrhage. Sixteen gifted brain surgeons worked on him for eight hours, and still Joseph Stalin stepped into eternity on March 5, 1953, to meet the Son of God: a Jewish rabbi from Bethlehem.

God has placed the responsibility of taking action squarely on your shoulders.

Jesus said to His church, "Whatever you bind on earth will be bound in heaven" (Matt. 18:18). The message is very clear. The initiative rests with you, not God! Stop asking, "When is God going to do something about my situation?" God has placed the responsibility of taking action squarely on your shoulders. Start praying in Jesus' name with a believer with whom you can come into agreement, and watch for powerful results.

What area of your life is under attack? Your marriage? Your children? Your business? Your finances? Your health? Your emotions? Your relationships?

Find someone with whom you can agree right now. If you take the initiative, the power of your prayer will move the hand of God to bring the perfect answer.

5

PRAY IN THE SPIRIT

God's secret weapon in prayer is praying in the Spirit. The apostle Paul writes:

> Likewise the Spirit also helps in our weaknesses. For we do not know not what we should pray for as we ought, but the Spirit Himself makes intercession for us with groanings that cannot be uttered. Now He who searches the hearts knows what the

mind of the Spirit is, because He makes intercession for the saints according to the will of God.

—ROMANS 8:26–27

Note that our weakness in this verse is in our minds. We do not know what we should pray for. We have a language barrier with heaven; therefore, the Holy Spirit makes intercession to God in heaven for us, saying, "Father, here is what Your child is trying to say."

Praying in the Spirit helps you hit the bull's-eye every time you get on your knees. The Bible says, "God is a Spirit, and those who worship Him must worship in spirit and truth" (John 4:24).

One particular weekend when I was attending Southwestern Bible Institute in Waxahachie, Texas, I traveled to Oklahoma to preach. Friday night, Saturday night, Sunday morning, and Sunday night I preached a weekend revival. After the Sunday night service, I showered and started driving back toward Dallas.

Several hours later, exhausted from driving and the strenuous weekend, I fell asleep at the wheel of my car. I woke up when my car jumped a railroad track. I thought I was flying a guided missile. I could see nothing but the stars and the moon over my steering wheel.

When my car finally came down to earth, it miraculously landed back in my lane on the two-lane highway. At that moment I saw a Texaco gasoline truck in the opposite lane, coming straight at me. I assure you I was instantly wide awake. Thankfully, that eighteen wheeler passed without hitting my little 1948 Pontiac, because my car had landed precisely in my lane on that two-lane highway. It was an absolute miracle! I looked at my watch to reorient myself, and it was three o'clock in the morning.

I got back to Dallas just in time to go to class. As I walked in the dormitory, the phone was ringing. It was my mother. She asked me, "Where were you this morning at three o'clock?" (Mom never takes long to get to the subject.)

Trying to dodge the issue, I said, "I was driving back from Oklahoma where I had been preaching all weekend."

"Son, God got me out of the bed at 2:45 A.M. this morning to pray for you because you were in grave danger. Where were you at three o'clock this morning?"

I told her the story in detail.

She said, "At five minutes after 3:00, the burden lifted from my heart, and I knew you were all right. But for those few short moments I knew your life was hanging in the balance."

6

PRAYER GIVES YOU THE POWER TO SHAPE THE DESTINY OF NATIONS

King Sennacherib of Assyria was the Atilla the Hun, the Napoleon, the Hitler of his time (701 B.C.). A skillful army general, he captured most of the fortified cities of Judah except Jerusalem. He and his Assyrian army were known as vicious warriors who posted the heads of their victims outside the conquered city gates. They also tossed infants in the air and caught the babies on their swords to kill them. As all conquerors, Sennacherib would not be content until he had all known territory under his control, particularly the sacred city of Jerusalem.

In 701 B.C., he marched his legions toward the city of Jerusalem for the purpose of slaughtering the Jews. Once he arrived outside the city, Sennacherib sent a message to King Hezekiah, promising to slaughter every citizen of Jerusalem the next morning. Terrified, Hezekiah pulled out his secret weapon: prayer. He laid Sennacherib's letter before the Lord and said, "Look what that heathen has written to You, O God." (See Isaiah 37:14.)

That night the death angel swept through the camp of the Assyrians. The death angel smote the sentry standing at his post. The death angel smote the infantry soldiers slumbering in their tents. The death angel smote the generals as they made their battle plans to destroy the sacred city of Jerusalem.

The next morning when Hezekiah looked over the fortified walls of the city of Jerusalem by the dawn's early light, 185,000 men were dead. Hezekiah prayed, and the destiny of his nation was determined, as it has been throughout Israel's history.

Prayer has influenced our own nation's history. During the dark days of the Civil War, when brother fought against brother and father fought against son, the United States of America was saved by the power of fasting and prayer. President Abraham Lincoln called for a day of fasting and prayer. His declaration "For a Day of National Humiliation, Fasting, and Prayer" began with this thought:

And, insomuch as we know that, by His divine law, nations, like individuals, are subjected to punishments and chastisements in this world, may we not justly fear that the awful calamity of civil war, which now desolates the land, may be but a punishment inflicted upon us for our presumptuous sins, to the needful end of our national reformation as a whole People?

He went on to say:

We have grown in numbers, wealth, and power as no other nation has ever grown. But we have forgotten God. We have forgotten the gracious hand which preserved us in peace, and multiplied and enriched and strengthened us; and we have vainly imagined, in the deceitfulness of our hearts, that all these blessings were produced by some superior wisdom and virtue of our own. Intoxicated with unbroken success, we have become too self-sufficient to feel the necessity of redeeming and preserving grace, too proud to pray to the God that made us! It behooves us, then, to humble ourselves before the offended Power, to confess our national sins, and to pray for clemency and forgiveness.

"It behooves us, then, to humble ourselves before the offended Power, to confess our national sins, and to pray for clemency and forgiveness."

—ABRAHAM LINCOLN

He then set aside April 30, 1863, as a day of national humiliation, fasting, and prayer and asked people in our nation to "abstain on that day from their ordinary secular pursuits, and to unite, at their several places of public worship and their respective homes, in keeping the day holy to the Lord, and devoted to the humble discharge of the religious duties proper to that solemn occasion."[1]

7

PRAYER IS A WEAPON GOD HAS GIVEN TO WAGE WAR IN THE HEAVENLIES

The New Testament church was under extreme persecution. King Herod had executed James, the brother of John. The king then arrested Peter and placed him in a maximum security prison, where he was guarded by four squads of four soldiers around the clock.

What was the church's response? They prayed to God without ceasing for Peter's deliverance. They didn't have political influence or financial wealth, but they knew the power of prayer.

What was God's response? Angels were released to help Peter escape from prison (Acts 12:11–15). Your prayer also has the power to release the angels of God to defend you, guard you, and guide you. King David wrote, "He shall give His angels charge over you, to keep you in all your ways" (Ps. 91:11). The phrase *to keep* is a military expression meaning "to guard by force." You have that power through prayer.

Uniquely enough, the church that was praying for the deliverance of their pastor, Peter, was shocked when it happened, so shocked that when Peter knocked on the door they thought it was his angel and not the man of God himself. The early church had waged war in the heavenlies, but they hadn't prayed with a sense of expectation that they would win. Do you?

And God finished this heavenly battle by judging Herod. Acts 12:23 says, "Then immediately the angel of the Lord struck him, because he did not give glory to God. And he was eaten by worms and died."

Prayer is a weapon of attack, and praise is also a weapon of attack. The enemy is Satan and his kingdom. Praise gives strength to the body of Christ to conquer the prince of darkness.

The power of praise

In Matthew 21:15, the religious leaders asked Jesus to silence the children who were praising Him in the temple. Jesus replied by quoting Psalm 8:2: "Out of the mouths of babes and nursing infants You have ordained strength, because of Your enemies, that you may silence the enemy and the avenger." The babes of Matthew 21 are the disciples of Christ. Praise is the source of our strength, and praise has the power to conquer the prince of darkness.

*Praise gives strength to the body of Christ to
conquer the prince of darkness.*

The power of the tongue is awesome. The Bible says, "Death and life
are in the power of the tongue, and those who love it will eat its fruit"
(Prov. 18:21). Simply said, in spiritual warfare, the side that uses its
mouth the most is the side that wins the war.

Consider the power of praise in Psalm 149:6-9:

> Let the high praises of God be in their mouth,
> And a two-edged sword in their hand,
> To execute vengeance on the nations,
> And punishment on the peoples;
> To bind their kings with chains,
> And their nobles with fetters of iron;
> To execute upon them the judgment written—
> This honor have all His saints.
>
> Praise the LORD!

Praise combined with the Word of God is a weapon in the hand
of every believer. It is also the instrument of judgment. The "kings
and nobles" spoken of in these verses are Satan's angelic princes and
authorities in the heavenlies.

Paul wrote in 1 Corinthians 6:2–3: "Do you not know that the saints
will judge the world?…Do you not know that we shall judge angels?"
We have the power through praise to bring judgment against powers
and principalities in the heavenlies.

These are the seven principles of prayer you must fully understand
to be effective in spiritual warfare. There are also seven reasons God
might not answer your prayer. If your prayers are not being answered,
use these reasons as a checklist.

SEVEN REASONS GOD DOESN'T ANSWER PRAYER

There is a right way and a wrong way to pray. There is not a Baptist way
and a Pentecostal way and a Methodist way. There is only the right way
and the wrong way. The disciples came to Christ and said, "Lord, teach

us to pray" (Luke 11:1). The very statement means that there is a right way and a wrong way.

1. We do not ask.

Jesus clearly said, "Ask and you shall receive" (Matt. 21:22).

Ask—do not attempt to solve your problem without God's guidance. Ask—do not visualize the answer. Visualizing the answer in your mind is mind control. Ask—do not stare into a crystal. That's idolatry. Speak your request and believe that God will answer. Jesus said, "For assuredly, I say to you, whoever...does not doubt in his heart, but believes that those things he says will be done, he will have whatever he says" (Mark 11:22).

2. We do not pray in Jesus' name.

John 14:14 says: "If you ask anything in My name, I will do it." You do not receive answers to your prayer if you pray in Mary's name or in Buddha's name or in Allah's name. You receive an audience in heaven by using the name that's above every name, the name of Jesus Christ.

3. We do not ask according to God's will.

First John 5:14 says, "Now this is the confidence that we have in Him, that if we ask anything according to His will, He hears us." Some people think God's will is mysterious. It's not! Isaiah said, "The way of the Lord is so simple a fool cannot err therein." (See Isaiah 35:8).

God's will is clearly stated in the Bible, and His will is consistent with His Word. Let's examine God's will in several different instances from His description of Himself in the Bible.

God is light. We know from reading the Word of God that God is light. The priest described Jesus as "a light to bring revelation to the Gentiles, and the glory of Your people Israel" (Luke 2:32). Jesus is a light.

That means He is against darkness. He stands against the *occult*, which means, "that which is hidden." He is opposed to witchcraft and Satanism and fortune-telling. He is opposed to horoscopes and mind control and the principles presented in current adult and children's literature that glorify witches and witchcraft.

God is life! His Word says, "I have come that they may have life, and that they may have it more abundantly" (John 10:10). That means God is pro-life. He's anti-abortion! You don't have to pray,

"If it be thy will," concerning abortion. God's Word makes it clear. Abortion is murder.

God is peace! He opposes fear and intimidation. He opposes manipulation and control of your life by other people. He opposes the torment that Satan tries to force upon you with fear. He opposes anyone trying to manipulate your life.

God is love! He opposes hatred and bitterness. He opposes racial strife and anti-Semitism. Genesis 12:3 states: "I will bless those who bless you, and I will curse him who curses you." That's God's foreign policy statement toward the Jewish people and the nation of Israel.

Walk through the pages of world history, and you will find that the nation or man who cursed the Jewish people or Israel was brought to the swift judgment of God. On the other hand, if you bless Israel, God will bless you.

God is forgiving! If you bear a grudge or if you have resentment against another, you are out of the will of God. If you rehearse bitter scenes in your mind and will not let them go, you are out of the will of God. Mark 11:25 says, "And whenever you stand praying, if you have anything against anyone, forgive him, that your Father in heaven may also forgive you your trespasses."

God is merciful! If you're as mean as a junkyard dog, you're out of the will of God. If you do not extend mercy, God will not show you mercy.

God is holy! The word *holy* means "pure." You don't have to ask God if you should read pornography on the Internet or watch it on HBO. You don't have to pray about going to X-rated movies or subscribing to *Playboy* magazine. It's not the will of God. Get it out of your house and out of your life.

God is authority! All that God does on Planet Earth He does through spiritual authority. If you rebel against God's delegated authority, you're out of the will of God.

He has made the father the head of the home. And the mother submitted to the father. And the children submitted to both mother and father. Our generation has teenagers raising their parents, which is utter nonsense. This is a dysfunctional family, as evidenced by the clear teaching of the Word of God.

---

*God is a giver! Giving is the only
proof that the cancer of greed has not
consumed your soul.*

God is a giver! Giving is the only proof that the cancer of greed has not consumed your soul. God gave His only begotten Son that you might have everlasting life. His Son gave His life, and His disciples gave their lives for the cause of the gospel. The day is going to come when all that you have is what you have given to God. What are you giving? To whom are you giving it?

4. We do not pray in faith believing.

Matthew 21:21 states, "If you have faith and do not doubt…if you say to this mountain, 'Be removed and be cast into the sea,' it will be done."

Going to God without faith is like going to Sears without money. Without faith it is impossible to please God. Faith starts out before you know how your prayers are going to turn out. Faith does not demand miracles. Faith creates an environment where miracles are the only possible result.

The Bible commands, "Have faith in God" (Mark 11:22). Note that the Bible doesn't say to *try* to have faith in God. You *try* broccoli. You *try* low-fat ice cream. You may not like it, but you try it. You don't *try* to have faith in God: You *have* faith in God. As I've said over and over again, the God that you serve has never failed. Therefore, it does not require great faith to believe that He will help you today with a crisis you're facing.

5. We do not pray specifically.

Be specific with your prayer request so that when your request is answered, you'll know God sent it. The Lord's Prayer gives us an illustration of this specificity: "Give us this day our daily bread" (Matt. 6:11). Notice three of the four specifics of good journalism, which every reporter has been taught: Who, what, when. "Give us" is who. "Our daily bread" is what. "This day" is when. Specific prayer is a prerequisite to answered prayer.

Every Christmas at Cornerstone we give Christmas gifts to the children of single mothers who are struggling to hold their families together. One particular Christmas, a physician in our city came to Diana and said, "I have a red bicycle that is very expensive. I never use it, and I never ride it. It's a shame that it's wasted. I want to give it to you to give to some special child this Christmas."

We put that red bicycle in our garage and prayed that God would indicate the exact child who should receive this bike. Our God is a faithful God. In a church of thousands, there was a single mother with an only son who was trying to get a paper route to help his mother with their finances. He was not just praying for a bicycle; he was praying for a red bicycle!

On Christmas Eve, we pulled up in front of their house with that red bike attached to the back of the car and pushed that shiny bike to the front door.

When the mother answered the doorbell, my wife, Diana, said, "We have a red bicycle for your son."

At that instant, the boy arrived at the door, threw his hands into the air, and burst into tears, screaming, "God has answered my prayer exactly! He sent a red bicycle just like I asked." Both mother and son burst into tears, thanking God for that specific answer to a specific prayer.

What are you praying for? Ask specifically so when you get it, you'll know God sent it.

6. We do not remove unconfessed sin.

King David wrote in Psalm 66:18, "If I regard iniquity in my heart, the LORD will not hear."

When people think of the word *repentance* in our humanistic society, they see the word as a put down. They think it is degrading and mean-spirited to ask them to repent. But repentance is one of the most beautiful words in the Bible. As I mentioned earlier, repentance means to return to the highest point.

A holy God cannot associate with sin. He's made it possible for sin to be removed from your life with a simple prayer. If you know that sin is in your life, ask Christ to remove it now. Then you are ready for an adventure of prayer that knows no limit.

7. We do not forgive other people.

The Word of God says, "And forgive us our debts, as we forgive our debtors" (Matt. 6:12).

I talked about forgiveness extensively in chapter five. I mention it again here because unforgiveness is a real stumbling block to answered prayer. If you know you still haven't forgiven someone, go back to chapter five and review the principles there. Then pray that God will empower you to forgive so you can be forgiven and your prayers can be answered.

God gets excited when you get down on your knees. He says, "Look, angels. Here he (she) comes. We're finally going to talk. Get ready to carry back My answer to earth. Listen to his (her) request and fulfill it according to his (her) faith."

The power of continuous prayer is a precursor to great and mighty accomplishments.

Chapter Eight

Secret Seven: The Undeniable Laws of Prosperity

Unleashing the Power of God's Abundance

I've found that prosperity is always linked to giving, and the most difficult spiritual lesson I've ever had to learn was the importance of giving. When you start out at the age of eight in a South Texas cotton patch with a sixteen-foot cotton sack, working like a slave for a dollar a day, you learn to hold on to your money with an iron grip.

When I was seventeen and leaving home to attend Southwestern Bible Institute in Waxahachie, Texas, I walked out of the door with seventy-five dollars, which was enough to pay for the first six weeks of school.

I had to bum a ride to Southwestern with Harvey Hayslip, who was also going to Southwestern from my father's church. Even though I had that 1948 Pontiac, I didn't have the gas money to drive to school. It was understood by all that I would have to get a job quickly and work my way through school.

I packed one suitcase and threw it into the trunk of Harvey's car.

I kissed my mother good-bye and shook hands with Dad, who demonstrated affection publicly about as often as lightning strikes on the Fourth of July.

We drove away from home the third Sunday in January of 1958 about 2:00 P.M., and I knew I would never be back. It was a sinking feeling everyone has to experience at least once in a lifetime.

Harvey and I drove in total silence as we left the city of Houston and headed toward Dallas. We were both wondering what lay ahead for us. Harvey wanted to be a pastor. At that moment I believed I would go to school for about two years, become an earth-shaking evangelist with twenty-four memorized sermons, and keep the whole world from going to hell. What a joke! The longer I went to school, the more I discovered how much I didn't know. And the more I discovered, the longer I stayed in school. Now, after two earned university degrees and over forty-five years of daily study, I'm still learning. The best remedy for conceit is to sit down and make a list of all the things you don't know.

We arrived in Waxahachie at about 6:30 P.M. and went directly to the men's dormitory. The good news: Harvey and I would be roommates. The bad news: Our dorm room was a twelve-by-eighteen, concrete-block room. We began to unpack. This didn't take long; I didn't have much.

The burning question eating at my brain like a starved lion was, *Where could I get a job?* In 1958, Waxahachie mainly consisted of five Assemblies of God churches, Carl's Restaurant, and a few gas stations on the main street. There was also Southwestern Wood Products, which manufactured church furniture and was located on the university property.

Most students who needed employment drove to Dallas to work for Plastics Incorporated or for one of the freight companies. I didn't have transportation. My job had to be in Waxahachie, and the closer the better.

I knew I had to find employment within six weeks. Once that seventy-five dollars was used up, I had to move out. Returning home was not an option for me. Plan B was to follow my older brother, Bill, into the army.

The next day, on Monday afternoon, I started looking for jobs. I looked every day for three weeks. I went to Southwestern Wood

Products, which was the absolute pinnacle of employment opportunity because it paid the fabulous sum of one dollar per hour, and I could walk to work while attending school. Southwestern Wood Products made church pews and pulpits out of solid Appalachian oak.

I knew this was a long shot. Since the company was so close to the campus and paid so well, there was very seldom a vacancy. Most all the employees attended Southwestern and were upper classman. Still, I was in a desperate situation, and long shots were the order of the day. The answer was no.

I tried to hire out as a dishwasher at Carl's Restaurant. I sought employment at the gas stations, pumping gas. An entrepreneurial job, like yard work, was not even an option since it was winter, and frozen grass doesn't need cutting.

I looked the second week...nothing.

I looked the third and fourth week...nothing.

The fifth week involved the same routine—six long days of pounding the streets and a chorus of no's. I even returned to Southwestern Wood Products, just in case. The answer was still no.

I was beginning to feel panicky. My parents had given me all they had, and I was beginning to look into the abyss.

The sixth week started, as always, with no job. That Tuesday I read a flyer on the school bulletin board that a car lot needed help to wash all their cars the next day, and they would pay fifty cents per hour. I was the first in line, even though the temperature was in the low thirties and the wind was blowing out of the north, cutting my face and hands like a knife.

Four hours later we finished washing the cars, and I walked back to the campus with two dollars in my pocket. I was wet, cold, and miserable. However, I was still willing to work doing anything that was legal, but there was no work to be had in Waxahachie.

That night I went to chapel on campus to hear Charles Greenway, a missionary to Africa. He spoke more like a Methodist than a Pentecostal: slow, deliberate, and with every word in every sentence anointed with the fire of the Holy Spirit. His passion for Africa filled the auditorium. He spoke for an hour and a half, which seemed like ten minutes.

Then came the offering!

Offerings had not been a problem for me in the past six weeks, because I was dead broke. Now I had two dollars in my pocket, and my German mind was made up: I needed this money more than that missionary did.

Suddenly, as clearly as the tolling of a bell on a cold Christmas morning, the voice of the Lord said, "Give that two dollars!"

My instant response was, "No!"

"Give that two dollars!"

My second response was more reasoned and more articulate: "Absolutely not."

"Give it!"

"I need it more than Charles Greenway needs it."

"Give it! "

The offering plate was coming toward me. I clutched the two dollars in my pocket like a drowning man would clutch a life raft.

"Give it."

I worked for this in freezing weather. I needed it. I *really* needed it.

The offering plate was now directly in front of me. As Billy Graham says, "It was the hour of decision." I pulled the two dollars out of my pocket like they were my eye teeth with roots a foot long. I placed the money in the offering and watched the basket pass down the pew like Moses' sister watched him float out into the treacherous Nile.

I would like to tell you I was covered with waves of joy that produced unspeakable ecstasy. It would be an absolute lie! The truth is when I got back to my room, it took all the self-control I had not to put my head in the toilet and vomit.

Little did I know, God was teaching me a lesson about giving I would remember for the rest of my life. When what you have in your hands is not enough to meet your need, what you have in your hands is your seed. However grudgingly, I had planted my seed in the sacred soil of the kingdom of God.

> *When what you have in your hands is not enough to meet your need, what you have in your hands is your seed.*

The next day, I awoke at daybreak, wondering what I'd look like in a military uniform. I had tried my best to find employment, and it just didn't work out. Now, I was dead broke again, thanks to my generosity last night.

Maybe I had missed the will of God in even thinking I should be in the ministry. Six months earlier I had received a letter from Senator Lyndon Johnson, stating that he was willing to give me an appointment to the West Point Military Academy. Perhaps that's where God wanted me to go.

Way down deep in my belly came this unspeakable urge to go to Southwestern Wood Products and ask for a job for a third time.

What did I have to lose? I got up, dressed, and waited for eight o'clock to arrive. No, I'm not the world's most patient person. F-I-N-A-L-L-Y, 8 A.M. arrived.

I walked across campus to the front door of Southwestern Wood Products. When I opened the door, the first person I saw was General Manager Bill Craig. He looked surprised to see me. Shocked might be more accurate.

I seized the initiative. "I thought I would give you people just one more chance to hire me."

Bill Craig laughed. Then he slapped me on the shoulder and spoke words I never expected to hear: "You're hired. One of our employees quit last night. You can have his job."

Suddenly, I had one of the best jobs a student at Southwestern could possibly have in Waxahachie, Texas. I went to work immediately, sanding church pews by hand for the fabulous income of a dollar per hour.

As I sanded the endless rows of pews that had been lacquered, Bill Craig's words suddenly echoed in my ear: "One of our employees quit last night!"

Last night? Last night—when I was in chapel listening to a missionary from Africa? Last night—when I was dragging those last two dollars out of pocket like they were a boat anchor? Yes! Last night when I gave my best to God, God gave His best to me. It was only a two-dollar gift, but it was all I had and all I had the opportunity to get in the foreseeable future. I knew I would not have gotten that job had I not given those two dollars.

At that moment, I knew as certainly as I know my name is John Hagee that giving is the secret to financial and spiritual wealth. My two-dollar gift to the kingdom of God changed the destiny of my life.

The words Jesus spoke concerning giving instantly became my financial compass for the future: "Give, and it will be given to you; good measure, pressed down, shaken together, and running over will be put into your bosom. For with the same measure that you use, it will be measured back to you" (Luke 6:38).

THE IMPORTANCE OF MONEY

Jesus Christ gave us thirty-eight parables. Sixteen of those thirty-eight parables deal with money management. More is said in the New Testament about managing your money than the instruction about heaven and hell combined.

Five times more is said about money than prayer. While there are five hundred plus verses on both prayer and faith, over two thousand verses deal with money and your possessions. Think about that. The Bible is the greatest financial manual ever printed. God's Word makes it clear that you will either master your money, or your money will master you.

God owns and controls all the wealth in the world—and He's willing to share His resources with us. Matthew 25:14 says, "For the kingdom of heaven is like a man traveling to a far country, who called his own servants and delivered his goods to them."

There are two revolutionary implications in this verse. First, it is God's money, and He has the right to do with it whatever He wants, whenever He wants. As the owner, He has rights. And second, as the steward, I have responsibilities.

Since all your money is God's money, every spending decision is a spiritual decision. Your checkbook is a spiritual reflection of your love of God. Look at it, and determine what it says about you.

Could the accounting go something like this? Your trip to Hawaii cost $20,000 dollars, and your tithe is $15 per week. Your new car cost $50,000, and your weekly offering is $5. You spent $150 shampooing your poodle, and your mission gift was $2.50.

Remember you are only a steward. God is the owner. You will give an account to God of how you managed His resources. What are you going to say on Judgment Day when you've invested more in your poodle than in the Prince of Glory and His work on earth?

What are you going to say on Judgment Day when you've invested more in your poodle than in the Prince of Glory and His work on earth?

I am often reminded of the movie *Schindler's List*. If you didn't see it, I urge you to do so. In my judgment it was Steven Spielberg's finest hour. By the end of the movie, Schindler had used all his wealth to protect a group of Jewish people from the Nazi horde.

As World War II came to an end and he was leaving the Jewish people he had saved from Hitler's holocaust, he was struck with remorse. Surrounded by his grateful Jewish employees, he realized with agony that he could have done more. He held a gold ring in the air and lamented, "This would have saved 10 more lives." He pointed to a luxury automobile and sobbed, "That would have saved 150 or maybe 200 lives."

Despite all he had done, tears were flowing down his face as he mourned the fact that he had kept for himself material possessions that could have saved more lives.

On Judgment Day, how many of us will have to say, "I kept for myself money that would have made an eternal difference in the life of another person"? How we manage our money has great importance to our prosperity, both here on earth and in heaven.

Since that day in Waxahachie, I have learned some other secrets of prosperity that I'd like to add to this all-important one: Prosperity is always linked to giving.

I

INVEST IN YOURSELF

God wants you to invest in yourself! The Bible says, "Lay up for yourselves treasures…" (Matt. 6:20).

Two words often confuse Christians, keeping them from success. Those two words are *self-interest* and *selfishness*. Self-interest is good; however, selfishness is a spiritual cancer. Unfortunately, too many Christians think the definitions are the same.

A quick look at *Webster's Ninth New Collegiate Dictionary* should clear up this misunderstanding. *Self-interest* means "a concern for one's own advantage and well-being."

On the other hand, the word *selfish* is defined this way: "Concerned excessively or exclusively with oneself; seeking or concentrating on one's own advantage, pleasure, or well-being without regard for others." The difference is a matter of extremes. Selfishness is an over-concentration on self, without consideration for others. Self-interest, however, is a natural, God-given concern for our own well-being.

It is in my self-interest to be saved. The options are heaven and hell. You don't have to be a rocket scientist to know heaven is the better choice.

It's in my self-interest to be happy because the Bible says, "A merry heart does good, like medicine" (Prov. 17:22).

It is in my self-interest to invest in the kingdom of God. Why? Because God controls the economy on both sides of the Jordan River. Matthew 19:29 states, "And everyone who has left houses or brothers or sisters or father or mother or wife or children or lands, for My name's sake, shall receive a hundredfold, and inherit eternal life." You don't have to die to get the interest on your investments in the kingdom of God. You get them in this life.

Jesus taught us to invest wisely by investing in things that are permanent. "It's not in your self-interest," He said, "to invest in something that moths can eat, or rust can decay, or thieves can carry off, or the IRS can tax out of existence" (Matt. 6:19, HIT PARAPHRASE).

Jesus taught us to invest wisely by investing in things that are permanent.

Are you investing in things that are not permanent? Are you investing in dewdrops, which are as pretty as diamonds until the sun comes out?

The truth is the earth is not permanent. The Bible tells us that someday the earth will burn with fire. Second Peter 3:10 says, "But the day of the Lord will come as a thief in the night, in which the heavens will pass away with a great noise…both the earth and the works that are in it will be burned up."

If I told you your house was going to burn down in two hours, would you leave all your valuables in the house? You would consider that insane. You would do everything in your power to get them out of the house as quickly as possible.

Invest in yourself by investing in the kingdom of God. Lay up for yourself treasures in heaven, because the kingdom of God is the only certain investment opportunity you have. Wall Street will collapse. The economy of America will eventually fold. But the kingdom of God will stand forever.

2

INVEST IN OTHERS

This is an undeniable law of prosperity, which I call "givers' gain." God has created a universe where it is impossible to receive without giving. "Give, and it will be given to you" is the law of God (Luke 6:38).

You do not qualify to receive from God—or from Neiman Marcus—until you give. You go shopping at Neiman Marcus and see a T-shirt you like, and you give the man three hundred dollars. Then you receive the T-shirt. If not, you're shoplifting.

You go to the grocery store and buy fifty dollars' worth of groceries. You check out, and the checker puts it in a bag that you can carry with one hand. You leave the store and throw the groceries into the glove compartment of your Toyota. You give before you receive.

Many people watch Christian television and shoplift every Sunday. Many have been saved, their marriages have been salvaged, their bodies have been healed, television counselors have lovingly led them out of addictions and out of emotional crisis. But they never do anything to financially keep that television ministry on the air. That's shoplifting.

Let me share this true story with you. His name was Fleming, and he was a poor Scottish farmer. One day while trying to make a living for his family, he heard a cry for help coming from a nearby bog. He dropped his tools and ran to the bog. There was a terrified boy mired to the waist in black muck, screaming and struggling to free himself.

Farmer Fleming saved the lad from what would have been a slow and terrifying death.

The next day, a fancy carriage pulled up to the Scotsman's sparse surroundings. An eloquently dressed nobleman stepped out and introduced himself as the father of the boy.

"I want to repay you," said the nobleman. "You saved my son's life."

"No, I can't accept payment for what I did," the farmer replied, waving off the offer.

At that moment, the farmer's own son came to the door of the family hovel.

Is that your son?" the nobleman asked.

"Yes," the farmer replied proudly.

"I'll make you a deal. Let me provide him with the level of education my son will enjoy. If the lad is anything like his father, he'll no doubt grow to be a man we both will be proud of."

And that's exactly what the nobleman did.

Farmer Fleming's son attended the very best schools, and in time he graduated from Saint Mary's Hospital Medical School in London. He went on to become known throughout the world as the noted Sir Alexander Fleming, the discoverer of penicillin.

Years afterward, the nobleman's son was stricken with pneumonia. What saved his life this time? Penicillin.

The name of the nobleman was Lord Randolph Churchill. The nobleman's son, the one dragged from the bog, was Sir Winston Churchill. His son had been saved by the son of the farmer, the doctor who invented penicillin.[1]

Until you give, you don't qualify to receive God's power to get wealth.

God Almighty controls the economy of the world, and He controls your income. The United States government is not your source; God is. Deuteronomy 8:18 says: "Remember the LORD your God, for it is He who gives you power to get wealth."

I get so tired of hearing people say, "The government gave me blah, blah, blah." Give me a break! Where do you think the government got the money? They got it from you. The government giving you something is like you giving yourself a transfusion from your right arm to your left arm, with 90 percent of your blood dripping out on the floor.

The stock market is not your source; God is. The IRA account you have is not your source; God is. Your rich aunt is not your source; God is.

In God's economy there is no such thing as a "fixed income." Your income is only controlled by your giving.

Consider the widow woman in the Old Testament. She gave her last piece of bread to Elijah, even though she and her son were about to die from starvation since this was a time of great depression in Israel. The prophet asked for her last slice of bread, and she gave it.

You get supernatural abundance when you let go of what's in your hand for God; then God will let go of what's in His hand for you.

As soon as she gave Elijah what was in her hand, God supernaturally caused the cruse of oil to fill and the mill barrel to be full. She had more than she could use, created by the supernatural abundance of God. That's what God wants to give you—supernatural abundance. How do you get it? You get supernatural abundance when you let go of what's in your hand for God; then God will let go of what's in His hand for you.

3
QUALIFY FOR GOD'S ABUNDANCE

When you read the Word of God, it clearly says that all of the gold and the silver in earth belong to the Lord (Hag. 2:8). Scripture also clearly says that "the cattle on a thousand hills" belong to God (Ps. 50:10). It's the Bible's way of saying, "God's abundance exceeds anything your mind can conceive." But how do you qualify to receive the abundance? First you must be one of His children.

The key of being His children
The truth is, you do not qualify for God's abundance until you become God's child. You cannot pray, "Our Father, which art in heaven," until you receive Christ. The Bible says, "Nor is there salvation in any other, for there is no other name under heaven given among men by which we must be saved" (Acts 4:12).

There are two families in the Bible. One is the family of God, for Jesus taught us to pray, "Our Father, which art in heaven." The other is the family of Satan.

On one occasion when Jesus was addressing the Pharisees He said, "You are of your father the devil" (John 8:44). So, very clearly in

Scripture, there are two fathers and two families and two destinations for every believer. Those two destinations are heaven and hell. So I ask you, whose child are you?

When God is your father, all His wealth belongs to you. He has promised to take care of His children. King David wrote, "I have not seen the righteous forsaken, nor his descendants begging bread" (Ps. 37:25).

When God is your father, all His wealth belongs to you.

Paul wrote in Romans 8:17, "…and if children, then heirs—heirs of God and joint heirs with Christ." We are not equal heirs, which means half and half, but joint heirs. Joint heirs means that all Christ has is mine, and all I have is His. At Calvary I brought my poverty, and He gave me the riches of Abraham. I brought my sickness, and He gave me health and healing. I brought my sin, and He gave me total forgiveness. I brought my rejection, and He adopted me and brought me into the family of God as an heir and a joint heir.

This inheritance excites me—and it should. Jesus expected us to be excited about the treasures of heaven. He said, "The kingdom of heaven is like treasure hidden in a field" (Matt. 13:44). The prospect of treasure excites people. I know from personal experience.

On one of our family vacations, I took my wife and children to the Texas coast. We were staying in the beachfront home of one of our church members in Rockport, Texas. These were the days of financial lack in the John Hagee house. This was a low-budget vacation.

The first day Diana and I took Tish, who was six, and Chris, who was five, to the beach to swim. As we were wading in the water, Christopher asked me, "Dad, did pirates ever sail in these waters?"

"Absolutely, Son, pirates were all over this coastline." I could see his interest accelerate instantly.

"Do you think there's treasure buried out here in this water, Dad?"

I had gone too far to turn back now so I continued the drama. "Absolutely, Son. I'm sure there's treasure in these waters."

"Let's search for the treasure, and we will be rich."

I agreed to search for treasure, and we waded back and forth in the surf until the sun set. I took my two discouraged treasure hunters back to the beachfront home. We ate supper, and I put them to bed.

Then I drove into town to a novelty shop and bought a little wooden chest about eighteen-inches long that looked like a pirate's treasure chest. I filled it with junk jewelry that cost me less than five dollars—rings, necklaces, and so on.

That night in the moonlight I went out and buried the treasure. I measured the steps from the flag that I put on the beach out in the water so I could find it myself the next day.

The next morning when Tish and Chris awoke I said, "Let's go search for treasure one more time."

They responded much less enthusiastically than the day before so I said, "I believe that if we'll be persistent, we'll find something today."

They gobbled their breakfast, and out the door we went one more time.

For about thirty minutes I let them search in the water, and when they both began to become discouraged, I shouted, "I think I see something!"

"What do you see?" one of them asked.

"I think I see a pirate's treasure chest."

"Where is it?" they both screamed.

I started walking the number of steps into the water from that marker on the beach. They were both right beside me, screaming with joy.

Christopher was the first to see the edge of the little treasure chest sticking up out of the water as the tide was going away from the shore. Tish saw it a nanosecond afterward, and they were like two dogs chasing the same fox. They darted after that chest and snatched it out of the water. They opened the lid and peered at the costume jewelry, which they were sure was worth a fortune. Then they ran toward the house, screaming with joy.

Once we all were inside, Tish slammed the door and locked it to make sure no thieves would get this rare treasure.

"Let's call the newspaper and tell them what we found," Chris suggested.

"Absolutely not," Tish replied. "People will come and steal the chest tonight, and we'll be poor again." Not bad logic for a six-year-old.

My son and daughter literally spent the rest of the day polishing that junk jewelry and spinning tales of fortune. That night they went to bed totally convinced they were two of the richest children on earth. There was such a sense of joy and happiness that I couldn't dare tell them it was not real. They kept that box for years until they knew it was not what they thought it was.

The point of this story is that treasure excites people. And this is the kind of excitement we should feel about God's kingdom and the wealth that is naturally ours. "It's like a treasure hidden in a field;" it is the "pearl of great price" (Matt. 13:44, 46). John the Revelator described our eternal home, which he saw in his vision on Patmos: "The foundations of the wall of the city were adorned with all kinds of precious stones" (Rev. 21:19).

That eternal kingdom has twelve gates of solid pearl with streets of fine-spun gold. Mansions left and right are designed by the architect of the ages for God's children. If that's poverty, I say, "Bring it on!"

THE NATURAL INHERITANCE OF GOD'S CHILDREN

All of the wealth of God belongs to His children. Note the scriptures below that testify to this:

"He who did not spare His own Son, but delivered Him up for us all, how shall He not with Him also freely give us all things?"

—ROMANS 8:32

"Trust…in the living God, who gives us richly all things to enjoy."

—1 TIMOTHY 6:17

"Therefore let no one boast in men. For *all things are yours*…and you are Christ's, and Christ is God's."

—1 CORINTHIANS 3:21, 23, EMPHASIS ADDED

These verses simply say that when you are God's child, you receive His abundance. God does not take responsibility for providing for the devil's children, just His own. Whose child are you?

The importance of tithing

Scripture is very clear about the importance of tithing and its relationship to prosperity. Malachi 3:8–9 reads:

> Will a man rob God? Yet you have robbed Me! But you say, "In what way have we robbed You?" In tithes and offerings. You are cursed with a curse, for you have robbed Me, even this whole nation. Bring all the tithes into the storehouse, that there may be food in My house.

Why tithe? Because the tithe is not a debt we owe, but a seed we sow. Remember my seed gift of two dollars—and God's resulting blessing.

Why tithe? Because the tithe is not a debt we owe, but a seed we sow.

Why tithe? Because God commands it. Refusal to tithe is rebellion against the Word and will of God.

Why tithe? Because you live under the financial curse of God when you don't. Remember the warning in Malachi 3:9: "You are cursed with a curse, for you have robbed Me." When you tithe, God gives to you. When you don't tithe, God takes it away from you.

Why tithe? Because God will give you an increase of income when you do. He challenges you in Malachi 3:10: "'Try Me now in this,' says the LORD of hosts, 'If I will not open for you the windows of heaven and pour out for you such blessing that there will not be room enough to receive it.'" Many people don't need to pray to receive blessings; they need to tithe. Unfortunately most people are divine tippers, not tithers.

Why tithe? Because God says, "I will rebuke the devourer for your sakes" (Mal. 3:11). "The devourer" is Satan. God promises to hold Satan on a leash and not allow him to steal your inheritance.

On one occasion Diana and I took our five children to the theater. Our routine was that I would be seated in the theater with the children while Diana bought the popcorn and Cokes. We had followed our routine, and I was sitting in the theater with four of our children, waiting for the movie to begin while Diana and our baby, Sandy, who was less than two years of age, stood in line to get Cokes and popcorn.

After a few minutes I heard Diana running down the aisle toward me. Her face was ashen white as she said, "John, Sandy is gone!"

"What do you mean she's gone?"

"Someone has taken our daughter!"

I jumped to my feet and sprinted up the aisle, ran to the lobby of the theater, and screamed like a wild man, "Shut the doors. Someone has kidnapped my daughter." I screamed until the security services came, the manager came, and I had the attention of everyone in that building. I did not care if I seemed deranged. My daughter's life was hanging in the balance, and I wanted to do everything in my power to save her.

We searched the theater and found nothing. It was one of the few times in my life that I felt terror literally grip my brain. My baby had been snatched right out of my hands, and I was totally helpless.

I told Diana to search the women's bathroom again. Even though she was sobbing and shaking almost uncontrollably, she walked obediently to the women's restroom and searched yet again. This time she found Sandy standing on the top of a commode.

As soon as Sandy heard her mother sobbing, Sandy said, "Don't cry, Mama. The lady told me if I wouldn't cry she wouldn't hurt me."

Diana brought Sandy to us, and I knew that this kidnapper had dropped her off in the women's restroom because she heard me screaming in the lobby. As soon as I regained my composure, I heard the voice of the Lord say to me, "I have rebuked the devourer for your sake today." That's the kind of return you get on your tithe to the kingdom of God.

The importance of work

Solomon wrote, "The soul of a lazy man desires, and has nothing; but the soul of the diligent shall be made rich" (Prov. 13:4). He is saying, "Go to work!"

The only place you find *success* before *work* is in the dictionary, where the letter *s* comes before *w*. God provides worms for birds, but He doesn't throw them down their throats. Fight poverty the American way: Get a job. The Bible says, "Six days you shall work" (Deut. 5:13). Giving money to the man who can work but won't work is insanity.

America has abandoned the principles of God, and we are also forsaking the work ethic of God. God the Father worked six days in the creative week, and then He rested. That principle has not stopped. It is God's will for you to work, and work diligently.

I have a secret! Work, wherever you find it, is monotonous; it's preparation and striving, sweat and stress. There is no meaningful employment without toil.

It's easy to get excited about someone else's job, but you need to get excited about your work. Life is not doing what you like to do; it's doing what you ought to do. Too many people today are looking for the right kind of work. God never made the job to fit the man. He found the man and gave him the job. You can put a pygmy on the top of Mount Everest, and he's still a little person in a big position. It is the man that makes the job; the job does not make the man.

The importance of being debt-free

Debt is not a sin, but it is dangerous. The Bible strongly discourages the use of debt in any form. Proverbs 22:7 reads, "The borrower is servant to the lender." David wrote in Psalm 37:21, "The wicked borrows and does not repay." This means both "never pays" and also "does not pay *on time.*" If you don't pay your charge accounts on time, God numbers you with the wicked. Why? Because you lied to your creditor about when you would pay him, and you are stealing his product.

Moses wrote in Deuteronomy, "You shall not oppress a hired servant...who is in your land...each day you shall give him his wages" (Deut. 24:15). The point is you must pay promptly.

We have become a credit card society, addicted to the abundance of material possessions. Yet Luke 12:15 warns, "Take heed and beware of covetousness, for one's life does not consist in the abundance of the things he possesses"

We are a "thing" society. With our credit cards, we buy things to wear, things for the house, things for the garage, and things for the car. Yet when we die, the only things in the boxes are going to be our physical bodies.

Romans 13:8 says, "Owe no one anything." The point is that when you borrow, you don't owe until it's due. When it's due, you must pay it in full. If you don't, you owe. And God says, "Owe no one anything."

Debt may keep you from providing for your own. Yet when Paul was describing how a Christian should treat other people, he said, "If anyone does not provide for his own, and especially for those of his household, he has denied the faith and is worse than an unbeliever" (1 Tim. 5:8). Debt can lead to wife and child abuse.

Greed is never satisfied.

I repeat, debt is not a sin, but it is very dangerous. In the Bible, your creditor could claim your possessions and send you to prison for personal debt. This still happens!

People go to jail every day over debt. It's not a literal jail, but it is a penitentiary where their fears, regrets, and depression over unpaid bills put them in an emotional prison from which there is no escape. They are tormented and can't function well at home or on the job.

Excessive debt is a symptom of greed, and greed grasps and claws. It clutches and clings for more, more, more. Greed is never satisfied.

You need to ask yourself five questions before going into debt.

Five essential questions

The first question is, *"Do I need this?"* God will help you meet your needs, but not your greeds.

The second question is, *"Does my wife or husband agree with me about taking on this debt?"* Diana and I do not spend over twenty-five dollars for anything without talking about it. Why? Because the Bible says, "Can two walk together, unless they are agreed?" (Amos 3:3).

When the bill comes due and there was not unity between the husband and wife when the purchase was made, there's going to be a fight. Have enough of these arguments, and you will be meeting in divorce court with a lawyer because of debt.

The third question to ask before going into debt is, *"Do I have peace of mind about this new debt?"* Husband, if you go out and buy a boat without checking with your wife, and you can't take a vacation that summer because you have made that expensive purchase, you will not have peace of mind. Instead you will be receiving a piece of her mind.

The fourth question is, *"How am I going to pay this back?"* Come up with concrete ways. Not foolish rationalizations like, "If I cut back on my food budget or lower the heat or air conditioning in the house, I can pay for this."

The fifth question is, *"What goals am I meeting with this debt that can be met in no other way?"*

Money is a test. Luke 16:11–12 says, "Therefore if you have not been faithful in the unrighteous mammon [money], who will commit to your trust the true riches? And if you had not been faithful in what is another man's, who will give you what is your own?"

Simply stated, you are a steward of God's wealth. You do not own it. You simply oversee it. Stewards do not steal from God, meaning their tithes and offerings. Neither do stewards waste God's money. Stewards invest, which is the story of the parable of the talents. According to Luke 16, if you don't manage God's resources well on earth, He will not release the riches of the kingdom to you when He rules on the earth. Stewards own nothing, but they control the fortunes of their heavenly Father.

The consequences of debt

Debt is a bondage that destroys your relationship with God. You sink yourself into debt and lose your job; then you get bitter at God because your car gets repossessed. It's not God's fault. It's greed's fault. Debt creates another god: the banker or the credit union. If you came before God with the same hat-in-hand humility that you adopt when you appear before the banker, there would be a worldwide revival tomorrow.

Debt also destroys friendships. Romans 13:8 says, "Owe no one anything except to love one another, for he who loves another has fulfilled the law." Anyone who has borrowed money from another person, especially another Christian, realizes the wall that immediately goes up in the debtor/lender relationship. Debtors and lenders are not really free to love one another.

If a friend asks to borrow money and you can't afford to give the money, then say a very bold, "No, I can't afford it."

The difference between the wealthy and the poor is this: The wealthy invest their money and spend what's left; the poor spend their money and invest what's left.

I often hear other people say, "I don't understand God's economic system." My response is, "You don't have to understand God's economic system for it to work." I don't understand how a black cow eats green grass, gives white milk and yellow butter, but I still drink the milk and eat the butter.

Isaiah 55:8–9 expresses it this way:

> "My thoughts are not your thoughts, nor are your ways My ways," says the LORD. "For as the heavens are higher than the earth, so are My ways higher than your ways, and My thoughts than your thoughts."

The importance of a plan

Are you going into business? Get a sophisticated business plan that covers all of the potential opportunity and at the same time all of the potential downside.

When my son John Christopher went into his first business venture, I asked him to put together a business plan. Once I looked at this plan, I saw that it had more holes in it than a cheap sponge, so I asked him to meet with me one year later. At that time we would discuss his future, I said, when he probably would have worked himself to a frazzle and earned nothing. He agreed.

One year later we met, and sure enough he had worked hard but lost money. His plan was not a good one. I asked him if we could set out a new plan together. That day we structured the economic road to success that he is presently walking. Today, John has fabulous prosperity because of his hard work, the blessing of God, and a good plan.

The importance of Christian partners

The Bible says, "Do not be unequally yoked together with unbelievers" (2 Cor. 6:14). God wants to open the windows of heaven and bless His children, but He doesn't want to enrich the devil's crowd with your inheritance. If you are starting a business of your own, choose Christians as partners.

And in the words of Solomon, "He who is surety for a stranger will suffer" (Prov. 11:15). That means do not sign a loan for another person for any reason unless you're fully prepared to lose all the money.

I have a friend who allowed a business acquaintance to charge a toaster, costing about thirty dollars, on my friend's credit card. This acquaintance was going through a difficult divorce, and her funds were limited at that moment, she said. When the credit card bill arrived, the acquaintance had not paid my friend, so she allowed that amount to stay on the card. This went on for several months, with the business acquaintance always promising to pay. Finally my friend paid the card, realizing that this acquaintance would never repay the debt.

Fifteen years later when my friend was checking her credit, she noticed that this balance on her card had been noted on her credit report. That thirty dollars had tainted her credit. Unfortunately she learned the truth of God's advice to be a surety for no one.

The importance of avoiding fear

How many times have I heard businessmen say, "I could have bought this property on Loop 1604 (where Cornerstone Church is located) twenty years ago for peanuts!" But they didn't because they feared the future. Fearful businessmen make poor decisions.

Fearful Christians are living in a state of practical apostasy.

Fearful Christians are living in a state of practical apostasy. God has said, "There is no fear in love; but perfect love casts out fear" (1 John 4:18). When fear knocks at the door of your soul, send faith to answer, and fear will not be there. If you're planning for the future, do so fearlessly. If God is with you, who can be against you? You can live your life without limits, but the moment you allow fear to get in your thoughts or your speech, you will never succeed.

The secrets of prosperity are invest in yourself; invest in others; qualify for God's abundance; and manage your greatest assets.

4
MANAGE YOUR GREATEST ASSETS

Your greatest assets are your spouse and your children. The Bible says that a father is to leave an inheritance for his children and his children's children (Prov. 13:22). I suggest that the eight essentials below should be a part of that inheritance. Although you may have heard these ideas before, I note them quickly here because they are so important to a successful Christian life.

1. Give the treasure of your time.

If you, Father, are watching the World Series on television or reading the *Wall Street Journal*, and your child comes in and says, "I need to talk to you," don't say, "We'll talk about it later." You've communicated to your child that he or she doesn't matter. The greatest gift you can give your children is your time.

2. Be a promise keeper.

When you tell your children you're going to do something, do it. Don't make excuses; simply do it.

For instance, if you tell your son, "This Friday night we're going to go to the football game," the boy will get excited and tell his friends that his father is going to take him. But if Friday comes and you say you're too tired to go, your child loses faith in you and learns to distrust you. Eventually that distrust will cloud the child's image of God. *If my earthly father doesn't keep his word,* the child reasons, *why should I believe an invisible God will keep His word?*

3. Get rest.

I'm fighting pangs of hypocrisy as I advise you to get rest. I must admit this is a "do-as-I-say, not-as-I-do" principle. My two parents considered a twelve-hour workday as part-time work (as you probably surmised from a few of the stories from my childhood), so I work seventy hours a week and have done so for forty years. However, in my years of ministry, I have seen great pastors, evangelists, and titanic businessmen become unraveled because they were simply exhausted.

Jesus "took the twelve disciples apart in the way" (Matt. 20:17, KJV). The truth is they *went apart* before they *came apart.* I assure you the stress level in Jesus' society was considerably less than ours. There is a biblical principle for resting one in seven days. There is also a biblical principle of resting one week in seven weeks and one year in seven years.

Psychologists are now saying that the marriages of Americans are being extremely stressed because of the tension of overwork. Take time to rest so that you can be the best for God and for your family.

4. Build a family creed based on faith in God.

When you as a father and head of the house pray with your children each night, your children see you put God first. When they see you give the first fruits of your labor to the church, they see you put God first. The Ten Commandments say, "You shall have no other gods before Me" (Exod. 20:3). Jesus said, "Seek first the kingdom of God and His righteousness, and all these things shall be added to you" (Matt. 6:33).

The point is very simple: When you put God first, your whole life falls into divine order. When you don't put God first, there's nothing you can do to get your screwed-up life to make sense.

5. Manage your time.

Every person wakes up every day with the same amount of time. You can't stop time, and you can't buy time. You only have so much time on this earth, and then you have to step off the stage of time into eternity.

How much time do you waste? And how much of your time do you let other people waste? My mother taught me to be time conscious. Over the years, the intensity of managing 18,000 church members, 485 full-time employees, 5 children, a wife, and 2 dogs has taught me to manage my time ruthlessly.

Time is more valuable than money.
You can get more money, but you
can't get more time.

One of the greatest time management secrets I learned was from the president of the United States Steel Company. As recommended by him, every night I make a list of everything I want to accomplish the next day, and I start by putting the most difficult task on the list first. I don't allow difficult things to wait until the end of the day, because I will dread them all day long. Instead I do the unpleasant things first, and I tell my staff I want to hear bad news immediately. I want to take care of problems instantly.

I encourage you to make a nightly list of the things you want to accomplish the next day. Then discipline yourself to accomplish that list, and you will be amazed at how much more you can do in a shorter period of time.

6. Learn to say no.

One of the most powerful and eloquent words in the English language is *no*. This single word can save your time, your money, your marriage, your health, and your sanity.

For instance, when you are tempted to spend money you should not spend, have the courage to tell yourself, "No, we can't afford this," and make it stick. When your closest friends tempt you to do things that are not beneficial to your divine purpose on this earth, say no.

In the Bible some people's lives were distinguished by their ability to say no. One example is Vashti, the queen of Persia. When King Ahasuerus invited Vashti into his elaborate banquet, she said no. She refused to come into the company of drunks for the amusement of her husband. She is remembered forever in history as the woman who had the courage to say no.

No is one of the most powerful words you can use in the pursuit of God's purpose for your life.

Do you have the courage to say no? *No* is one of the most powerful words you can use in the pursuit of God's purpose for your life. Your time is your life, and if you don't learn to say no, you will waste your life doing what others insist you must do instead of what God wants you to do.

7. Bless your children.

The power of the blessing is a concept that I have portrayed in a six-hour videocassette series. Briefly, the power of the blessing is demonstrated in Scripture when God blessed Adam and Eve in Genesis 1 and Abraham in Genesis 12. Jacob continued this tradition when he blessed his twelve sons, speaking a blessing into each of their lives that became a self-fulfilling prophecy. (See Genesis 49:1–28.)

When the spiritual authority over a child speaks a divine blessing over that child, the result is still a self-fulfilling prophecy. A father puts his hand on his son or his daughter and speaks his desires for the future of that child's life, and he literally releases that child to be all he or she can be.

I encourage every father and mother reading this book to bless your children on a regular basis so you can release the anointing of God into their lives to accomplish the divine destiny God has sculptured for them from the beginning of time. For further study I encourage you to get "The Power of Blessing" video series from our television ministry.[2]

8. Work at staying physically fit.

I had been in the ministry many years before I began to see my body as "the temple of the Holy Spirit" (1 Cor. 6:19).

When I played football at the university, bones were broken and muscles were torn. In some cases I played those football games with sedatives to dull the pain so I could continue to play. What I put my body through was nothing short of sin. In the autumn of my life, those sins of my youth are talking back to me in the aches and pains of my physical body.

Once you see your body as the temple of the Holy Spirit, you should be concerned about what you eat and drink and its effect upon your longevity. Charles Haddon Spurgeon was one of the greatest preachers who ever stood behind a pulpit, but he died at the age of fifty-eight. How much more could he have blessed the world if he had lived to be seventy?

It's your future; be there for it. Take care of the physical body God gave you because it is a treasure. You will not recognize the value of your health until you lose it.

The secrets of a successful life are invest in yourself; invest in others; qualify for God's abundance; manage your greatest assets; and be patient in waiting for your prosperity.

5

BE PATIENT IN WAITING FOR YOUR PROSPERITY

Everything God does on earth comes from the principle of seedtime and harvest. Genesis 8:22 says: "While the earth remains, seedtime and harvest…shall not cease."

If you plant apple seeds, you get apples. If you plant peach seeds, you get peaches. The Bible says, "Whatever a man sows, that he will also reap" (Gal. 6:7). If you sow wild oats, you will reap wild oats. You can't sow wild oats for twenty-five years and go home and pray for crop failure. It doesn't work that way. Your wild oats will come up, and God will let you eat the crop.

Ecclesiastes 3:2 says: "A time to plant, and a time to pluck what is planted." The truth is, without seedtime it's impossible to have harvest time. If you give nothing, you get nothing. God can increase what you give a hundredfold, but nothing times nothing is nothing.

I often hear people say, "Pastor, I have nothing to give." That's absolutely wrong. The apostle Paul wrote in 2 Corinthians 9:11, "Now may He who supplies seed to the sower, and bread for food, supply and multiply the seed you have sown and increase the fruits of your righteousness."

But you must be patient in waiting for your harvest.

I was born in the country, and I love planting seeds in soil and watching them grow. I have also owned a farm or a ranch for many years. There's something about watching a seed grow in soil that makes you feel like you're in partnership with God.

On one occasion I planted a wheat field. I prepared the ground well. I planted the seed properly. But as I've already said, I am not the most patient person on the planet. One day I was inspecting my field, and I did not see the wheat popping through the soil, so I took a stick and began to dig up the seed so I could see if the seeds were germinating. And true to countless millennia of God's faithfulness, they were. Then I heard a voice within me say, "You are digging up your harvest, because of your impatience. I have never failed you, and I will not fail you. Cover the seed up."

Are you destroying your harvest with your impatience?

Jesus said in Luke 8:15: "But the ones that fell on the good ground are those who, having heard the word with a noble and good heart, keep it and bear fruit with patience." And the apostle Paul wrote in Hebrews 10:36, "For you have need of patience, that after you have done the will of God, you might receive the promise." Paul wrote again in Romans 8:25, "If we hope for that we see not, then do we with patience wait for it?" (KJV).

You can kill your harvest with a lack of patience.

You can plant your seed properly and abundantly in good ground, but you can kill your harvest with a lack of patience. Esau sold his birthright for a bowl of pottage because of his impatience. He saw the bowl of pottage his brother, Jacob, had made and said, "Look, I am about to die; so what is this birthright to me?" (Gen. 25:32). He wasn't anywhere close to death, but his impatience destroyed his inheritance.

If you invest a thousand dollars in the kingdom of God today, don't look for a hundredfold return before the sun sets. Impatience will kill your harvest.

6

CONQUER THE POVERTY COMPLEX

Some of God's children have a poverty complex. It sounds like this: "Jesus was poor. I'm poor. I'm like Jesus." That's absolutely wrong, because Jesus wasn't poor.

Unfortunately many people teach and preach that Christ was poor, and that poverty is a sacred position. Some go so far as to say there must be a moral doctrine of poverty for believers. This is utter nonsense.

The Bible does say in 2 Corinthians 8 that Christ "for your sakes became poor." But the question must be asked, when did He become poor? And the answer is this: He became poor at the cross when He took my poverty. In every other biblical reference, He is the King of a kingdom that rules the world, and Christ was not—and is not—poor.

The difference between living a life of prosperity and a life of poverty is a matter of choice. Not chance, but choice. Not circumstance, but choice. Moses said to Israel, "I have set before you life and death, blessing and cursing…choose" (Deut. 30:19). The truth is that blessing is a result of choice.

God's children have historically been prosperous.

In Genesis 13:2 the Bible says, "Abram was very rich in livestock, in silver, and gold." Notice this is not spiritually rich; this is materially rich. Ecclesiastes 5:19 states, "As for every man to whom God has given riches and wealth…this is the gift of God!"

Solomon wrote in Proverbs 10:22, "The blessing of the LORD makes one rich, and He adds no sorrow with it." Solomon was extremely wealthy. Archaeologists have discovered that the hinges on Solomon's horse stables were gold plated. Solomon was wealthy enough to send care packages to Bill Gates, the founder of Microsoft.

King David gave one hundred million for the building of the temple in one offering. That's not bad for someone who started out with five rocks and a slingshot.

I have had people quote Mark 10:25 to me, which says, "It is easier for a camel to go through the eye of a needle than for a rich man to enter the kingdom of God." In Jerusalem, you easily see what Jesus meant by "the eye of a needle." It is not the same needle that is used in sewing. Instead Jesus was referring to the Needle Gate.

The old city of Jerusalem was surrounded by a protective wall that had gates so people could enter the city. About five feet down the wall from every gate was an arch called the Needle Gate. If you came to the city at midnight, all the main gates were closed so you had to enter through the narrow gate, the Needle Gate.

Those who entered the city at night had to strip their camel of all its baggage and pull the animal through a very tight passageway into the city. Then the rider went back outside the city wall to carry his baggage through the tunnel, reload the stuff onto the camel, and take it to his home inside the city.

This biblical picture is a portrait of stripping yourself of unnecessary attachments. The apostle Paul expressed this principle when he said, "Lay aside every weight, and the sin which so easily ensnares us" (Heb. 12:1).

If you want to picture this narrow gate more completely, go to the Russian Orthodox Church in Jerusalem, which has preserved one of the old city gates with its Needle Gate. Then remember the real meaning of this verse. Jesus was talking about the Needle Gate, not a needle that sews our garments. A camel could go through the Needle Gate if it was stripped of unnecessary baggage.

Jesus was not poor. John 19:23 states that Jesus had a seamless robe so valuable that Roman soldiers gambled for it at the cross. It was a designer robe, the very best.

Jesus had enough money available to him that He assigned one of His disciples to carry the "money box" (John 13:29). When you have to have a secretary-treasurer to carry the excess money, you're not poor. If you're walking around with your lower lip trembling,-saying, "Jesus was poor; I'm poor; I'm spiritual because I'm like Jesus," you're simply in deception.

I have heard people say, "Pastor, I feel guilty about having nice things." Jesus didn't! He enjoyed nice things! He doesn't care how many things you own as long as those things do not own you.

He doesn't care how many things you own as long as those things do not own you.

If wealth is a negative thing, why would God the Father give it to His Son, Jesus Christ? John the Revelator writes in Revelation 5:12:

"Worthy is the Lamb...to receive power and riches and wisdom and strength and honor and glory and blessing." Note that there are seven blessings in this verse that are given to Jesus Christ, the Son, and to His church, and one of those blessings is riches.

When the woman with the alabaster box approached Jesus, the Bible is clear that it was "very costly" (Matt. 26:7). It cost the woman one year's wages to break that twelve-ounce box of alabaster over the head of Jesus. The aroma of that perfume was legendary: It was said that this perfume could be smelled from Jerusalem to Bethlehem, a distance of approximately eight miles. The rich aroma filled the room, and people were shocked by the sacrifice.

Judas, who had a poverty complex, shouted, "You should have given it to the poor." Jesus cut him off at the knees, saying, "Leave her alone. She has done what she could" (Matt. 26:10).

Why was this gift so important? We often teach that Jesus was alone the last hours He lived on earth. That's wrong!

When Jesus was in the Garden of Gethsemane, the disciples slept as the sins of the world were being placed upon His back. He sweat drops of blood, but the aroma of that perfume was there, saying, "Someone loved You enough, Jesus, to do her very best."

When Herod's men of war spat on Him, crowned Him with thorns, and mocked Him with a purple robe, saying, "All hail, King of the Jews," that aroma was there, saying, "Someone loved You enough, Jesus, to do her very best for You."

When Jesus laid down on the Roman cross on the crest of Calvary and was nailed to the cursed tree, that aroma was there, saying, "Someone loved You enough to do her very best for You."

Jesus gave His very best for you. Are you giving your very best for Him?

7

GOD GIVES WEALTH TO THOSE WHO PASS THE BLESSING ON

God does not have trouble getting money to us; He has trouble getting money through us. God said to Abraham, "I will bless you...and you shall be a blessing" (Gen. 12:2).

Abraham is our spiritual father. Galatians 3:29 states, "If you are

Christ's, then you are Abraham's seed, and heirs according to the promise." Abraham was a mighty man of wealth. And God used that wealth to birth the nation of Israel.

Over thirty years ago, I performed a pauper's funeral. It was two weeks before Christmas. When I arrived at the cemetery, I saw three little boys sitting alone under the tent. Their ages were eight, nine, and ten. And their clothes were dirty. Their shirts had holes, as well as their pants and their shoes. Their hair was uncut. The funeral was attended by their schoolteachers and a school principal. Not one family member was present.

I did not recognize these three boys at that moment. But they occasionally attended the church on Nacogdoches Road. They had the same mother, but each of them had a different father. None of them knew their mother; instead a godly grandmother who loved them with an everlasting love had raised them. We were burying her in a wooden box in a pauper's grave, but she meant the whole world to them.

After the funeral, I met the principal and asked, "What's going to be done with these boys?"

"I have called the authorities, and they say all facilities are full, and these brothers are going to have to be split up."

"It's Christmas time. They've just lost the only human being on earth who loved them. We've got to come up with another answer."

We talked under that tent for thirty minutes, and there seemed to be no solution. There are times when you must decide to do something rather than just let suffering humanity go on suffering. I took those three boys home with me. The next day, I went to their house, an eight-by-twelve shack, to get their clothes. The house was full of fleas because a German Shepherd dog had also lived there. The clothes in their closet were so filthy and riddled with holes, I threw them in a barrel and burned them.

The next day, I went to Dillards and purchased new clothes for those boys. I could write a book on the experiences we had with these three boys in the years they stayed with us. I kept them for three years until a member of their family retired from the military and could give them a home.

At a critical moment in their lives, I was able to be a bridge over troubled waters that helped their lives stay on course. It took abundance to do that. God will give abundance to those who will use it to bless other people. James 4:3 says, "You ask and do not receive, because you ask amiss, that you may spend it on your pleasures."

God also gives wealth to those who make world evangelism a top priority. Deuteronomy 8:18 says, "Remember the LORD your God, for it is He who gives you power to get wealth, that He may establish His covenant which He swore to your fathers, as it is this day."

How can the world hear about a God of covenant without a preacher? And how can a preacher be sent unless someone has the abundance to send him? Not one missionary can be sent and not one church can be built without financial abundance. Not one crusade can happen without financial abundance. Not one television program or telecast can be made without abundance.

God's abundance is to be used to teach the gospel because every man and woman, every boy and girl without Christ will spend eternity in hell. Winning the lost is God's top priority, and if you will invest in winning the lost, God will give you abundance you cannot contain.

If you will invest in winning the lost, God will give you abundance you cannot contain.

Scripture says that your prosperity gives God pleasure. David wrote in Psalm 35:27: "Let the LORD be magnified, who has pleasure in the prosperity of His servant." The Bible says, "Beloved, I pray that you may prosper in all things and be in health, just as your soul prospers" (3 John 2).

You will unleash the power of God's abundance if you observe these seven undeniable laws of prosperity. God will multiply your treasure supernaturally, abundantly, and miraculously. And you will discover the true secret of a successful life.

Enjoying the Jubilee
of Success

Y ou have just finished reading seven secrets of a successful life with seven applications to each secret, making forty-nine Bible truths that will reshape your divine destiny.

Forty-nine in Scripture led to the Year of Jubilee where all debts were forgiven and all possessions were restored. One can almost hear the silver trumpets blasting the arrival of this celebration throughout the land of Israel. If a man had sold himself into slavery, when those trumpets sounded he went free. His shackles were broken. His indenture canceled.

Property was also returned to those who had sold it, which tended to prevent the amassing of immense wealth by some and the extreme poverty of others, giving all a chance for success.

Let's look at the changes you should have made throughout this book. These changes will cancel your debts and allow you to receive God's blessing. You will enter into your year of jubilee.

You have replaced your negative attitude with an *I can* philosophy. The word *but* is no longer a part of your vocabulary. Instead the words *I can do all things through Christ who strengthens me* echo in your mind. Rather than your attitude being your worst enemy, it is now your best friend.

You have made the Perseverance Principle a part of your life. "It's always too soon to quit" is a motto that has become part of your daily walk. You have vowed to become an overcomer. You will never...never...never give up!

You have decided to overcome your temptation to devalue yourself, and instead you have accepted my challenge to discard the mask you're wearing and live in the sunshine of God's love, to love your neighbor as yourself and to begin to see yourself as God sees you.

You have adopted the secret of self-mastery. Worry, fear, anger, depression, resentment, unforgiveness, and unrepentance are no longer your bedfellows. By passion, by conviction, and by unswerving determination, you have decided to conquer your supreme and most subtle enemy: yourself.

You are aware that your communication with your God, your family, and your associates should be level one communication. You probably can't do that every day in every situation, but you are determined to try to give a part of your heart to those around you, whether it is to one person or to a million.

You know the power of prayer, and when you pray you ask God for things so staggering, so big, that God slides to the edge of His holy throne and says to the angels, "Did you hear what that kid asked for? Do it, angels! Faith like that excites Me. Get down there with the answer."

Finally, you practice the undeniable law of prosperity: "giver's gain." You know that how you manage your money has great importance to your prosperity, both here on earth and in heaven. Your checkbook is, in fact, a spiritual reflection of your love of God.

These seven secrets lead to true success. I like the way Booker T. Washington measured success. He said, "I have learned that success is to be measured not so much by the position that one has reached in life as by the obstacles, which one has overcome while trying to succeed."[1]

What obstacles have you overcome to succeed?

Consider Prince Charles of Great Britain. He is a handsome representative of British royalty, but what has he overcome to reach the pinnacle of power he so richly enjoys?

The answer is nothing!

He was born with the proverbial silver spoon in his mouth in a

horse-drawn carriage of gold. His most outstanding accomplishment to date is learning how to ride a polo pony without falling off. He's paid millions each year to do what his mamma tells him to do. By Booker T. Washington's definition, Prince Charles's success factor is modest.

Contrast his life with that of a member of my congregation named Margaret. You haven't read about her in the newspapers or heard her mentioned on television. Paparazzi didn't track her to take her picture. But she does belong to a royal family, and her name is written in the Lord's Book of Life.

A Child of the King

When the church was young, I made all the house calls—when I wasn't cutting the grass or cleaning commodes with a Johnny mop. Anyone who signed a visitor's card would get a visit from me.

One July day in San Antonio when the temperature was sizzling in the high nineties, I went to Margaret's home. Two of her young daughters answered the door, dressed in swimming suits.

"Good morning, are you going swimming?" I asked the girls.

They both responded in unison, "No." I noticed they were eating popcorn.

"Is your mother home?" I asked.

Almost magically Margaret appeared at the door and invited me to come in. Although it was sizzling hot outside I noticed the air conditioning was turned off.

I introduced myself and asked, "Is your husband home?"

"I'm recently divorced," Margaret replied. "My husband was a university professor who left me for one of his students." But Margaret had not allowed this betrayal to destroy her self-esteem or make her bitter. She pointed to her daughters and said, "He also left his beautiful children." Then her lips began to quiver. "I'm sorry" she said, "I don't have the air conditioning on. I have it turned off because I can't afford the utility bill."

Then it dawned on me! The children were eating popcorn because they were out of food. The girls were wearing swimming suits because they were so hot; this was the coolest thing they had.

"I'll be right back!" I told Margaret. I drove to the church, got a check, and went to the supermarket where I filled my Volkswagen with groceries to take to Margaret's house. I told the secretary to call the San Antonio Light and Power and get Margaret's utilities turned back on. We would guarantee the bill.

During the many years after that, Margaret's love and loyalty to God and to the church never wavered. Her daughters grew up to become beautiful women of God. Then doctors told Margaret she had cancer. Undaunted, she faced this challenge like all others she had known: head on.

I went to see her in the Baptist hospital in the final hours of her life, a moment in time I shall never forget. As I walked into the room, she was reading her Bible. Her hair was gone due to the chemotherapy, but her face was covered with a glow that filled the room with the glory of God.

I took her frail hand and gently kissed it. I looked deeply into her dark eyes, and there wasn't a trace of fear. I knelt beside her bed and asked, "Margaret, how are you doing today?"

She smiled courageously and said, "Pastor, today when I awoke I realized this was the best day of my life. Last night I did not know if I would see this day. But it's a gift from God, so I'm going to celebrate.

"I'm going to celebrate the blessings God has given me. I'm going to celebrate the burdens He's given me to carry and the hardships that have made me stronger.

"I'm going to celebrate today, Pastor, by hugging and kissing my children passionately. I'll give a sincere compliment to those who are cast down. I've stopped worrying about what I don't have because I have today.

"Tonight when the stars come out and the moon glows, I will look at them as long as I can. I don't know if I'll see them tomorrow. With my last breath tonight I will thank God for this beautiful day. It's been the best day of my life."

It was Margaret's last day, and she lived it to the glory of God, just as she had lived her life. That's true success.

I can only imagine her reception in heaven. I can see the omnipotent, almighty King of kings running toward her. I can see Him taking her in His arms, holding her head to His chest, and laughing with joy as He greets her and says, "My daughter's come home."

And I'm sure after the Lord hugged her, He stepped back, gave her a long and loving look, and then say, "Well done, good and faithful servant. You have been faithful over a few things. I will make you ruler over many things. Enter into the joy of your Lord."

That's true success. May each of us one day hear those words of love and congratulation from the King of kings and the Lord of lords.

CHAPTER 1
Success Is for Everyone

1. Paul Lee Tan, Th.D., *Encyclopedia of 7,700 Illustrations* (Rockville, MD: Assurance Publishers, 1979), 832.
2. John C. Maxwell, *The Success Journey* (Nashville, TN: Nelson Publishers, 1997), 5.
3. Tan, *Encyclopedia of 7,700 Illustrations*, 830.
4. Ibid., 824.
5. Adapted from Denis Waitley, *Seeds of Greatness* (Grand Rapids, MI: Revell, a division of Baker Books, 1983), 242.
6. Jamie Buckingham, *Coping With Criticism* (South Plainfield, NJ: Logos Publishing, 1978), 96.
7. Author interview with Red McComb.

CHAPTER 2
Secret One: The Mystery and Power of Your Mind

1. James S. Hewett, *Illustrations Unlimited* (Wheaton, IL: Tyndale House Publishers, 1988), 41.
2. Hewett, *Illustrations Unlimited*, 129.
3. Taken from http://www.khof/inductees/cunningham.html (accessed October 26, 2003).
4. Tan, *Encyclopedia of 7,700 Illustrations*, 956.
5. Your Ultimate Success Quotation Library, cybernation.com.
6. Ibid.

CHAPTER 3
Secret Two: The Seven Perseverance Principles

1. Waitley, *Seeds of Greatness*, 215–223.
2. Tan, *Encyclopedia of 7,700 Illustrations*, 999.
3. This description of Edison's invention was found at http://gci/gospelcom.net/dw/1997/03/12/ (accessed October 23, 2003).
4. More information about the Paradoxical Commandments by Kent M. Keith, copyright © 1968, 2001, may be obtained at www.paradoxicalcommandments.com.

CHAPTER 5
Secret Four: Mastery of Your Supreme and Most Subtle Enemy

1. John Hagee, *From Daniel to Doomsday* (Nashville, TN: Thomas Nelson Publishers, 2000).
2. Used with permission from *Bright Side,* May 1999. Copyright © Campus Crusade for Christ, Inc.
3. Adapted from http://www.christian-bookshop.co.uk/free/biogs/spurg2 .htm (accessed October 24, 2003).
4. The information about Max Jukes and Jonathan Edwards was adapted from http://self-discipline.8m.com/generational_discipline.htm (accessed October 24, 2003).

CHAPTER 6
Secret Five: Level One Communication

1. Gordan Lindsay, *Forty Signs of the Soon-Coming of Christ* (Dallas, TX: Christ for the Nations, 1969), 20.

CHAPTER 7
Secret Six: The Power of Continuous Prayer

1. Derek Prince, *Shaping History Through Prayer and Fasting* (Grand Rapids, MI: Fleming H. Revell, 1973), 5–8.

CHAPTER 8
Secret Seven: The Undeniable Laws of Prosperity

1. Alice A. Bays and Elizabeth Jones Oakbery, "The Power of Kindness" (American Religious House).
2. You may order "The Power of Blessing" video (S0240) by calling 1-800-854-9899 or by writing John Hagee Ministries, 239 North Loop 1604 W, San Antonio, TX 78232.

EPILOGUE
Enjoying the Jubilee of Success

1. John Maxwell, *Your Road Map for Success* (Nashville: Thomas Nelson Publishers, 2002), 15.

Joseph's Journey: From the Pit to the Palace

Life is a journey and every one of us is on it. Joseph's journey is your journey. Everything Joseph experienced, you will experience. You begin your journey with the favor of God and a dream. The beauty of the dream is shattered by the reality of the pit... and you will have pits in life you can choose to stay in or climb out of. Just when you think things can't get worse... they do. You quickly find out who you are when you are in the pit. The pit is not your destiny! Your destiny is the palace. Pastor Hagee will walk you through God's plan from devastation to restoration and perfect revelation for the future.

S-0231   **Joseph's Journey: From the Pit to the Palace Series**
8 Audio Tapes $42 US/$55 CAN
8 Video Tapes $120 US/$156 CAN
8 CD Set $63 US/$82 CAN

Prophecy Of The Seven Feasts

The word "feast" in Hebrew is "mo-ed" and it means a set time or an appointed time. Another Hebrew word connected to the Seven Feasts Of the Lord is the word "mikrah" which means rehearsal or recital. The point is this - God is showing us through the Seven Feasts an elaborate rehearsal of the future that will occur at a set time.

What do these Seven Feasts have to do with you? Why is it important for you to know about these Feasts in order to prepare for the future? Pastor Hagee walks you through each one in vivid detail. Everything that God will do... He has done. The future has been revealed through the past.

S-0338   **Prophecy of the Seven Feasts Series**
7 Audio Tapes $37 US/$48 CAN
7 Video Tapes $110 US/$143 CAN
7 CD Set $55 US/$72 CAN

To Order Call: 1-800-854-9899 US or 1-416-447-4000 CAN
or visit us online: www.johnhagee.net

GAIN A DEEPER UNDERSTANDING OF YOUR SPOUSE!

In *What Every Man Wants in a Woman / What Every Woman Wants in a Man*, best-selling author and pastor John Hagee and his wife, Diana, offer a man's and woman's point of view on understanding your partner and creating a happy marriage. This unique, easy-to-read flipbook book will invigorate your marriage.

$19.99/1-59185-557-8
(Hardcover)

Strang Communications, the publisher of both Charisma House and *Charisma* magazine, wants to give you 3 FREE ISSUES of our award-winning magazine.

Since its inception in 1975, *Charisma* magazine has helped thousands of Christians stay connected with what God is doing worldwide.

Within its pages you will discover in-depth reports and the latest news from a Christian perspective, biblical health tips, global events in the body of Christ, personality profiles, and so much more. Join the family of *Charisma* readers who enjoy feeding their spirit each month with miracle-filled testimonies and inspiring articles that bring clarity, provoke prayer, and demand answers.

To claim your **3 free issues** of *Charisma,* send your name and address to: Charisma 3 Free Issue Offer, 600 Rinehart Road, Lake Mary, FL 32746. Or you may call 1-800-829-3346 and ask for Offer # 93FREE. This offer is only valid in the USA.

www.charismamag.com